Under the editorship of

DAYTON D. McKEAN

University of Colorado

The Urban Political Community

PROFILES IN TOWN POLITICS

GLADYS M. Marie KAMMERER

CHARLES D. FARRIS

JOHN M. DeGROVE

ALFRED B. CLUBOK

THE UNIVERSITY OF FLORIDA

HOUGHTON MIFFLIN COMPANY · BOSTON

CONTENTS

119435

LIST OF TABLES

PREFACE

The Social Science Research Council in 1960 made a group research grant in the field of American government and political behavior to Gladys M. Kammerer for a study of council-manager tenure and turnover in Florida in relation to community political stability. Associated with her in this project were the other co-authors of this set of profiles. The summer of 1960 was spent in intensive field studies of ten council-manager cities by this research team.

Our cities for field studies were selected from those at either extreme from all Florida council-manager cities plotted on a continuum as to average tenure for managers. Other factors, aside from highest or lowest average tenure for managers, also guided us in selection of the field study cities, and these factors were geographic distribution and economy of the town, i.e., touristic, industrial, agricultural processing, or retiree colony.

Those whom we defined as "influentials" in the politics of each town were interviewed by means of a structured interview guide. The "influentials" always included the city manager, the mayor, members of both the majority and minority factions of the council, civic leaders such as the chamber of commerce president or executive secretary, and the local newspaper editor or city hall reporter. In addition, we interviewed past city managers, mayors, and councilmen, and other city officers who were major figures, such as the city attorney, as these persons were available and still resident in the community.

The agreement was remarkable among our interviewees in the information and interpretations provided despite such obvious factors, always to be noted, as rivalries and even feuds among various interviewees. We, therefore, concluded that our interviewees were providing us with honest reports and appraisals despite the fact that much of the information conveyed was "disreputable" by American middle-class standards. When our interviewees provided us with information that correlated, we concluded that the validity of our data was established and that "closure" had been attained.

All cities are disguised by fictitious names, as is commonly done in such studies. Similarly, the identity of our principal interviewees is not revealed. Instead, the most common surnames are used to mask their identities.

Although a monograph focused on our central problem of city manager tenure and turnover — *City Managers in Politics* — was produced in due course, we believed that we had mined a rich lode of ore for students of political behavior that should be presented on its own. Hence our determination to write political profiles of our study towns that might serve as useful readings for the undergraduate student of political science. It is with that purpose in mind that we present this volume.

July 1, 1962

GLADYS M. KAMMERER
CHARLES D. FARRIS
JOHN M. DEGROVE
ALFRED B. CLUBOK

1

Introduction

The study of local government within the political science curriculum has, for many years, been a political stepchild. We realize that writers of textbooks on local or urban government often assume that courses in "politics" are normally separate offerings and that such writers purposefully omit any intensive analysis of the political process in order to avoid duplication. Although we realize that the nature of the curriculum is in large part the reason for the political stepchild status of local government, we believe that is hardly fair to the student.

The standard texts devote many pages to such topics as the structure of the mayor-council or council-manager forms of government, to personnel administration, budget and fiscal administration, or police and fire protection. These topics, however, are often treated as if the city were, in miniature, an administrative state possessed of neither politics external to the administrative organization nor palace politics within the organization. The texts normally contain a chapter about political parties and interest groups, about elections and, perhaps even about bosses, but once these chapters are concluded, the student usually finds that politics has been disposed of in the text.

Some of the factors which underlie the "political sterilization" of the study of local government are readily apparent. The graft, corruption, vice, and bossism which were often obvious and prevalent in the American urban community early in the twentieth century led to vigorous municipal reform movements. The reformers had reason to be shocked by the facts of urban life. It was not pleasant to contemplate the fact that the prerogatives and, indeed, the routine functions of government could be and were sometimes sold by politicians and bought by members of the business and criminal communities. Some political scientists, understandably, joined the reformers in order to contribute whatever they could to redeem the city and to save local democracy.

As a result of the reform movements, then, came a series of plans and devices designed to change the face of urban politics. Political scientists became either the designers or the advocates of commission government, the strong mayor plan, the council-manager plan, nonpartisan elections, etc. Underlying these plans for structural change, however, was a basic assumption which shaped the course of the study of local government for many years. The reformers and the political scientists assumed that it was politics that made the scheme of local government go awry. If politics was something evil, then it was a thing to be avoided.

To break the hold of the politician, the reformer became the advocate of nonpartisan elections. But even the most fervent advocate of reform had to admit that the election process itself, whether partisan or nonpartisan, was a political act. In order to eliminate politics, then, the reformer had to play with words. For instance, the decision of a city council could be called a policy rather than a political decision. But if some political scientists found it hard to distinguish policy from politics, the reform-oriented political scientist could find one area which he, at least, believed could be divorced from politics. The executive or administrative side was the area that could be saved.

As a consequence, the council-manager plan become the favorite of the reform-oriented because it seemed so clearly to allow for the differentiation of the political side from the administrative. The plan called for a small city council elected at large in nonpartisan elections to serve as the city's policy-making body. The mayor, usually chosen by the council rather than the voters, was merely a presiding officer and ceremonial head of the city. The council was denied the exercise of administrative authority over city employees, and its appointive power was limited to the selection and dismissal of the city manager. While policy-making was to be the prerogative of the city council, administration was to be the exclusive territory of a professionally trained manager. Presumably, the city manager would be guided in his actions by the twin goals of honesty and efficiency.

Under the terms of the Model City Charter municipal elections were made nonpartisan, and reformers reiterated over the years the dictum that streets and sewers are not Republican or Democratic — or political. It was, therefore, easy for political scientists to concentrate on the "management" side of local government to the exclusion of all things political. Budget-making and personnel, organizational analysis, cost analysis, public reporting — all of these processes were viewed by political scientists as tasks in themselves without reference to the political context in which they were carried on. The notion the reform-oriented political scientists had of local politics as a source of corruption of governmental functioning was carried over into the "scientific management" school, which was becoming popular contemporaneously with the reform movement. From our standpoint, then, the reform-oriented political scientist, in reaction against what he believed to be the corruption of urban life, rejected the concept that politics served a legitimate function in local government. There is little wonder, therefore, that students in American universities who were interested in politics were hesitant about entering traditional courses on local government.

If, however, politics is viewed not as something "unclean," not as something a "good citizen would not get mixed up in," but rather as a process of making significant community-wide decisions, or as a process of deciding who gets what, when, and how,[1] then the student leaves the "lost world" of municipal government and re-enters the world of politics.

If politics flows from differences over policy, such issues as sewer construction, street construction and maintenance, zoning, land use, subdivision regulations, property assessment, tax rates on real property, garbage and trash collection, parking facilities and traffic routing, urban renewal, and public housing are the basic ingredients of urban politics. When a community, for instance, decides to adopt a strict zoning ordinance or approves the construction of low rental public housing, some people lose and some people gain. When debate arises in a community over any of these problems even though a unanimous decision may ultimately emerge, we are in the realm of politics. The issues which face the decision-making apparatus of a community may not seem as exciting as a question of regulation of labor unions or the railways, but to the inhabitants of a community, to those whose interests are affected by the decision, the issues are real and important. Political decisions can, in fact, decide the fate of the community. The decision of a group of citizens in a small farming community to seek industry in order to revitalize or diversify the economy of the community can translate itself into a struggle of competing factions or cliques to control the political structure of the community, and the outcome of the struggle can determine the future course of the community. The public or visible struggle might be over the question of tax rates or expansion of city services such as water, electricity, or fire protection. The political struggle might never come into public view, but a most important community political decision is being made — what kind of town is ours to be?

In this book we present the political profiles of eight communities

[1] Or as the process for the authoritative allocation of values within a jurisdiction, according to David Easton.

ranging in population from about 5,000 to 60,000. By metropolitan standards these are all relatively small communities. We deliberately selected small communities for study. The smaller community presents in a simpler fashion, and, therefore, in ways easier for the beginning student of politics to unravel, many of the same kinds of political questions and controversies found in larger cities. For example, zoning battles, sewerage programs, recreational facilities, and concessions to industry constitute types of issues common to all sizes of cities. Furthermore, because of the overlay of tradition and institutionalization, the larger city usually has less choice among alternative development paths than does the small city. Chicago today can hardly decide what kind of city it wants to be. This decision (whether made positively or by inaction — still a decision) was made years ago. On the other hand, the small city may still have the possibility of choice. Shall it remain a retail center for a farming hinterland or shall it try to attract industry or open its doors to the subdivision developer in hopes of becoming a dormitory suburb of a neighboring larger community? The doubling or trebling of the population, a by no means uncommon phenomenon outside large central cities since the end of World War II, may possibly force the community to re-evaluate its style of living, for new and different kinds of people often make demands which the older inhabitants are not prepared to meet.

In the profiles presented we hope to acquaint the reader with the political process at the local level — with the forces that produce significant community decisions. However, we believe that this set of profiles offers more than that. The student of political science is accustomed to the term "comparative government." The term normally connotes the study of the government and politics of selected Western European countries. Yet local government in the United States offers an ideal area for the study of comparative politics.

The reader may well ask at this point, "Is not one city in the United States fairly well like another city?" The answer we would give is "no." The politics of a tobacco community is likely to be different from the politics of an industrially expanding community or a dormitory suburb. When we use the word "different," we are not simply indicating that issues will differ. This is obvious. Rather, we believe that the communities may have different styles of politics. The rural, face-to-face community probably will play the political game in a different manner from that of the dormitory suburb or the industrial community. Some textbooks in government have used the comparative method to a limited extent, but their authors seldom did more than compare the theoretical virtues of the mayor-council and council-manager plans. We propose instead to hold the form of government constant and to compare communities in terms of their style of politics.

We have selected for presentation eight communities which utilize the council-manager form of government. In this manner, then, we hope to control for the variations in the political process produced by differing institutional arrangements within a generally similar structure.

In order to provide for the reader a focus common to all of the communities, we have structured the presentation of the profiles around the problem of city manager terminations and tenure. In each profile, therefore, we are interested in explaining why city managers are fired or, on the other hand, enjoy long tenure.

In selecting the involuntary termination of city managers for study, we have assumed that there is no sharp distinction between politics and administration, at least at the level of the city manager. Politics in this context is defined as the process of making significant community-wide decisions. From this standpoint, unless a city manager confines his recommendations to matters on which there is overwhelming agreement in the community, then any recommendation he makes contains the possibility of raising or defining an issue. Consequently, in making "policy" recommendations the city manager is acting politically. In this context the city manager is a participant in the political process of the community whether he plays an active role in initiating policy, a passive role by merely drawing council attention to emerging problems, or a neutral role by refusing to commit himself publicly on a controversial question. Our research experience shows that a refusal of a manager to commit himself can be interpreted by opposing groups as taking a position antagonistic to their own.

We found the decision to hire or fire a city manager to be one of the first order in city politics and possibly to symbolize almost as much as a council election. Given the crucial role of the managership in the council-manager plan, the selection or the termination of a manager resembles in form and relative importance the selection or rejection of a prime minister in a parliamentary system. The student in reading the following profiles, then, should be constantly aware of the place of the manager in the political structure of the city and search for the factors underlying his strength or weakness in the political process.

We have developed a number of concepts which we have utilized consistently throughout the profiles. We believe these concepts will help the student organize the materials in order to relate managerial terminations to the political process of the community.

Leadership clique. In our use of the term, "leadership clique" corresponds roughly to what other writers have called "crowds" or "leadership factions." The leadership clique shares with a political party one major objective — acquiring and maintaining control of the community for the realization of whatever policy goals the clique may have. It is not necessary to assume that a leadership clique is "organized" in a formal sense, and it is immaterial whether it centers on a single strong personality or operates collegially. Most leadership cliques operate from an identifiable power base in the community. A clique might represent the interests of the bankers, the downtown merchants, the real estate developers, the dormitory suburbanites, the old families, or in a broader sense the free-spending liberals as opposed to the budget-balancing conservatives. A leadership clique might desire political control of a community because the members of the clique make, or can make, their living from politics by selling in both a big and little way the favors which a government can bestow. A clique which allows gambling and prostitution to flourish in return for payments can be thought of as representing the interests of organized crime, but leadership cliques of this sort often are in the business of taking "kickbacks" from contractors and suppliers of materials. The leadership clique, in this sense, can be thought of as playing a broker's role.

Political style. Two types of political style were found in the case study cities: monopoly and competition. *Monopoly,* according to our definition, prevails when one leadership clique regularly wins all, or practically all, council seats regardless of the changing identity of candidates backed by the clique and when there is no continuing opposition from a rival leadership clique that regularly sponsors candidates or coopts successful candidates. A monopoly style of politics, indeed, can prevail under the following conditions: no opposition; "personal" opposition by candidates not affiliated with a clique; or formation of a temporary opposition group constituted for a particular election and either dissolved upon its defeat or disintegrated by the cooptation of its successful candidates into the ruling leadership clique. The student should note that the major characteristic of monopoly politics is a lack, during the time period studied, of continuing opposition from another leadership clique. Conflict prevails at a level low enough to be accommodated by the ruling clique. *Competition,* as a style of politics, exists when at least two leadership cliques compete on a *continuing* basis for elective office. We do not require an alternation in the political control of the community. One clique could consistently win control of the city council, but, as long as the opposition clique exists and challenges in elections, we use the term "competition" to describe the community's style of politics.

Power exchange. The replacement of one leadership clique by another is described as a power exchange. Power exchanges can occur at the time of an election, or they can occur after an election if council members defect and join another clique. When one clique replaces another, although a condition of monopoly existed both before and after the exchange, we would call such an exchange a "revolution." In other words, monopolistic control replaces monopolistic control. On the other hand, we would use the term "alternation" to describe power exchanges in a competitive system.

Power play. The term "power play" refers to the withdrawal of a leadership clique's support from a city manager whom the clique previously had supported. Our data suggest that power plays occur as acts of reprisal against managers who cooperate with opposition leadership cliques or as manipulations undertaken by leadership cliques to forestall defeat. Frequently they take the form of firing the manager before an election in order to shift blame for an unpopular policy to the manager and away from the clique in power.

Professional-local status. Finally, we classified managers by their professional-amateur status and by their local boy–outsider status. We consider as a local boy any manager who was born or went to school in the city or in the county containing the city where he presently holds a post as manager. All other managers we consider outsiders.

We consider a manager as a professional if he had collegiate training in political science, public administration, engineering, or business administration (fields usually regarded as preparatory to city management career development) and had adult career experience in public administration at any level of government. All other managers we consider as amateurs.

When reading the profiles, what should the student look for? First, the student should identify the leadership clique structure of the community. What interests — economic and social — do the cliques represent? Second, the student should attempt to evaluate the political style of the community. Is the community's style of politics monopolistic or is it competitive? Did the community undergo a change in its style of politics during the study period? What factors led to the change? Finally, the student should try to relate manager tenure and terminations to the community's style of politics and to the occurrence of power exchanges. What happens to managers when power exchanges occur? Do power exchanges occur more often in monopoly or competitive communities? Do amateur or professional managers have a longer average tenure? Do local boys or outsiders appear to have a longer average tenure? What kind of community tends to hire professional and outsider managers? What kind of community tends to hire amateurs and local boys?

Although in the concluding section of this book we provide a generalized statement based on a statistical analysis of interview data which answers many of the above questions, we believe that the reader will benefit if he attempts independently to analyze the materials presented. We hope that through this process of analysis he may gain insight both into the "real world" of local government and into a more precise method for the study of comparative politics and administration.

2

Orange Point

Orange Point is located in the southern part of the state about two miles inland from the Gulf of Mexico. Its 1960 population was about 8,000. Although this area of the state has grown considerably in population since the end of World War II, Orange Point has grown more slowly than neighboring communities.

The community is physically divided by a major federal highway. To the east of this highway the land is sandy but fairly high. West of the highway, however, the land is low with a water table only a foot or two below the surface. As one moves from the highway west towards the beach, the land becomes progressively lower and swampier. Twelve to eighteen inches of standing water, even close to the highway, are not uncommon during the rainy summer months. Sand flies and mosquitoes breed in the swampy area, and when the winds are off the Gulf, huge swarms of the insects are blown into town to make life uncomfortable even for people born in the area and accustomed to the nuisance.

Most of the town's population lives on the high sandy ridge which forms the eastern part of the town. The topography of this part of the city has made building construction possible without sewerage. In the low area west of the highway the land remains largely undeveloped, since construction is not feasible until the people of Orange Point decide to install both storm and sanitary sewers.

Orange Point is a shabby community as compared with others in the southern section of the state: the homes are old, the downtown area is decaying rapidly, and there is very little new construction. Orange Point is often referred to as the "slum" of its area by the inhabitants of the surrounding cities.

As settlements go in southern Florida, Orange Point is a relatively old town. The community was established by the Gold Branch Railway Company as a real estate development. Its first settlers were

9

farmers, and Orange Point early developed into a thriving farming community. With the development of the refrigerated railway car, Orange Point became a major center for winter vegetable crops. The mid-1940's brought a very rapid decline in agriculture. By the mid-1950's agriculture was dead in Orange Point. Forty per cent of the labor force in Orange Point had been engaged in agriculture in 1940. By 1950 only 16 per cent of the labor force was still farming. Salt water infiltration into the vegetable fields, the rising cost of labor, fertilizers, and insecticides, as well as a number of damaging frosts, brought an end to agricultural production in Orange Point.

Orange Point's population has grown slowly but steadily since 1940. In 1940 its population was about 3,000; in 1950 about 5,000; and in 1960 almost 8,000. The new population, however, has not brought much wealth into the community. Some retired persons have moved into the town, but apparently they have brought little more than Social Security payments with them on their retirement trek from the North. Most of the others moving into the community appear to be working class people who, as with the retired, have not brought much wealth to the community.

Since the death of agriculture, Orange Point has been fragmented in terms of the solution of its economic problem. The major question facing Orange Point today — and it has been confronted by the same problem since the mid-1940's — is what type of city shall Orange Point become. The town appears to be no closer to an answer today than it was ten years ago.

In a way, the death of farming came too late for Orange Point. While it remained a farming community, cities to the north and south expanded very rapidly as service, tourist, and retirement centers. Orange Point remained as a center of rural culture in an area that was rapidly urbanizing. By 1950 Orange Point was hemmed in on three sides by the annexations of neighboring communities. By the time Orange Point's preoccupation with agriculture had passed and the city fathers became cognizant of the beach as an economic asset to the city, the community's potential beach had been annexed by a neighboring community, and Orange Point was forced to buy a two-mile strip for a public beach.

The death of agriculture, of course, produced a drastic change in the occupational structure of the community. Apparently, most of the labor force which had depended upon agriculture for a livelihood was forced to turn to common labor. The surrounding communities do have some fair-sized industries, and some of the displaced agricultural workers have found employment there. Orange Point's Negro population, which comprised almost one-half of the town's population in 1950, was hit hard by the death of agriculture. The Negroes were primarily tenant farmers or farm laborers. The vast majority of them turned to construction, yard work, or common labor.

Orange Point, as is the case with many communities, would like to attract industry. A few small manufacturing firms have located in the town, but they provide only a limited number of jobs. The major economic asset which Orange Point has acquired in the last ten years has been a dog track. Although the issue of permitting dog racing produced a bitter struggle in the community, the track does provide some seasonal employment, and the city receives about $50,000 a year from a head tax at the track.

Orange Point's economic future appears to be less than rosy. The town is divided on the solution of its economic problems. Some people in the town would like to see Orange Point become a tourist center; others are attracted by the magic lure of "light, clean industry"; still others, perhaps more realistically, believe that Orange Point can never be more than a "nice place to live" and would like to see Orange Point become a retirement center or a dormitory community for the neighboring larger cities. No solution has been agreed upon by the community leadership. In fact, there is a great deal of pessimism in Orange Point about the future of the town.

II

The death of farming produced a drastic change in the political life of the community. In the period when agriculture provided a viable economy, the town council and local politics appear to have been dominated by a few old farming families. Following the sudden and drastic collapse in agriculture in the mid-1940's, the growers lost or abdicated control of Orange Point's city council. The agriculturalists were replaced by a clique of young men primarily interested in the monetary gains they could make from governing Orange Point. The graft was petty — as one respondent phrased it, "nickel and dime stuff" — but it was widespread.

In 1950 two ambitious and competent men, Frank Barton and John Burkhart, joined forces in what apparently began as a reform movement to take control of the city government. Frank Barton's grandfather had been one of the original settlers in Orange Point, and the Barton family had become wealthy from agriculture. As early as 1940, when most of the wealthy people in Orange Point still thought solely in terms of crops as constituting the base for Orange Point's economic future, Barton had decided that Orange Point could and should receive its share of the lucrative tourist trade in that section of the state. He built the Orange Point Hotel in 1940, hoping to capture some of the tourist trade. Aside from the hotel, Barton had interests in the Orange Point Bank and owned a large amount of land in the Negro section of the community.

John Burkhart, on the other hand, had no connection with agriculture. He was born in Pennsylvania and was a successful liquor dealer in Pittsburgh before coming to Orange Point in 1940 upon his retirement from business. There are persistent rumors in Orange Point that Burkhart was connected with organized crime in Pittsburgh. He began his political career in Orange Point by serving on the local zoning board. In 1949 he served on a charter revision committee which succeeded in changing the form of government from mayor-council to council-manager.

Burkhart ran for the city council in 1951 as a member of a slate which included Barton and his son-in-law, George Kay, vice-president of the Orange Point Bank. The slate, strongly backed by Frank Barton, won the election. Although Kay had obtained the highest number of votes in the council election, and, by charter provision, should have become mayor, he stepped aside in favor of Burkhart.

Once elected to office, Burkhart proceeded to build a small-town political machine along classic lines. The machine was maintained by a series of friendships and obligations he built up: — friends were helped and enemies punished. City business and services became a series of favors which he could provide or not provide as he saw fit. If the trash behind a store was not picked up regularly or often enough, the storekeeper's chance of ameliorating this vexing problem would be considerably enhanced by calling Burkhart and asking for a favor. The man who wanted a street paving contract in Orange Point increased his chances of obtaining the contract by calling him. Contracting work for the city became a political prize to be captured by means of friendship with Burkhart. A number of contractors became staunch Burkhart supporters, and the contractors advised their employees to do the same.

The Burkhart machine was also supported by a Negro bloc vote. Bloc voting for the Burkhart machine is immediately apparent from even a cursory examination of election returns in Orange Point. For instance, in the 1959 primary election, Burkhart received 180 votes in the all-Negro precinct, and his running mate received 134 votes, while the opposing slate's two candidates received only 21 and 17 votes each.

Before Burkhart took office, Negroes did not vote in Orange Point elections. Burkhart, however, encouraged Negro registration and voting. Burkhart is not a transplanted "Northern liberal," nor is he an integrationist. Negro registration and voting were encouraged in order to build and maintain a political machine. Almost unanimous agreement prevailed among those interviewed that the Negro vote is a bought vote in Orange Point. The usual figure mentioned was two dollars a vote. Fish fries and election eve rallies where liquor flowed quite freely have been standard practices in the Negro section of the town.

The police were an important element in securing the Negro vote. During the period of Burkhart's control of the city from 1951 to 1959 no numbers racket raids were made in the Negro section of town. The police quietly campaigned for Burkhart among the Negroes. In 1959, when the Burkhart machine was seriously challenged, the Chief of Police stood at the entrance to the Negro polling place, which was in a combined fire and police station attached to the city hall, and openly asked the Negro voters to cast their ballots for Burkhart unless they wanted the Chief to lose his job.

In return for their votes, Orange Point's Negroes have received very little in the way of capital improvements. A few streets have been paved and lighted and a Negro recreation center was built. Most of the promises made to the Negro community, however, have not been kept. On the other hand, Negroes have received some protection from police interference and brutality. In a small Southern town protection from the police can be an enormous asset to the Negro community.

Burkhart is a working boss. Usually he is at city hall by six o'clock in the morning, and he stays all day. Apparently he knows more about the town than anyone else. He knows the routes of every trash truck. He knows where every water main is located. On any question that arises in Orange Point Burkhart normally can muster more facts and figures than anyone else in the community. Even Burkhart's opposition has had to admit that the man works very hard in his role as boss-mayor of Orange Point. Furthermore, everyone interviewed stated that Burkhart had accomplished many things which were beneficial to the community. It was Burkhart who built the new water plant and new city hall. Burkhart fought and won the battle for the dog track.

Some people in the community believe that Burkhart's strength as boss of Orange Point stems from the fact that he is retired and, therefore, can and does devote his full and undivided attention to running Orange Point. This explanation appears to have considerable validity. In a sense, Burkhart seems to have overwhelmed Orange Point with his energy. However, two other factors appear to have contributed strongly to the Burkhart bossdom. First, with the death of agriculture,

Orange Point became and has remained a fragmented community. The community is split in terms of its future, and no group, aside from the Burkhart clique, has emerged which would provide direction or leadership for the community. Neither the would-be industrializers, the retired, the real estate dealers, nor the business community were sufficiently committed to a specific set of goals to form a lasting opposition to the Burkhart regime. Second, we speculate, without actual supporting evidence, that race track money has backed the Burkhart machine. There is little question that Burkhart is tied to the track. When the possibility of the track being located in Orange Point was first brought into the open, Burkhart opposed the idea. He then made an abrupt switch and fought vigorously for the track against the strong opposition of the fundamentalist churches. The track issue was forced into a referendum where it won by a three-to-one margin. Burkhart negotiated for the city with the track backers. Aside from the head tax the city receives, the track provides its own trash and garbage collection. The track has proved to be an economic asset to Orange Point.

With the battle won in the referendum, Burkhart was put on the track's payroll as a "public relations" man. Burkhart is singularly unfit for this job as he totally lacks a sense of diplomacy. Many respondents believe that Burkhart's authority in Orange Point would never have been challenged if he had learned to say "no" graciously. Burkhart admitted that other track interests in the area tried to bribe him to stop the Orange Point track from coming into existence, and there is no reason to believe that the Orange Point track did not act in the same way. We would speculate that the race track interests would like to see a tame and controllable town as well as a tame and controllable police force and that Burkhart, as boss of Orange Point, could supply both of these.

The coalition between Burkhart and Barton was strained by 1955. Barton, however, did not openly oppose Burkhart, but rather appeared to have retired from politics for a time. Barton's break with Burkhart was apparently the culmination of an accumulation of many things. Burkhart was beginning to act dictatorially, and strong objection to his behavior was beginning to appear in the community. Aside from general irritation with Burkhart's arrogant behavior, Barton objected very strongly to one of Burkhart's schemes. Barton had donated a twenty acre site to the city to be used as a public park. Burkhart, however, determined that Burkhart Memorial Stadium should be constructed by the city as the most appropriate structure for the park. Barton vigorously opposed the expenditure of funds for the stadium, and apparently his opposition to the scheme developed enough pressure in the community to force a referendum on the issue of the stadium.

Although the vote went against the stadium, Burkhart decided that the referendum had been meaningless and proceeded to have plans drawn for the structure. Burkhart for a number of years had secretly set aside a reserve of money by failing to spend the entire annual street paving appropriation. Through this maneuver the city had about $200,000 available at the time of the referendum. Burkhart concluded, therefore, that the availability of the money prevented the referendum from being binding. Once the plans were drawn, construction began with the pouring of a concrete slab for rest room facilities. At this point opposition in the community became so strong and vociferous that Burkhart was forced to call a halt to the project.

The break between Barton and Burkhart became an open one in the 1957 election when George Kay, Barton's son-in-law, again was high man in the election but this time refused to step aside for Burkhart to take the post of mayor. In 1958 Burkhart's control of the city council slipped a little further when two non-Burkhart men were elected to the city council, and in 1959 Burkhart himself was beaten in the city council race by the slim margin of 25 votes. Burkhart's defeat can be attributed to the defection of some of his Negro supporters and to rather strong opposition in the white community to his position on a sewer issue.

In 1958 Burkhart became enamored with sewers. Everyone in Orange Point agrees that sewers — like mother and apple pie — are good, necessary, and American, and furthermore that the west side of the town cannot be developed without installing a sewer system. However, most of the population lives on the east side of town on the sand ridge where septic tanks work well. Consequently they did not wish to see their taxes go to the construction of a facility they did not themselves need.

Burkhart still had the $200,000 that he had intended to spend on the stadium, and he proposed to use this sum along with property assessments, to pay for the sewers. Strong opposition developed in the town to his proposal, and the anti-Burkhart candidates in the election vigorously criticized the sewer program.

Frank Barton took the anti-Burkhart forces into the Negro section of the community and introduced them to Negro leaders. Money was forthcoming from Barton and from the Orange Point Bank in which Barton holds an interest. Underlying the sewer issue there was a strong undercurrent of a simple "beat Burkhart" philosophy.

Burkhart's defeat left only one Burkhart supporter on the council, a senile politico, who everyone, including Burkhart, admitted took his orders from Burkhart but often became confused in their execution and voted the wrong way if the motion before the council was changed after he had received his voting instructions from Burkhart.

Although the Burkhart clique was left with only one representative in the council, the city clerk remained a strong Burkhart supporter. The new council realized that the clerk's loyalties ran to Burkhart and that she reported faithfully to Burkhart everything that occurred in City Hall, but the council did not believe that they could very well dispense with her. Burkhart had run Orange Point for eight years essentially as a one-man show, and the clerk was the only person who knew where any official papers or files could be found in City Hall. The council believed, and probably correctly, that if they discharged the clerk, chaos would result.

Between the 1959 and 1960 elections Burkhart constantly harassed the new council. He played upon their inexperience, ineptitude, and lack of unity. The new council had been united on only two things: the desire to take control of Orange Point from Burkhart's hands and their opposition to the sewer proposal. They lacked unity in the sense that they had no positive policy. In the 1960 election, again with solid Negro support, Burkhart and his slate were returned to office. Again he became mayor of Orange Point and held a three-to-two majority on the council.

Throughout the period of the Burkhart bossdom, Orange Point, by charter regulation, had a council-manager form of government. In terms of charter provisions Orange Point's council-manager system differs very little from that of other cities operating under the same form of government. The charter, adopted in 1950, created a council of five, all elected by popular vote for a two-year term. Three councilmen are elected in even-numbered years and two in odd-numbered years. The man who receives the highest vote each year is by custom supposed to take the post of mayor. The council uses a number of committees to oversee specific functions of city administration. The council normally has committtees on finance, streets, fire and police, parks and recreation, and utilities.

The city manager in Orange Point is charged with supervising and coordinating the work of the department heads, although the council rather than the manager has the final authority for selection of department heads. The manager, however, does have the legal authority to fire department heads. Although charter provisions are important in the sense that they structure the broad institutional framework within which the political process operates, it is the political life of the community which shapes the role played by the officeholders under the city charter. In Orange Point the actual roles of the mayor, the council, and the city manager appear to have been structured more by the fact of bossdom than by the provisions of the city charter.

When Burkhart served as the mayor of Orange Point, the office of the mayor was the single most important position in the city government. When Burkhart did not hold the office, its status significantly declined. Orange Point had three mayors from 1957 to 1960: Kay, Becker, and Brown. None of the three men had significantly greater roles in Orange Point's government than any of the other councilmen. In a similar manner, the actual role played by the city manager under the Burkhart regime was far different from the role played by the manager after Burkhart lost control of the city council. The role of the city manager in Orange Point under Burkhart approached that of an errand boy. With the defeat of Burkhart, the role played by the manager somewhat approached the role normally assumed to be appropriate for a city manager.

The life of a city manager in Orange Point has been short and normally unhappy. Between 1950 and 1960 the city had eight managers. According to the city charter, a manager was subjected to a six months' trial period, during which period he could be fired without a public hearing. Burkhart's standard operating practice during this period was to fire managers before their six-month probationary period expired. During the interval between firing one city manager and hiring another, the city clerk, who was a Burkhart protégé, would become the acting city manager and handle the "inside" work at City Hall while Burkhart would supervise the "outside" work. The period between the firing of one city manager and the hiring of another apparently was as long as political considerations would permit.

The physical facilities at City Hall during the Burkhart period tell a great deal about the role of a manager in Orange Point. During the Burkhart period the manager did not have an office of his own but had his desk in a large "bull pen" type of room, with the desk of the city clerk on one side and Burkhart's desk on the other. This arrangement obviously left no room for privacy. The City Hall had only two telephone lines into it. If both were in use, there was no way for citizens to reach the police or fire department except by calling a neighboring community and asking it to radio the message to an Orange Point police car. No way existed to insure the privacy of a telephone call, for anyone could pick up an extension phone. An ex-city manager stated that when he wanted to make a private call, he would go outside of City Hall and use the pay phone at the side of the police station.

Burkhart viewed city managers as "flunkies." He believed he knew what should be done in Orange Point and apparently believed that no man with the title of city manager attached to his name could possibly make correct decisions in Orange Point. Burkhart rationalized his position by stating that the city, because of its low salary scale, could only attract youngsters just coming out of school, or the retired and incompetent. Orange Point, then, could only be a training ground for the beginning manager, and Burkhart would be the trainer. Burkhart's reply to a difference of opinion between himself and a city manager was that if at any time a manager does not know how to do something, "By God, I'm going to tell him how to do it, because *I know how to do it.*"

There was unanimous agreement in Orange Point concerning the reason for the high turnover of its city managers. That reason was Burkhart. Given Burkhart's political domination of Orange Point, his almost unlimited interest in everything that went on in the city, and his firm belief that Orange Point was his city, no city manager, whether professional or amateur, could exist for any length of time. Of the eight city managers in Orange Point between 1950 and 1960, three were professionals who lasted no longer than the amateurs.

By 1958 Orange Point's city managership had turned over six times in seven years, although one of these was a voluntary termination. In 1958 Orange Point was again without a manager, and Burkhart approached Robert Franks, who was an assistant to the city manager in a neighboring community, and offered Franks the job of manager of Orange Point. Franks accepted, and claims to have gone to Orange Point with his "eyes open." The newspapers in the surrounding communities had covered the comings and goings of Orange Point's city managers rather thoroughly. Simply reading the local newspapers would have informed Franks of the Orange Point situation.

The Burkhart machine was in trouble by 1958. Dissatisfaction with Burkhart's high-handed operations was growing. In 1957 the Hawthorne Fabricating Company had investigated Orange Point with the thought of locating a sizeable plant in the city. After conversations with Burkhart, the company had decided to locate at Red Snapper Beach instead. There were persistent rumors in town that either Burkhart's overbearing attitude had driven the company away or that Burkhart had tried to "shake down" the company for money payments. Barton had broken with Burkhart, and Kay had refused to step aside and allow Burkhart to become mayor following the 1957 election. Finally Franks appeared on the scene as an efficient manager and, from our point of view, a good politician. Franks, almost immediately after taking office, began to undercut Burkhart's control of Orange Point, for Franks began to regularize city services. The Burkhart machine thrived on favors, and Franks' operation eliminated the opportunities for favoritism. No longer did the store owners have to call Burkhart to have their trash picked up. They could call Franks and, not only get the trash picked up, but also have some assurance of regular service. Franks grew in popularity in Orange Point, and Burkhart came to the conclusion rather quickly that Franks had to leave. Apparently, however, Burkhart believed that Franks was so dangerous that the ordinary firing procedure was not appropriate. Accordingly, a complicated plot was hatched to get rid of Franks. The necessity for the plot rather than a simple, quiet, behind-closed-doors firing (Franks was still in his probationary period) was a good indication that politically Burkhart was slipping.

Arthur Bane, the city's recreation director and a Burkhart man, was put to work digging into Franks' past and watching him. Franks had written a novel about gangs in the slums of Los Angeles, which appeared in paperback with the usual amount of sex on the front cover and in the book. Bane was to have stood up in the local Baptist Church and have denounced authors of pornographic literature. Bane had persuaded Mrs. Kay to rise at this point and ask if he had read Franks' book, thereby suggesting that it was pornographic. Kay returned to town before the dramatic event could occur as planned and, realizing the nature of the conspiracy afoot, kept Mrs. Kay away from the church. But the newspapers had been informed that something was scheduled to "break" that Sunday morning and had sent reporters to the church. When Bane rose in church to make his remarks about pornographic literature, there was no ally present to carry the plot through. The newspaper reporters pressed Bane, but he became evasive. Bane finally consulted with Burkhart outside of the church and then gave the Franks story to the press. In addition to the open accusations made to the press questioning Franks' moral standards, there were other accusations made in private, which were never substantiated, that Franks was merely using Orange Point as a stepping stone to attempt the ouster of the manager of a neighboring city, High Acres, and his own succession to that managership. A series of closed council meetings was held, and Franks was fired.

After Franks was fired, the Burkhart crowd decided it would be safer to obtain a home town boy as city manager. Frank Short, a retired businessman, applied for the job. Short had no experience in government; his only experience in management was as the owner of a small trucking line in Iowa. Short worked a year under Burkhart and then worked against Burkhart in the election campaign in 1959.

The anti-Burkhart forces that captured the city council in 1959 were unhappy with Short. He was not bright — he could not remember things from one day to another, and was a constant source of embarrassment to the new council. He presented the budget to the council without having the slightest knowledge of its internal composition. Apparently all of the new council members would have liked to fire Short, but the city managership had been an issue in the 1959 campaign, and they did not believe it would be politically feasible to fire him. The new council did, however, get rid of Burkhart's recreation director and his Chief of Police. Their decision to retain his city clerk was made in part as a result of their recognition of the incompetence of the city manager.

In 1960 when Burkhart and his slate returned to office, he fired Short. Burkhart has refused to appoint a city manager and has taken over that position himself. In his public statements he has made clear that he believes the preceding administration left the city in a chaotic state, and that he will not appoint a city manager until the mess in Orange Point is cleaned up. Burkhart is both mayor and city manager of Orange Point, despite charter provisions prohibiting such combination.

Manager tenure in Orange Point is fairly easily explained. Orange Point's first city manager was fired when the Burkhart clique took control of City Hall. During the Burkhart period one manager retired voluntarily because of ill health. Five managers were fired by Burkhart. Finally, the latest city manager — Short — was fired when the Burkhart clique returned to power in 1960. There is little doubt that Short would have been fired by the anti-Burkhart forces when they captured City Hall if it had been politically feasible. The anti-Burkhart forces, however, had their hands tied by their own ideological commitments. It is an enlightening commentary on council-manager government and politics in Orange Point that the manager who achieved the longest tenure record was judged by everyone to be grossly incompetent.

III

To guess at Orange Point's political future is like crystal-ball gazing, a highly uncertain occupation. It is probably safe to assume that as long as Burkhart has control of City Hall, he will keep the managership for himself as a much simpler arrangement than to go to the trouble of hiring and firing managers, as formerly. Of course, there is always the possibility that a member of the Burkhart clique will be given the post of manager. But long tenure for another person in the manager post would be hard to imagine, for Burkhart apparently looks upon any individual with the title of city manager as a potential threat to his authority.

One can expect Burkhart's machine to break down when he passes from the political scene. Burkhart has run his organization as a one-man show. No leadership appears to exist below him.

If this analysis is correct, then the political stability which Orange Point possessed during the early and middle years of the Burkhart regime will probably pass with the passing of Burkhart. Given the very difficult problem of economic survival which Orange Point must face, we would assume that political instability and its attendant managerial instability will be the rule in Orange Point.

3

Floriana

Floriana, a food processing center, takes its name from its agricultural origin. The fruit marketing carried on extensively until just a few years ago has now declined in importance. It was a cotton center in the nineteenth-century before citrus became Florida's most important agricultural commodity. Because of its agricultural connections, Floriana was early linked by rail to the major Florida cities, especially to the core city of the Standard Metropolitan Area in which Floriana is located.

Although the town traces its history to an Indian village connected with tobacco growing, its modern history dates from the period of cotton culture and its present name from the time the railroad was built through the town. It was incorporated in 1885. Despite such catastrophes as a yellow fever epidemic and a great fire, each of which nearly destroyed the town, it recovered and grew slowly and undramatically. In 1960 it had a population in excess of 15,000, a gain of some 6,000 over its 1950 population, but almost half of this gain came from an annexation in the middle of the decade.

In appearance Floriana belies what one should logically expect of its name. It is a town of unredeemed ugliness and in its appearance is fairly typical of a number of central Florida agricultural processing towns. The downtown not only lacks architectural distinction but has unusually narrow crowded streets for a small city. But to say that Floriana is ugly hardly does it justice, despite the accuracy of that description for its residential and downtown areas. Civic pride and some appreciation for the values of contemporary architecture have induced Floriana to construct, away from the center of the city, a city hall and a public library that far surpass in esthetic value those of almost any other Florida city of approximately the same size.

The surrounding countryside consists largely of the grove lands common to central Florida, but it is marred by extensive limerock operations that are, in general, always disfiguring to a countryside. Commercially Floriana is tied more closely to a town three times its size located only eleven miles to the east than it is to the very much greater metropolitan city lying twenty-two miles to the west in the same county with Floriana. Possibly this reversal of the usual set of ties is due to a feeling of kinship by essentially country people for their counterparts in another agricultural processing center rather than the "city slicker" types of "Sin City," their larger neighbor. There is nothing in the entire area around or within Floriana to attract tourists.

The economy of Floriana today rests on two very different industries: food processing and limerock mining. Several large out-of-state food processors operate sizeable plants in the town and, indeed, contribute to the town's problems in the form of industrial wastes as well as to its employment. The original fruit which gave the town some early note is still grown in the environs of Floriana and still marketed in the town, but with lesser significance today in the town's economy.

The 1950 census shows that the part of the labor force in manufacturing remained almost the same as in the previous decade although the total labor force grew about as much as the population. During the decade of 1950–1960 the total number in manufacturing doubled. Approximately one-fifth of all workers now are employed in manufacturing, primarily in several fairly large food processing plants. There is one small steel fabricating plant. Only 13 per cent of the total labor force is engaged in agriculture.

Floriana merchants, however, are distressed by the city's failure to grow as a shopping center. But for Floriana this is understandable. For one thing, it is a unit in one of the state's largest Standard Metropolitan Areas, only twenty-two miles by four-lane highway from the central core city of this area. As previously mentioned, another fair-sized city with several large shopping centers is only eleven miles away on the new interstate highway. To offset the two pulls away from Floriana, the local retail merchants division of the Chamber of Comerce has tried to push a "Buy in Floriana" campaign.

Two banks, a savings and loan bank, and the local branch of the electric utility company of the area constitute the principal business offices in town. There is a weekly newspaper.

Realtors play little or no part in the community's economy; developers, as such, are vitually unknown. The lack of a number of these persons sizeable enough to constitute an interest group has had marked results in the political programs undertaken by Floriana. Not the least of these results, which will be referred to later, has been the absence of organized opposition to the construction of public housing units for both white and colored tenants. The lack of a real estate-developer "axis" is most unusual for a Florida town.

The people of Floriana show a population-age distribution close to the norm for the state, with only 11 per cent sixty-five years of age or older. This is no retirement town, as it is no tourist town. Negroes make up 28.9 per cent of the population and for the most part find employment in limerock quarrying as well as in farm labor.

Like most small towns, Floriana has its leading family, which has long controlled the older of two banks in town — the County Bank — the leading insurance agency, and in the past the Chamber of Commerce. The same family has provided the city with a mayor, a circuit judge, and several attorneys. The money of this family was derived from citrus groves and its bank, the only one in Floriana able to weather the Depression. Such "aristocracy" as is represented by this family, the Thomases, embraces the older families of the town, a few professional men, and some of the retail merchants. They are quiet, sedate, and for the most part pillars of the town's leading churches.

However, a social as well as economic and political polarization has taken place around the leadership of a newer bank, the Floriana National Bank. Led by an industrial building contractor whose principal work and income are not in the town, the Floriana Bank "crowd" embraces a younger group of businessmen who not only wish to push industrialization but who also represent 90 per cent of the membership of the local country club.

II

Although Floriana is a council-manager town, its charter is somewhat different in structural details both from the Model City Charter and from other Florida manager charters. There are five council members elected at large on a nonpartisan ballot for three-year overlapping terms that run on a 2-2-1 schedule. Temporarily, following the 1955 large-scale annexation undertaken by the city, two additional council seats were created, for one term only, to represent the newly annexed areas. The major charter difference, however, lies in the provisions for selection of a mayor. This is done annually in Floriana by a separate popular election followed the council election, with the names of all five councilmen placed on the mayoral ballot. By custom, and obviously by pre-arragement prior to 1960, all but one of the councilmen made it known publicly that they were not interested in being mayor, and the vote distrubution typically reflected these facts. The occasional contest for mayor, apparently for purely personal reasons of *amour-propre*, was considered not "cricket." But in 1960 intensive competition started for the mayor's post.

The office of mayor under the charter is not powerful, as the mayor's principal duty is presiding over the council for the short term of one year. In practice, however, the mayors of Floriana until 1960 tended to be re-elected for a number of consecutive terms, a fact which reflected their leadership over policy.

The council selects a city attorney and a municipal judge as well as the city manager. All executive departments except that of law are responsible to the manager. The city owns and operates its own water system and formerly owned its own gas distribution system. The charter gives the manager power to make all executive appointments under him with the approval of the council, which is given virtually automatically.

The manager of Floriana, Elmer Sands, is a local man without much formal education or any work experience outside Floriana who worked his way up from a bookkeeper position. He has been city manager for twenty-two years, an almost phenomenal length of time to hold a city managership except for the significant circumstances of Sands' local origin and his acceptability to Floriana's ruling group.

Who does what on policy proposals in Floriana is not an easy question to unravel simply because the perceptions of different actors in the process of policy-making differ. According to Manager Sands, both he and the council members initiate policy. Sands claimed to bring up policy proposals in private conversation with council members and publicly at council meetings, when he presents major alternatives and gives the relevant facts about each. One councilman, a relative newcomer on that body, saw the manager as a man who "knows everything that is going on and sort of runs the council." In contrast, the Chamber of Commerce president saw Sands in a negative role, as the chief veto-wielder, a "nay-sayer," frequently killing new ideas because he has not changed with the times. The local utility district manager, however, saw Manager Sands not as a policy originator but as an executor of plans that originated with the mayor or the council.

In the public relations process of promoting a new policy, Manager Sands, by his own admission, plays no part, nor does he think he should. His claim is that he leaves public relations to the mayor and council. His public recommendation to vote "yes" on sale of the city-owned gas utility was exceptional, but this question was apparently "safe" anyway, with a low turnout and lop-sided majority. Sands also claimed, apparently accurately, that he had never encouraged people to run for the council. The most he admitted doing of a political nature was to let a few friends know privately how he "felt" on specific candidates for council. Candidates have solicited his aid during election campaigns, but Sands claimed to have consistently rebuffed them. "I make the budget," Sands has stated categorically. Actually this statement requires considerable qualification. The manager, prior to 1960, reviewed departmental estimates, put them together into a tentative budget, and discussed this informally with the council in four or five private meetings. When the budget finally went before a public meeting of the council, it was routinely adopted. But in 1960 Manager Sands sat informally with the council to obtain their proposals on various items. Then he collated these proposals with the usual departmental estimates and held one private meeting with the council before the public adoption meeting. The manager claimed to have dropped some council-sponsored items from "his" budget, but it was not clear whether these would or did get back into the final budget as adopted.

Floriana has had a fairly strong tradition against interference by either the mayor or the council with the manager's day-to-day administration. "That's Sands' job," all councilmen agree. The manager confirmed this attitude, but he did describe the problem some new councilmen have presented to him when they failed to understand this delegation, particularly with respect to personnel matters and complaints. The manager has been able to hold both employees and council to acceptance of him as the exchange center for communication with the other.

Although it is difficult to characterize the way Sands plays the role of manager, he appears to be a status-quo-preserver and idea-smotherer, playing his policy role principally in non-initiation of policy ideas. During a weak mayoralty, he gives to new councilmen the impression of "running" the council. But in relative terms the Floriana councils have probably been for years councils that wanted to preserve the fiscal and substantive status quo. As a result, Sands has reflected council negativism. During an occasional strong mayoralty, Sands has associated himself with the mayor, both for implementation and braking of mayoral ideas. Although Manager Sands is reported by his supporters to be a "darling," as having "a way with people," and a man who "knows Floriana government through having risen from the ranks," the impression still persists that one of his major functions is that of fiscal nay-sayer or "not-so-much"-sayer.

III

The question of the kind of town Floriana is to be was presumably settled a long time ago in a way not typical of most Florida towns in the same area of the state. To Florianans tourism or a retirement colony never appeared to offer any real alternatives that entered into any discussion of the town's destiny. In modern times the town was never visualized as anything but an agricultural marketing-processing and limerock quarrying center. What else could there be?

The question of town destiny became more than theoretical to some of the younger, more aggressive Chamber of Commerce members in Floriana. Indeed, several years ago visions of other types of desirable industry began to dance in their eyes like the visions of sugar plums in the dreams of Dr. Clement Moore's toddlers the night before Christmas. So obsessive have these "visions" become that today the persistent line of political demarcation in the town has become the division into those who are well satisfied with the present industrial growth and want to move very slowly and cautiously in any other direction, and those who want to diversify industrially and search aggressively for substantial, clean industrial prospects in order to grow more rapidly in economy and in population. In other words, the differences between these two groups are merely differences of degree and not of utterly disharmonious concepts.

The internal politics of the Chamber of Commerce shows in microcosm the political division of the city itself. Long dominated by the County Bank executives and the retail merchants' division, essentially a group of older men, the Chamber was entirely satisfied with the food processors' dominance in the town and the processors' methods. But the newer Floriana National Bank recruited as its financial group the younger and more ambitious downtown merchants not entirely happy with the existing state of business in town. Acting as an aggressive faction within the Chamber, they established a Development Committee to stimulate an active campaign for additional industry. An important addition to the group was the local manager of the electric utility company who was quite naturally interested in new industrial customers. Their push to take over the Chamber culminated in capturing the presidency and the recruitment of a new secretary, an aggressive young native son who had worked on the staff of the United States Chamber of Commerce in Washington and was induced to return to Floriana.

Other conflicts that may be perceived as "problems" and as interrelated with the basic one of speed and type of industrialization are: (1) sanitary disposal of industrial wastes from the food canneries, and (2) getting a younger, better-educated manager more attuned to the aggressive younger businessmen. The first of those emerged as a full-blown problem during the summer of 1960, raised, surprisingly enough, by the Chamber of Commerce. Manager Sands tried to postpone action on the second by hiring a young assistant manager in 1960–61. Inevitably, the second "problem" will break out into the open if the political group in favor of more rapid industrialization gets a clear majority on the council.

Among the current issues before the town, the one that has caused most stir and revealed the dichotomy in its politics has been the controvery over disposal of industrial wastes that broke out in the summer of 1960. The *Floriana Citizen*'s headline of its story of this controversy was: "Industrial Waste in City Canals Creates Long, Hot Discussion — Odors, Health Hazard, Cost of Correcting Bring Hassle." Another parallel story was headlined: "Mayor Is Opposed to Tough Attitude." A meeting of the city council with a firm of consulting engineers employed by the city was attended by the members of the Development Committee of the Floriana Chamber of Commerce. The engineers in their remarks preliminary to a discussion of a new master sewer plan described the unattractiveness of the canals loaded with decaying vegetable and citrus wastes. But in the heat of the debate their description triggered off they never got to present their sewer plan. Instead, Chamber of Commerce Development Committee members referred to bacteriological reports they had which established the existence of a health menace.

The industrial wastes must be put through a special treatment plant or process before the waste can be discharged into the canals, if the present health risks and nuisance of bad odors are to be eliminated. The existing sewage treatment plant at Floriana cannot handle this type of waste, which is essentially liquid garbage, and the construction of a special treatment plant by the city alone would place an excessive financial burden on local property owners in the opinion of all persons concerned in this dispute. The Development Committee spokesman and the Chamber executive secretary voiced two other solutions: (1) construction of treatment facilities by the food processors entirely at their expense, or (2) construction of special treatment facilities by the city on a cost-sharing basis with the food processors. As the argument grew warmer, the councilmen and engineers warned that several central Florida cities which had tried to make food processors conform to strict waste disposal regulations had lost their plants. The Chamber spokesmen countered with a double-barreled set of arguments to the effect that they were sure local industries would take a "reasonable" attitude and be willing to share costs and that the city's existing lack of policy on industrial waste was obstructive to the Chamber's efforts to attract new industry. The Chamber claimed that it needed an explicit policy it could explain to new industrial prospects in order to push ahead with its "development" program.

Because this dispute broke out openly during the summer, the mayor could postpone any effort to come to grips with it until the end of the vacation period. This he did. But some considerable delay, with lengthy discussions preceding disposition, was in accord with his temperament as well as his sense of political timing.

The industrial waste controversy both epitomized and illustrated the nature of the political cleavage in Floriana. The stand taken by the Chamber of Commerce executive secretary and the Chamber of Commerce Devolpment Committee was that of the aggressive, "go-faster-with-industrialization" groups polarized around the Floriana National Bank. The slower, more cautious, "don't-let's-rock-the-boat" stand of the mayor and of Manager Sands also, were characteristic of the older County Bank crowd whose spiritual leaders were the Thomas family of Floriana.

This controversy was not without irony. Normally local Chambers of Commerce do their best to stop public measures that regulate business interests. But Floriana's aggressive young Chamber manager called for strong anti-pollution measures. The city government defended, if not the right to pollute, at least a policy of going slow against pollution. The Chamber attitude and that of the Floriana National Bank supporters of the Chamber's stand seem explicable only in terms of attachment of great value to an explicit policy on waste to assist in the Chamber's No. 1 objective for the town — rapid industrialization. This was a case of "first things coming first," as the Chamber saw it. Therefore, the Committee, in effect, by opening up the whole debate publicly, tried to force a policy decision quickly. City councilmen indicated privately that they were prepared to go "halfway" on solution of this problem in trying to work out some kind of cost-sharing formula to finance the necessary disposal facilities.

But there was more than met the eye in this issue as far as the Chamber executive secretary was concerned. Some persons on the city council and in local business believed he had made an error in judgment in calling for the city to abolish pollution. Presumably he was stating an extremist, publicly popular position from which the Development Committee could recede and still get at least "half a loaf" in concrete achievement as well as in clear policy. The very extremity of the secretary's position would make an ultimate agreement very attractive to local industry even if it had to pay part of the disposal costs. In the meantime the city council had been "boxed" by the extremity of the Chamber's position. Also some of the County Bank slate on the council might lose their seats in the next election because of their "tenderness" to industry on this issue. But these were the fairly obvious advantages that might accrue from the secretary's leadership.

Another motive of the executive secretary may well have been to secure the managership for himself. At best, Sands thought that the Chamber secretary was "measuring himself for size" in the city manager's office, and some of the County Bank slate on the council — perhaps prompted by Sands — echoed this impression. The secretary could very well appeal to the Floriana National Bank crowd, if they ever got a majority on the council, as college-educated, young, aggressive, articulate, policy-oriented in the direction of their own values of a speeded-up industrialization.

Other issues in Floriana may be viewed in two ways. In local terms there are no real issues in Floriana. "It's personality differences that matter," or "We have our disagreements, but they're not *that* serious," were standard local descriptions of town attitudes on issues. In our terms, as a study team, we perceived some real issues which became more overt beginning in 1959. The usual way to get elected before the 1959 election had been to announce for office in a set of innocuous statements carried in the local weekly paper and then rely on one's friends to carry on a telephone campaign.

Some Florianans believe that the traditionally issueless campaigns have been socially functional rather than dysfunctional. For example, the district manager of the electric utility, also an influential member of the Chamber of Commerce Development Committee, stated as his belief that campaigns centered on issues lead to "knock-down and drag-out" fights that would not die down after election day but produce sharp and lasting divisions in a town too small to endure them. By implication, an issue politics is possible and possibly functional only in jurisdictions where the contestants have little likelihood of confronting each other face to face. *Vide* Aristotle and Plato. Is Floriana a truncated *polis?* Can those persons be all wrong who believe that issue politics, especially when carried out through parties with definite platforms, tends to insure more impersonal campaigns?

Zoning is a relatively new concept to Floriana. The city did not have a zoning ordinance until 1954 and certainly shows it. As Mrs. Marlow, the former owner-publisher of the *Floriana Citizen* puts it, "When I want to show out-of-town guests a nice neighborhood in Floriana, I hardly know where to take them." According to Manager Sands, the present zoning system was laid out by a planning consultant hired by the city for that purpose. This was prior to the extensive annexation program, and the zoning system has not changed since annexation. Zoning was reported noncontroversial, but Mrs. Marlow, the city manager, and others admitted that the council had been lax in granting requests for variances. Finally the council created a separate Planning and Zoning Board to hear such cases and do the detailed work on them, thereby "taking the heat" off themselves.

Since this board was established several years ago, the number of variances granted has dropped.

No subdivision regulations have been adopted in Floriana.

The planning and zoning board is also expected to develop ideas for long-range planning of the town. Its major present focus has been the zoning of lands adjacent to Interstate Highway E (which runs roughly parallel to and inside the northern boundary of the city) and the access approaches between Floriana and the highway. Both bank groups appeared to be interested in zoning this area, but the battle lines had not yet been drawn as to what types of zoning restrictions each group wanted: commercial of a particular type, light industrial, landscaped parkway, etc.

Floriana had not developed a so-called "master plan" for town development despite the fact that an industrial park had been set aside, and there had been considerable effort to get public buildings out of the most congested downtown areas. No one as yet talked in any terms beyond mere zoning.

As indicated above, a public housing program was established in Floriana with no controversial overtones. This step was taken in 1957 and involved clearing about thirty acres, condemning 105 sub-standard units, and building 200 units in four projects, two for whites and two for Negroes. The city attorney was especially influential in moving this project along to completion, both through special influence he had with the local Congressman and through effective speaking before local civic clubs in support of the program. The mayor appointed to membership on the housing board a group of people who worked together especially harmoniously. At no time did local "slum lords" or realtors appear before the council to object to public housing. The council members and manager appeared to be well satisfied with the new housing project, as the old shacks had yielded virtually no taxes, and the payments in lieu of taxes from the housing project represented a gain of at least five times the old "take," a far greater amount than the council had anticipated.

Manager and councilmen were all inarticulate in explaining the absence of controversy over this housing project. It is possible to speculate along several lines. One is that in the absence of a potent realtor lobby in Floriana, there are no respected or feared community leaders to distribute virulent propaganda, pay for newspaper advertising, and generally "scream" against socialism. The slum landlords were apparently not powerful because they were not substantial property owners and, therefore, not to be taken seriously by the city council, which has been impressed only by those persons it considered to represent substantial property interests. Furthermore, the slum properties were yielding very little revenue to the city, and all interests were impressed by the need to increase the revenue from impoverished parts of town, especially when most of the cost for such revenue raising could come from federal income taxes rather than property in Floriana. Finally, the metropolitan core city has long had several sizeable successful public housing projects which may have impressed Florianans favorably. In any event, the city is now moving ahead with "221" urban renewal low cost housing.

As with most cities, property assessment and millage are both rather serious problems. Floriana has no control over its property assessment because that is not done locally in Eastern County, but rather it is done centrally by the county assessor for all municipalities within the county. The assessment level was 50 per cent of market value. Floriana had no interest in either re-assessment or an across-the-board increase in the assessment ratio, despite the fact that the city had reached its maximum permissible millage under the charter. Another municipality in the county pushed for an increase in the assessment ratio, and in 1960 the county assessor gave a blanket raise to 60 per cent of market value.

About 60 per cent of the homes of Floriana were considered below the "break-even" point by the city manager and mayor. This, in view of the homestead exemption of the first $5,000 from ad valorem real estate taxes for owner-occupied homes (granted by the Florida Constitution) meant that these homes yielded little or no taxes to meet the costs of services rendered. The sensitivity of the city council, dominated by the retail merchants, to the issue of revenue levels is certainly understandable. But the council also represented some of the larger property owners tied to the County Bank. In contrast, the Floriana National Bank clique reacted more affirmatively to an increase in revenues and spending and mentioned the need for inventiveness in popularizing these steps with the public.

The biggest thing that had happened to Floriana during the decade of the Fifties was the annexation of an area inhabited by 2,500. As is usual in Florida, this move first required special legislation, in this case to provide for a referendum in both the city and the annexed area. Eastern County's three representatives were for this special bill, but the state senator was persuaded with difficulty. The bill differed from most in Florida in its provision for a single vote in the entire area — city and annexation area — to determine the outcome. The city won by a vote of 1178 to 737. The annexed area was temporarily granted two extra councilmen to ease the transition. In the 1956 city election the two new councilmen from the annexed area ran against the long-time mayor and a city councilman and defeated them. All persons interviewed coincided in attributing the outcome of this election to resentment by the voters in the annexed area against the vigorous advocacy of annexation by the two defeated councilmen. During the ensuing regular three-year council term one of these new councilmen was co-opted into the County Bank group and, in turn, received its nod for election support in 1959. The other new councilman, who was generally characterized as a "misfit," too outspoken, and a "chronic obstructionist," did not seek re-election.

Although Florianans interested in their local politics describe the annexation and its political aftermath as a straight-out fight between "insiders" and "outsiders," there was no answer available as to why the County Bank clique, firmly in the saddle in 1954–55, wanted the annexation program in the first instance. One hypothesis is that this bank group perhaps wanted to get the town into a new census bracket which might make real estate mortgages more inviting to insurance companies and other potential purchasers of such paper. The city then supplied fire protection service free to residents outside its limits. It still gives this service today, especially to the homes of "downtown people," who through their business connection are deemed to have a stake in Floriana. The present officials of Floriana all concurred in a belief that lands in the annexed area were underassessed and still are underassessed, but it must be remembered that property assessment has since 1946 been administered by the county assessor. Therefore, the status of assessment was in no wise changed by annexation. Furthermore, as has been mentioned earlier, Floriana officials have not displayed any interest in pushing the county assessor into a higher assessment ratio. Another plausible explanation is that perhaps the County Bank clique foresaw with the new bank industrialization and hoped for support from the resident voters in the newly annexed area, who were mainly rural or low- to middle-income residential, to slow down the rate of projected or feared industrialization.

Eastern County leaders, including its legislative delegation, have had some interest in county home rule. This interest has had repercussions in Floriana politics through the influence of one of the county legislators who practices law in Floriana and who has ties with the Floriana National Bank clique. Two members of the council in 1959, when the county home rule question first emerged, were personally friendly with this legislator and publicly supported him, even with reservations, on the county home rule question. The County Bank faction, however, has been openly and flatly against county home rule. In the 1959 councilmanic campaign, the support of home rule by the former of the two councilmen mentioned was twisted by his opponents into having been intended as support for a "Metro" (federalist) arrangement of the Dade County type, which is intensely disliked by everybody in Floriana. The second of the two councilmen referred to above did not think that the Floriana National Bank clique really sponsored county home rule but that this had just been inferred from the fact that the legislator sponsoring such home rule served as attorney for the bank. The legislator, according to this councilman, simply pushed hard for county home rule to perfect his ties with the county court house crowd and his fellow legislators from Eastern County. Others, however, like the mayor, do believe that there is a tie between the Floriana National Bank clique and county home rule and that this is not just political gamesmanship by the legislator. The legislator is assumed by many in Floriana to have become a county-wide man — that is, with appeal to the large central core city electorate. Although he had indicated some desire to run for Congress as soon as Eastern County could get a seat of its own in the new congressional redistricting, when the seat was allocated, another legislator beat him to the filing. Therefore, his stand on county home rule may have been real political gamesmanship for rather high stakes, with little serious intention of upsetting any Floriana arrangements.

Although city officials describe the city as having sewers in 95 per cent of its area, this figure is not entirely accurate, as they admit that the area annexed in 1955 has not been extensively provided with sewers. Also "isolated" houses are admittedly not on sewers. Where sewers have been built, sewer rentals are assessed against all adjacent property owners, whether they continue to use septic tanks or not. There is a sewage treatment plant that is rapidly approaching capacity and whose future expansion is tied in with the industrial waste problem described above. Storm sewers are provided only in the business district and a few residential areas. A twelve-inch rainfall during a thirty-six hour period in March 1960 caused extensive flooding. Little except talk ensued by way of corrective measures to prevent such flooding in the future.

Streets in the residential areas are in rather poor condition. Until recently the city paving was done on the formula of the city bearing one-third of the cost and assessing two-thirds against adjacent property owners. The city recently changed the formula to one-fourth city, three-fourths property owners, and this has effectively stopped requests for paving. Curbing or guttering is not usual on residential streets. Subdivision developers within the city have been required, since the beginning of 1960, to put in water mains, sewers, and residential paving. They must build the cost of these improvements into the sales price of their houses.

Floriana has only modest aspirations to be a tourist center. During the winter of 1959–60 only 300 tourists registered. These people had come mainly from northern agricultural areas and wanted a "quiet place" (also, no doubt, an inexpensive one) to stop. As to retirees, there are possibly about 150 retired families in Floriana living on incomes of around $250 per month. According to the mayor, they are not active in politics. The city has moved only slightly into a retirees' recreation program. The manager declared that Floriana retirees have their own ideas about city government, for he had obviously felt the effect of "sidewalk superintendents," and he was pessimistic that retirees might have the same effect on Floriana in the future as they had had on other nearby cities taken over by them.

On such matters as race, religion, labor relations, and northerners vs. southerners, Floriana has no obvious problems. Negroes comprise nearly 30 per cent of the population but have only recently manifested any interest in governmental activities. Estimates of Negro registrants in city elections ranged from 5 per cent to 15 per cent of the total. But it is clear that this bloc is growing and was first appealed to successfully by the Floriana National Bank clique candidates beginning in 1959. Negroes occasionally show up at council meetings requesting improvement, and by 1960 they started something of a push for a Negro Flor-Teen (teen-age) recreation program. The council reacted favorably to this in order to head off any alternative push for an integrated parks and playground attempt. Up to the summer of 1960, no attempts at lunch counter sit-ins or other integration activities had been made by Floriana Negroes. As the discussion of public housing had indicated, Negroes have received a share of such units, and there seems to have been no attempt or desire to discriminate against them.

Other blocs are nonexistent. Only about 10 per cent of the population is Catholic, and no Catholic has ever run for the council. No North vs. South feeling exists, as tourism and retirees are too unimportant to make a difference in sectional cleavage. Consequently there is no Republican vs. Democrat feud. Indeed, Republicanism is totally missing from Floriana politics. Similarly, there is no labor bloc, for although a substantial portion of the people around Floriana are laborers, the area is largely open shop. Organizers have tried unsuccessfully to organize the citrus processing plants and a steel fabrication plant, the latter having the largest payroll in the city and being presided over by a former city councilman. The labor efforts in the steel plant went to an election which the union lost. Although the limerock quarrying industry has experienced some labor turmoil in the past, little interest in labor organization seems to motivate the Floriana workers in it.

The general placidity on such questions as those just cited extends to the form of government. According to both mayor and manager.

there has been no serious attempt to change from council-manager government. The mayor recalled that many years before there were some people against the system but that had not been true for years. "We like it," he declared categorically.

Sin, too, is no issue in Floriana despite the existence of a spicy reputation for the nearby central city. Floriana has practically no bolita (numbers) operations, and no one gets excited over "friendly games" at the fraternal lodges. The church element is against Sunday liquor sales, which are decided by referendum in justice of the peace districts. Floriana's district is dry on Sunday, but it is adjacent to a district which permits a Sunday-selling store. The council approves of the opposition to Sunday sales voiced by the "church element" of the town. Present zoning regulations in Floriana prohibit additional liquor outlets, although permitting those that existed before the passage of the zoning ordinance, and the council will continue to control liquor outlets through zoning.

Serious controversy, which followed the lines of political cleavage in the city, began to develop in 1960 over Floriana's youth recreation program. Dissension arose because the city manager was reluctant to provide a salary increase for the director of the program for white youth during the middle of the fiscal year; indeed, he threatened to lock up the Flor-Teen, if she resigned, until a new director could be obtained. The civic clubs which had started the entire program became much exercised over his attitude.

The Floriana National Bank group embraced a number of these club leaders, and it became vocal on recreation items in particular. This clique had declared itself in favor of a consolidation of all recreation and park activities under one director who should be paid an adequate salary. This became the first issue that sharply differentiated the two bank cliques in city politics.

The failure of the council to move into the van on public improvements other than a new city hall is best illustrated by its attitude on the new public library building. Agitation for a new library to replace the small old structure in use was started in 1957 by the Floriana Women's Club. In 1959, after the city had sold its gas distribution system, the council offered to make some of the funds from this sale available for construction of a new library building, to be supplemented by a millage levy. A referendum was required by general law of the state on the question of adding a millage levy for the library, and the campaign for the levy of one-half mill was left to the Women's Club to promote. The levy was carried by a popular vote of 551 to 190.

Reference to the sale of the gas distribution system requires a word of explanation. A butane air-gas distribution system was established in 1937 as a "convenience" to the citizens. The city bought butane in carload lots, mixed it with compressed air, and sold it through city mains. According to the city manager, the system regularly ran a deficit. When the natural gas trunk line came down the peninsula, a branch line was built to the lime rock quarries near Floriana. Three firms interested in setting up or buying up small local distribution systems offered to buy the Floriana system. The city thereupon employed a Jacksonville engineering firm to appraise the city's system. The next step was acceptance by the city of a franchise offer from a company in a nearby county that owns a number of local distribution systems in that part of the state. The question of sale of franchise to this company was submitted to referendum and approved by a vote of 255 to 11, a vote that indicates considerable apathy on this question.

Under the terms of the offer, the entire price of the franchise, including the city's plant, was $275,000 plus a franchise tax of 6 per cent per year on sales. The initial payment to the city was $40,000, and the remainder was to be paid over the twenty years of the franchise. The firm has an option to buy at the expiration of the franchise period.

IV

The development of a rival political clique in Floriana, with the rise of the Floriana National Bank group, brought to the level of open discussion in the city the question of a possible firing of the manager. At least, some of the Floriana Bank clique were willing to talk of this possibility.

Despite Manager Sands' twenty-two years of service and his popularity with the ruling clique of Floriana, a wide range of opinion was encountered on the question of his possible firing. First of all, the councilman who had been mayor for a number of years expressed strong support for Sands and declared that there had been no attempt made to fire Sands since 1952, the year he went on the council. It was this councilman's belief that Sands would stay on as manager "as long as he wants to," and that Sands seemed happy with the "nice salary increase we gave him." The former owner-editor of the *Floriana Citizen* had heard of no move to fire Sands and did not believe one would develop. She expressed fondness for the manager, describing him as an amiable man, "a darling, and so nice." She also stressed his rise from the ranks and agreed that he "knows something about every phase of government."

During the interview with Sands, he expressed agitation when we asked him whether any attempt had been made to get him fired. He attributed the attack by the Chamber of Commerce and its executive secretary as, in effect, an attempt to "get my job" — an ambiguous phrase that probably clouded some of our later questions and his answers. Sands appeared to mean at times that the Chamber secretary wished to see him fired and not to become city manager himself; in other instances Sands hinted at fear that the Chamber secretary sought the managership.

We probed hard on this question in all other interviews. The most articulate anti-Sands man was the Chamber of Commerce president. During the two weeks preceding our interview (going back to the meeting between the Chamber and the city council over industrial waste disposal), he claimed to have heard strong "rumors" that Sands must go. It was, it seems, because of his own connections with the probable sources of these "rumors" that he was able to furnish a rather detailed bill of indictment, to wit:

1) Sands "hasn't changed with the times";
2) He lacks the professional training necessary to run a town the size of Floriana;
3) Because Sands is getting older, he naturally wants to "take things a little easier; you can't sit down or take Wednesday afternoons off in a growing city";
4) The City Council and the mayor rely more on the judgments of the manager than on their own, and in so doing they let him kill ideas to which he is opposed; and
5) Complaints have been made that Sands drinks too much. (Since the Chamber president reported Sands to be not a member of the cocktail party set, the implication is that he is a "private" rather than a "social" drinker.)

The Chamber president frankly discussed Sands' age and his own estimate of Sands' present financial reserves; those reserves, he thought, would permit Sands to retire early and live comfortably. The Floriana National Bank crowd wants a professionally trained manager and would accept, in fact probably seek, an "outside" man whose very "outsideness" the County Bank clique would oppose. The "outsider" in the president's opinion should not be from outside the state or even from just anywhere in Florida but from a city in one of the several counties adjacent to Eastern County.

The district manager of the electrical utility and vice-chairman of the Chamber's Development Committee reported at first that he had heard no rumors about changing managers and that most people were "pretty well satisfied with Sands," who he said was always available to talk over problems and "won't go out and tell what you've said."

Sands, he believed, was limited by Floriana's budget and with a larger budget would do better. But upon further probing, the utility manager admitted that he had heard several rumors that particular people wanted Sands to go. He had tried to dispel these rumors, he said, since he thought people were pretty well satisfied with Sands. In his own opinion the Chamber secretary "steps a little heavily at times," and is "a little on the strong-willed side." When probed as to the source of the rumors, the manager said they came from people who are foremost in wanting to "improve" the city and who believe that Floriana has not gone far enough.

A younger councilman affiliated with the County Bank clique admitted to having heard rumors that the Chamber secretary had his eye on somebody's job. But in this councilman's opinion there was no serious or legitimate complaint against Sands as manager. A constituent — he couldn't remember who it was — wanted him to get rid of Sands, but this councilman knew of no community leadership opposition to Sands. He himself did not believe that Floriana could hire anyone with Sands' knowledge of the community.

It seems quite clear that we visited Floriana at just about the time a serious movement was starting to get rid of the manager. It did not seem to us that the Floriana National Bank clique could accumulate the necessary council majority to do this until the elections of 1962. Only one councilman was due to come up for re-election in 1960 (he is strong County Bank clique man), and he was re-elected. The young insurance man on the council who was adjudged by us to be a County Bank man was regarded by the mayor and the manager as an uncertain quantity, but as "leaning the County Bank way." This councilman described himself as a "slow growth man, directly the reverse," he put it, "of the Development Committee," but he admitted that he had "never told that to anybody." Nevertheless, the Floriana National Bank clique correctly identified him as opposed to them, and they nominated a bank vice-president to oppose him successfully in 1961. This gave the Floriana Bank clique only two of five votes on the council.

One way the Development Committee might try to hasten the removal process is to move, via rumor-circulation, against Sands on the "tippler" charge. In that event, there would be some chance that he would resign before a complete council overturn. But actually Sands clearly tried to strengthen himself against the range of criticisms by getting the council to go along with appointment of a young man as assistant manager. That this move would help him in the long run was questionable.

The Sands case seems to present certain classic features: a nonprofessional "local boy" of long tenure becomes identified eventually with the policy positions of a long-standing, almost unanimous council majority, and in the view of a possibly emerging new council majority, he will "have to go" in favor of a Chamber-approved, professional manager. If the businessmen rule, this is one way they effect their rule.

V

Floriana presents some interesting possibilities for speculation at the present time concerning the trends in its clique structure. The emergence of a new *business* leadership clique centered around the Floriana National Bank has, beyond a shadow of a doubt, that effect on the sphere of council-manager decisions and relations. The old County Bank clique is being seriously challenged and may yet be forced out of majority control. If so, it would appear that a change in managers would be inevitable.

Reviewing once again the contending business cliques, we can see the differences more clearly. Centering around the older County Bank, which alone of Floriana banks successfully weathered the Depression of the Thirties, is a group of older and more conservative businessmen. Ringleaders of this County Bank clique, by virtue of larger property holdings and bank stock, are the Thomas clan of Floriana. At first this clan and their "aristocratic" bank friends ruled alone, but beginning during World War II, the downtown retail merchants compelled the County Bank group to come to terms with them politically, and the merchants have been dominant in the County Bank clique ever since. The merchants have helped to induce likely prospects to run for council. Furthermore, the Chamber of Commerce up to the mid-fifties appeared to have been quite thoroughly dominated by the Thomases and their County Bank group. The policy of the then Chamber and the city council was to "go slowly" on additional industrialization and do nothing to disturb the industries already located in the town.

Added to a conservative attitude toward municipal expansion was a restrictive policy on bank loans. Credit was tight, and the County Bank, having a monopoly on the town's banking business, refused to expand, change its methods, and so on. Quite consistent with its bank policy was the attitude expressed by its men on the city council who opposed higher assessment rates and higher millage rates.

But tight money policies on the part of the County Bank helped to breed their own counter-activity. In 1956 a new bank was organized by certain dissident businessmen: the Floriana National Bank. It advertised aggressively and introduced new services. The older County Bank had to start advertising, building a new bank structure, loosening the strings on loans, putting in new services, and in general modernizing its business approach. This business rivalry has been intense — so intense that it has swept out into the Chamber of Commerce, into civic programs, into city council politics, and into the social life of the town.

For example, the country club originally organized by the County Bank group and long dominated by it, now has 90 per cent of its membership from the Floriana Bank clique, a much younger and presumably livelier group of men. The city's recreational program for teen-agers is being fought out between the two bank cliques, as was mentioned above. A different way of life is advocated and lived by the two different groups, according to one of the more articulate spokesmen of one of these cliques. This man explained that the conflict between the two bank cliques divides the city from top to bottom: in image of the city sought, in recreation, in social behavior, in attitude toward new industry, etc.

The line-up of the two cliques is roughly as follows: *County Bank group:* the directors of the bank (a category which overlaps some of the following); the few remaining leaders of the old families; some people in industrial firms processing agricultural products (vegetable or citrus); many of the downtown merchants; at least three of the present city council, and, of course, the city manager, Sands. *Floriana National Bank group:* the directors of the bank (a category which overlaps some of the following); the state legislator resident in Floriana who is both attorney for the bank and a director of it; the editor of the *Floriana Citizen* (the widow of the former owner and editor who sold the paper about five or six years ago to the present owner is a member of the County Bank group); the executive secretary of the Chamber of Commerce; the president of the Chamber; many members of the Chamber's Retail Merchants Division and of its Industrial Development Committee; some officials of new industries in town; a large-scale industrial building contractor who is president of the Floriana National Bank; the local district manager of the privately owned electrical utility; and two councilmen. The first of these to be supported by the clique is a native of Italy in his forties, owner of the major downtown restaurant, who seems to be "on the make" politically, as demonstrated by the fact of his candidacy for county commissioner in 1962. The second of the councilmen is a bank-vice-president, as mentioned above.

The aggressiveness of the Floriana National Bank clique in city politics is well demonstrated by its introduction of new techniques and dimensions into campaigns. Not only did the restaurateur personally canvass the entire city and organize to cover the city with telephone committees; more significantly, he also sought the Negro vote actively. Most important of all, he insisted upon discussing issues when he successfully ran for mayor in 1960. This entire pattern was followed by his banker colleague.

The major issue which divides Floriana's present elite from its counter-elite is the perennial one — what kind of town should Floriana be; at what rate should Floriana grow and what direction(s) should the growth take? Although County Bank people uniformly asserted that they are not against further industrialization, it is still possible to tease out some major differences either in direction or in emphasis between the two bank cliques. For example, the differences are slow growth vs. rapid growth; modest vs. "crash" programs for attracting industry; agricultural processing industries vs. a diversified industry program, relatively low vs. relatively high levels of municipal taxation and spending; relatively low vs. relatively high public program consciousness; and a tendency to react to emerging problems vs., one might almost say, a tendency to create new problems by initiating or trying to initiate "big" programs.

Culturally, the conflict would appear to be based in part at least, on real differences in attitudes between rural (or rather rural-interested) people and urban-oriented people. One can also say that is a conflict between religious fundamentalists who are primarily "sin" conscious and people attracted toward the cocktail hour and a slightly more sophisticated way of life. These distinctions are real even though Floriana is itself far from being able at present to offer confirmed urbanites an urbane, cosmopolitan way of life.

In terms of the present conflict, the formation by the Floriana Chamber of Commerce of its Industrial Development Committee and the Chamber's success in getting the city council to establish an industrial park are of obvious significance. Equally significant is the fact that although the Committee and the park have been in existence for four years, and although the Chamber is led by a "dynamic," "aggressive" executive secretary, only one industrial firm has located in the park, and that is a firm already based in the town. The frustration on the part of the secretary and of this committee has been extreme.

For the time being, tactical advantage appears to lie with the County Bank clique. That clique has publicly opposed a "get tough" policy on industrial waste disposal and intimated that the Chamber appeared to be trying to drive industry away or prevent it from coming to Floriana rather than to attract it. The opposition clique has been unable to solve the problem by coming up with a solution that would cost the city and the plants little money and not drive the smallest of the plants away. However, the very persistence of this issue might ultimately cause the defeat of the County Bank clique.

There are at least three reasons why the Floriana National Bank clique may gain more council seats. First of all, the Floriana National clique, in sponsoring the candidacy of the Italian restaurant proprietor in 1959, were able to muster about seventy-five people from the downtown area who, as a delegation, waited upon him in his restaurant and asked him to run. This development indicated a serious effort by the Chamber-Floriana National people to try hard to split the old County Bank downtown mercantile coalition. They also tried to effect this split by means of stepping up the activities of the Chamber's Retail Merchants' Division through a "Buy in Floriana" campaign to try to improve the position of Floriana as a year-round trading center.

Second, the Italian restaurateur set a style of campaigning that, by Floriana standards, was unusually vigorous. For some ten years County Bank candidates, after announcing their candidacies, ran a few decorous newspaper ads, and then waited for votes to roll in from voters familiar with their names and reputations. In contrast, active pursuit of all voters, including Negro voters, may quite possibly replace the mere "merchandising of personality" in Floriana. In campaign activity the Floriana National Bank men are much more adept and modern than the "old guard," and because they are issue-oriented, they have maximized every issue within their grasp. When the restaurateur successfully ran for mayor in 1960 and defied the old system of not contesting the incumbent, he issued a platform for the first time in Floriana's history of mayoral campaigns. Significantly, the platform seemed to have "something for everybody," including street paving, lights, etc., in Negro as well as white neighborhoods.

Third, the Floriana National Bank clique, through their first man on the council, tried very hard to win over the city employees from what we presume is the long time support by the latter of the County Bank clique. The Italian restaurateur, after coming on the council, devoted a good deal of his time to personnel matters. He conducted many interviews with city employees on their problems and tried hard to establish himself as their champion. He pushed hard for a retirement plan and for significant salary increases and on these matters was sometimes for two years, as he put it, in a minority of one on the council. The County Bank clique reacted in a minimal way as the city manager pointed out that an employee pension plan, administered by a private insurance company, was "in the cards."

The entire matter of the future of city manager Sands, of course, hinges on the future of the contest between the two bank cliques. Presumably Sands is safe so long as the County Bank clique remains in majority control. But if that clique should lose another seat in 1962, then Sands may well find himself very hurriedly retired. It is not probable that he would be temperamentally in harmony with any of the faster-moving, more aggressive Floriana Bank clique leaders.

Who will have control of the town a year, two, or three years hence? As Floriana moves closer to deciding what kind of town it will be, the Floriana National Bank clique grows stronger and is perhaps reaching out now into county commission politics. If Central Florida, in which Floriana is located, is any guide, it will not be hard to guess that Floriana will ultimately decide it must make serious and aggressive efforts for more industry. In that case, the Thomases, the County Bank clique, and their manager Sands will fall from control. But it is unlikely that the new political clique will obtain monopolistic control, as the very polarization of politics around the banks would seem to insure competitive politics as well as competitive banking.

4

Center City

Center City is the core city of a rapidly developing Standard Metropolitan Area which achieved that benchmark classification in 1960. Although the city increased in population from 1950 to 1960 by some 30 per cent, its 62,000 residents constitute only about one-third of the total within the entire metropolitan area. The population of the area showed an increase of well over 50 per cent during the decade of the 1950's. Founded during the early years of the nineteenth century, the city grew at only a modest rate until the post-World War II period.

As Florida cities go, Center City is an old town, rich in tradition. The hustle and bustle associated with a river port have helped to develop a rather cosmopolitan atmosphere in the community. In addition, it had a lively history in the nineteenth-century struggle over the destiny of Florida. Moreover, a nearby military base that goes back many years has helped to flavor the life of the town.

I

Center City has a rather diversified economic base. The adjacent sizeable military installation and a second base in the general area have long contributed heavily to the town's economy. Within the last two decades, a large chemical industry has been established in the immediate area for the processing of wood products. Almost a dozen national firms operate plants in the chemical processing category. Port facilities are still a significant factor in Center City's economy, but shipping has declined in importance. Average weekly earnings in the surrounding county are well above the state average and near the national average. Manufacturing accounts for the largest proportion of the nonagricultural labor force of about 50,000, with government a very close second. Together they constitute about 40 per cent of

45

total employment. The various trades account for another 20 per cent of the total nonagricultural employment in the county.

Nonwhites, principally Negroes, make up about one-third of Center City's inhabitants. More than 7 per cent of the population is over age sixty-five. In the county, in contrast, the percentage of the population over sixty-five is about 5 per cent, and Negroes comprise only some 20 per cent of the total. Comparable figures for the entire metropolitan area are about the same as those for the county.

II

The electoral system used by Center City during the study period followed a pattern somewhat at variance with the usual practice under the council-manager form of government. Ten councilmen were elected from five wards for terms of two years, with one member elected at large and one from within the ward. The nonpartisan election system called for a primary and a general election. If no candidate received an absolute majority in the primary, the two high men opposed each other in the general election. The entire council came up for election every two years. All candidates had to live in the ward from which they ran. The structure of the council permitted rapid change in control by rival political factions, should such factions exist.

The mayor is selected by the council, but he need not be a member of that body. The council may choose any citizen of the town who is a qualified voter. During the earlier part of the fifteen-year study, the mayor was, in fact, chosen from outside the council, but in recent years a council member has customarily been named. Under the charter the mayor has only ceremonial powers.

The salient feature of Center City's institutional pattern is its civil service system. A Civil Service Board composed of three men exercises most of the hiring, firing, and promotion power ordinarily held by the city manager or the council. The three-member Civil Service Board is composed as follows: one is named by the city council, one by the city employees, and the third member is named by the other two. Rules and regulations are made by the Board covering hiring and firing in almost all positions. In practice, all top posts under the control of the Board were filled by strict seniority until 1961. The Board had the power to order promotion by examinations, but this procedure was almost never used until required by a change in law in 1961. Even if used, the promotional examination was open only to employees at the level immediately below the echelon involved. If no one at the lower echelon passed, then the examination could be thrown open to the public. In the rare instances in which this actually took place, a panel of the three top names was sent to the city manager, who could then exercise some choice in making an appointment. However, the manager's power was virtually meaningless because seniority dominated the process. The manager, however, had the power to name two department heads, finance and law.

These rather novel institutional arrangements have been accompanied by an equally novel political style. City employees have become the stable center between rival political forces and have obtained a power of their own. At the same time, the calibre of city employees, particularly of the police chief, became the subject of considerable controversy. The degree and manner in which city employees are involved in the political process will be detailed below. Suffice it to say here that their political role is of major proportions. The general political climate within which city employees function has led to some instances of interference by individual councilmen in day-to-day administration, but such action has been surprisingly limited, given the strength of the city employees in the political life of the community.

III

The manager in Center City, Spencer Hill, found himself in the delicate position of being charged with the responsibility for administering the affairs of the city with very little *legal* power to control the employees over whom he wished to exercise authority. His considerable success in exercising such control stemmed largely from Hill's skill in operating within a complex political situation. Manager Hill saw himself as the source of most policy initiation in the city, and council members substantially confirmed his view. However, there was a general consensus that Hill did not get upset if his proposals were rejected; that he was perfectly willing to "put them on ice for awhile" if a council majority was lacking. This was sometimes the case, but by and large the council seemed disposed to accept his program proposals. One council member in office at the time of our initial field interviewing stated that Hill often rescued the council from a difficult political situation by taking public responsibility for the setttlement of an issue "too hot for the council to handle." On the other hand, an ex-councilman described Hill's behavior in these terms: "When things get hot, it's not on his shoulders; he just ducks his head and the council takes the rap." This former councilman went on to remark that Hill's dominant role in the political process was really not his fault: "I think Hill is a good man. His biggest trouble is his own council. They let him do everything he wants to. Another thing, the councilmen don't have the time needed to be good councilmen. Therefore, a lot of things go by default to the city manager."

Hill's program orientation and his determination to play a meaningful role in the political process can be illustrated by his presentation of the budget. His control of the budget, of course, was one source of at least potential control over department heads, and he used it effectively. At one time a more or less hostile council instituted the practice of allowing department heads to appear and argue for funds that Hill had cut out of their original request, but this practice was soon ended. The council itself saw that Hill could take the "heat" of budget struggles better than they. Hill himself saw the budget as considerably more than a mere control device; it also represented one of his best opportunities to marshal public support for his favorite programs. Asked whether he consulted the council beforehand on what he put into the budget, Hill answered with an emphatic "no," and went on to comment, "You can't get unanimity on a ten-man council anyway, and if you ask advice and then don't use it, you're an S.O.B." Perhaps of more significance, he noted that the presentation of the budget was the manager's best chance to speak to the public.

Although Center City's charter gave the mayor no powers other than the usual ceremonial duties prescribed by council-manager plan doctrine, in actual practice there was some evidence that the mayor attempted to play a larger role in policy-making than did regular council members. The physical arrangements in city hall have encouraged such a development, in that the mayor has an office directly across from the city manager. Colonel Carl Jackson, mayor during the latter part of the period of the study, spent about an hour each day conferring with the manager. Their discussions usually centered on various policy problems rather than on routine administrative details. Members of the council as well as Manager Hill agreed that while the incumbent mayor wanted to become a policy leader, he had been a nearly complete failure in his efforts to do so. Hill judged Colonel Jackson's handling of his relations with the council and with influential groups in town to be poor. The mayor often became involved in personal and rather bitter wrangles and seemed intolerant of criticism. According to Hill, neither of the two mayors who served during the fifteen year period of the study attempted to interfere in routine administrative matters.

IV

Center City is characterized by a general consensus on the kind of community it should be. The post-World War II period produced rapid population growth and an expanding and rather diverse economic base. A general agreement prevails that the same kind of development should continue for the future. Few bitter struggles over policy issues such as streets, sewers, or recreation facilities are evident. Yet there are vexing problems confronting the town — some at the surface, others at the moment submerged but threatening to emerge into prominence in the near future. The problem of integration falls in the latter category, and to a lesser degree so also does the question of the effect of water and air pollution on Center City's nearby waterfront recreation facilities. Immediate problems center around a struggle between two competing political factions referred to locally as "Conservatives" and "Liberals," and the matter of the civil service system and the political role of city employees.

The conservatives and the liberals have been the major political factions competing for control of the council in Center City. They are not parties and do not "slate" candidates in the nonpartisan election system, but alignments to these two factions are well understood. The conservative faction is composed of the "haves" in the community — people who had already made their money or who come from "old" families. For the most part they are rentier, professional, or managerial types, described by one local political figure as "coupon clippers." Within the spectrum of Center City politics, the conservatives are the "small spenders." The conservatives, liberals would tell one, are primarily interested in maintaining the status quo.

The liberals are people on their way up economically. For some, Center City politics has been a channel for economic advancement. Liberals are willing to spend more money than are the conservatives. Change and development are seen as beneficial to the town as well as to the liberals' own financial future. From the conservatives' point of view, liberals have sought political power mainly as a way of reaping the financial benefits of petty graft. The occupations of many liberal council members have been those of contractors, building trades, and businesses involving close interaction with city government. Such callings have presented ample opportunities for favoritism in contract awards and the like.

The differences between the conservative and liberal factions in Center City politics can be clarified through a number of examples. In the matter of tax sources, the conservatives supported a general reassessment of property while the liberals opposed it. A crucial difference in terms of political power concerns salaries and fringe benefits for city employees. The liberal faction supported generous treatment of city employees, but the conservatives were more inclined to frugality. Another dimension of the city employee problem has involved attitudes toward inefficiency and even graft on the part of city employees, especially in the police department. The tolerance of the liberals, coupled with periodic scandals usually centered in the police department, has hurt them in their struggles with the conservatives.

Center City's political picture shows that the two distinct political factions compete for control of the council, with each winning on occasion. Since 1945, liberals and conservatives have alternated in control of the city hall. From 1945 to 1947, the conservatives controlled the council. In 1947 the liberals won the election and remained in a majority on the council until 1951, when the conservatives recaptured control. In 1953, the liberals won and remained in majority control until 1961. Contrary to our findings in most cities with competitive politics, the Center City manager did not rise and fall with each power exchange. Spencer Hill was hired by the winning faction in 1947, and he survived the three power exchanges that took place between then and 1960. He could have remained on in 1961 despite the power exchange that occurred in that election.

The city manager, Spencer Hill, and the city employees, operating through their civil service system, must be included in an identification of political factions in Center City from 1947 to 1961. City employees could not only determine the outcome of council races by voting as a cohesive bloc, but their support of Hill as manager was unequivocal.

The political climate within which Center City made a decision in the 1930's to substitute the council-manager form of government for the commission type is pertinent to the style of politics that developed in succeeding years. Pressures for the change came largely from the "respectable" business elements in the community who were determined to throw out the "political hacks" (hacks at least in the judgment of "respectable" business elements). The existence of petty graft and a lack of adequate municipal services were the standard complaints. The opponents of any change, led by a young lawyer with county and state political ambitions, were not successful in blocking the reformers, but they did succeed in inserting into the charter the provision for the Civil Service Board to control hiring, firing, and promotion. Apparently the assumption of the status-quo group was that it would probably be able to maintain control of city politics through the civil service group. An unanticipated consequence of this action has been the emergence of the civil service employees as an independent political power, the most cohesive and powerful single force in the political life of the community. A political power play, then, took place at the time the manager plan was adopted which produced an institutional arrangement that, in turn, formed a base for an important element in Center City politics. The adoption of the council-manager plan did not produce the hoped-for improvement in either the political "tone" of the community or the quality of services that the proponents of change had argued would ensue. The manager for much of the period (1932–1947) was described by various sources as "inefficient," "not big enough for the job," "petty," and "a man with no program for solving the problems of the city." Dissatisfaction with the manager led to a slate of candidates in 1947 who pledged themselves to fire him if they were elected. The slate was successful, and they did fire the manager, but they had given little thought to finding a replacement.

Spencer Hill, an engineering graduate of the state university, was then employed as city engineer. He had previously served as acting manager, and the council decided to offer him the job on a permanent basis. Hill accepted on condition that he would retain his civil service status by receiving a leave of absence as city engineer while he "tried out" the job of city manager. This arrangement continued for two years. Hill came to his post with imposing political assets to complement his administrative experience gained as city engineer. A member of a distinguished old family well placed in the local aristocracy, he also retained his many connections with the employees which stood him in good stead in the years to come.

The council elected in 1947 found it possible to unite on only one issue — the decision to fire the manager. They were soon locked in a five-to-five deadlock on the choice of mayor. This dispute was finally settled by selecting as mayor a distinguished retired general from outside the council. The new manager and the new council then turned their attention to the problems of Center City. The council quickly identified itself as liberal — that is, willing to spend money — and gave Hill support in his effort to launch several major municipal programs. An extensive street paving program was deemed the most pressing need by Hill and accepted by the council, but Hill soon found that the local banks either would not or could not lend the money the city needed to get the program under way. Hill then displayed his ingenuity by persuading a bank in a nearby town (but in a different state) to make the necessary loan. It was Hill's opinion that the local bank never forgave this financial coup and opposed him until he resigned in 1961, but no evidence could be obtained to verify Hill's impression of the lasting character of bank hostility.

A providential Securities and Exchange Commission ruling at almost the same time as the bank loan forced the local private utilities company to divest itself of a gas system, and Hill quickly developed a plan to acquire the system for the city. When the utility company displayed reluctance to sell to a public agency, Hill "persuaded" them otherwise by well-placed references to a pending city demand for a new franchise calling for more revenue from the company's electrical operations in the city.[1] Public ownership of the gas system turned out to be quite profitable for Center City; in 1960 the profits amounted to over $2,000,000. With the gas utilities profits available to back additional revenue certificates, Center City, under the skilled guiding hand of Hill, was able to expand the street program and embark on various other improvement programs including a major remodeling of the city hall, a new fire station, and a new jail and police head-quarters.

The "reform" council elected in 1947, which, it soon developed, was controlled by the liberal faction of Center City, supported Hill in his efforts to move his programs forward to improve city services. The first power exchange after Hill assumed the manager's post came in 1951. The circumstances leading up to the conservative victory and Hill's ability to survive the exchange shed considerable light on the political process in Center City.

The liberal group controlling the council during the 1949–1951 period followed a familiar pattern, in the words of Manager Hill, "sticking their noses into administrative affairs, particularly police business." The petty graft in which they indulged was exemplified by the police captain who was fired for demanding "payola" from a veteran's group in exchange for protection in the operation of slot machines. The council was tied in with other instances of "graft and shady dealings," and at one time Manager Hill's efforts to correct some of the excesses aroused their antagonism sufficiently to produce a concerted but unsuccessful effort to get the necessary majority to fire him. Hill persuaded the council, in the face of widespread public indignation, to hire a team of nationally recognized outside experts to make recommendations for changes in the police department. The consultants' report called for major alterations, including an end to the Civil Service Board of hiring, firing, and promotion, and the trans-fer of this power to the manager. Solid opposition by the city em-ployees to any change in the existing civil service system was enough to cause a hasty filing away of the report, where it remained until the next police scandal. Hill did not press the issue. Faced with the power of the city employees in Center City politics, he was not strong enough to do so.

The petty graft of the liberals, exemplified by the police scandal,

[1] A franchise had been granted in perpetuity years before which provided for no return to the city.

stirred so much public indignation that an unusually large vote was cast in the 1951 election. The 1951 election result was a conservative sweep. The only two councilmen who escaped defeat were generally agreed to be "in the pocket of the conservatives." One liberal councilman attributed his defeat to a strong mobilization of what he described as an old guard group of moneyed people in town who were always sympathetic toward the conservatives but usually took little part in city politics.

The incident that roused the old guardsmen to action involved an elaborate financial scheme by the council to launch a grandiose river-front development involving the construction of wharf facilities, a multi-storied building, an auditorium, and a pier. The liberal council had arranged financing and construction with a large firm in a neighboring state interested in using the wharf facilities. Under the tentative agreement, the firm was to underwrite the cost of a significant part of the facilities and lend the city the remainder of the funds necessary. The lending operation was to be handled through a new bank the out-of-state firm would establish in Center City. The old guard asked for time (thirty days) in which to raise the money themselves, but the liberals later described this move as simply a delaying tactic during which the old guard discovered the plans for the new bank. The liberals contended that this threat to old-guard dominance of Center City banking caused the old guard to throw its full support behind the conservatives in the 1951 election.

A combination of factors, therefore, caused the 1951 power exchange. Manager Hill was not an issue in the campaign, and the new council, controlled by the conservatives, made no effort to dislodge him. Hill had displayed the skill and sensitivity that enabled him to survive a competitive political environment for almost fifteen years. When confronted by a police scandal, he had moved with vigor to correct the situation, and had even made an effort to correct what he felt to be an underlying deficiency in the civil service system when he persuaded the council to bring in outside experts who, he was sure, would recommend a modification of the existing system. While the liberal council failed to carry through the suggested reforms, Hill had made the effort for reform and thus had made a good impression on the general public and on the conservatives, in particular. At the same time, he had pushed for a number of long-needed developmental programs, in which he had the general support of the liberal council. Although conservative leaders might attribute the council motivation for such programs mainly to a desire for wider opportunities for petty graft, in any event Hill and the council had agreed on the need for the programs, if for different reasons. Hill had also pushed for a comprehensive program to improve salaries and working conditions for the city employees, thus nullifying to some extent the opposition he aroused by pushing for reform in the civil service system. At any rate, he did not crusade for the civil service change. He initiated the study, supported the recommendation, and when the council refused to accept it, he dropped the matter.

The power struggle during the 1951–1953 period, climaxed by a return to power of the liberal faction, was further to test Hill's skill as a participant in the political process. This contest clearly revealed the power of the city employee group.

Two factors combined to produce political forces that turned out the conservatives in 1953 and returned the liberal faction to power. One factor involved a property reassessment designed to correct the extremely low valuations which, in turn, allowed hundreds of homes to escape all property taxes. The council elected in 1951 engaged a well-known private firm to carry out a thorough reassessment of all real property. The contract called for the payment of a $50,000 fee. The assessment firm apparently did a technically competent job, but the council lacked a public relations program. Widespread fear swept the community as rumors of vastly increased taxes spread. The liberal faction seized on these fears and plunged into the task of seeing that they were widely communicated. One veteran member of the liberal group, also one of their most accomplished political leaders, noted: "I followed those reassessment people around and said to every property owner who would talk to me, 'Look what they are doing to you, and look how terrible it is.' " The liberals ran a slate of four candidates in 1953 pledged, among other things, "never to put this re-evaluation into effect." There was a general agreement that the reassessment played a major role in the defeat of the conservative faction.

The second important factor in the campaign of 1953 centered around wages and working conditions for city employees. As noted above, Manager Hill had been successful in winning council approval of generous salary increases and favorable working conditions prior to 1951. The conservative faction controlling the council during the period 1951–1953 tried to halt this trend and even insisted on its reversal in at least one instance. The five-day week was ended, and over the protest of the manager, the city hall was kept open on Saturday morning. The council also resisted any increase in salary or fringe benefits. As Manager Hill put it, "The whole group of city employees moved against that council, and all of them that ran again lost out in 1953."

Center City's election of 1953 was a good example of the political power of the city employee group. Although their opposition was not the only factor involved in the conservatives' defeat, there was general agreement that it was the most significant one. Dual questions present themselves about the political power of the employees' group: What is the source of its power, and what are the techniques it utilizes; and what is the range of issues that are likely to mobilize the latent giant?

V

Center City in 1960 had 900 employees, 600 of whom are unskilled maintenance employees. They must reside within the city, and they operate with smoothness and efficiency as a political organization through the framework of the civil service system. Under that system, there is an executive committee supposedly made up of one representative from each department. In fact, however, there is usually one representative from each division, which results in a committee of about thirty. Within this group there is a smaller informal "steering committee" which provides the employees with their "front line" political leadership. The fire, police, and personnel departments have all played particularly strong roles, with the police department perhaps the strongest single leadership unit in the political activities of city employees.

The employee political organization has not followed the practice of open political support of or opposition to candidates. One of the most basic political facts of life in Center City is that any would-be candidate for council seeks out the representatives of the city employees and in a private session gives his views on the issues that concern the employee group. Should a candidate not do so, he may be "buttonholed" and forced to take some stand, or he may simply be adjudged hostile to the objectives of the employees.

A crucial question, of course, is the range of issues considered vital by the employee group. On this there was a widespread consensus — that employees were interested strictly in "bread-and-butter" questions such as wages (including overtime pay), working conditions, fringe benefits, and above all, the maintenance of the civil service system itself under which hiring, firing, and promotion were in the hands of the Civil Service Board rather than the council or manager. Once a candidate's views on these critical issues were determined, the leaders passed the word to the employee group on whom to support.

A description of the organizational framework, the techniques used, and the issues involved tells us little about the relative significance of the city employee vote in Center City politics. That importance hinges on the size of the employee vote in relation to the total vote and the ability of employee leaders to stimulate a large turnout of their people voting largely as a bloc. Also employee strength is in no way diluted inasmuch as the residence requirement maximizes their voting strength.

Estimates of the size of the city employee vote (employees themselves and those who could be counted on to vote with them) ranged from 3,000 up to 6,000 in normal elections in which the total vote usually ran around 9,000.[2] Citizen apathy was such that Center City usually had a low voter turnout, sometimes as low as 6,000 out of a registration of around 10,000–15,000. (Variation in registration also reflects particular apathy in some elections.) Furthermore, city employees were not concentrated heavily in any one ward, so that their influence seemed to be felt about equally in at-large and within-ward elections. The testimony of a number of veteran Center City political figures as to the motivation and importance of the city employee vote sheds considerable light on the question.[3]

One council incumbent, a veteran political leader in the city, commented, "The city employees control any given election. I would lose the next election if I made this statement in public." Another believed that in the past most councilmen who were elected were supported by the city employees. He went on to explain his strong position in city politics by stating that he was born on the wrong side of the tracks, lived near the main headquarters of the city streets and utilities building, knew most of these men from his childhood, and had a large number of relatives who worked for the city. He considered these connections with the city employees his most valuable asset as a political figure. Manager Hill himself, whose involvement in all this will be discussed below, identified the city employee group as the controlling factor in Center City politics and described them in these terms: "They are so secure in the city that they will buck anybody."

The power of the city employee vote in any given election is closely linked to the size of the turnout, and its variation is also related to the chance for victory of the conservative and liberal factions. The evidence supports the conclusion that the conservatives were the minority faction in Center City politics during the period 1945–1960. When everything went along smoothly, the liberals, who could usually count on the solid support of the city employee group, could anticipate

---

[2] As of 1960.

[3] We do not claim to have precise measures of the importance of the city employee vote. The measure we have stems from the perceptions of political leaders in the community as expressed to us in interviews and the analysis by the present city manager.

victory. When scandal filled the air, however, the conservatives were usually able to take advantage of the larger turnout resulting from an aroused citizenry and win. Thus in 1951, about 50 per cent of some 12,000 registered voters turned out to give the conservatives a victory. In the larger turnout, the city employee vote could not dominate the situation as fully as it could in quieter times. It might be said further, although only as speculation, that the kind of people aroused to moral indignation by police scandals and other revelations of graft would be middle-class, puritanical types who would be more likely to support the conservatives in any event. However, in the liberal victory in 1953, only about 40 per cent of a total registered voter list of some 10,000 went to the polls, a decrease of some 2,000 registrants and voters in the two-year period.

The power of the city employee group in politics, coupled with its apparent concentration on "bread and butter" issues such as wages, fringe benefits, and working conditions, would lead to the assumption that Center City employees fare better in such matters than employees in cities of comparable size and economic base. The data available suggest that this is, indeed, the case.

Table 1 shows that among our cities, two of which are significantly

Table 1

Comparable Salary Data of Center City and Other Florida Cities[a]

	National	Pop. 62,000 Center City	Pop. 90,000 City "A"	Pop. 60,000 City "B"	Pop. 90,000 City "C"
Av. Monthly earnings	$372	$350 (approx.)	$355	$304	$324
Av. no. of employees	866	900 (approx.)	1215	712	1561
Hrs. per week	40	40	40	40	40
Overtime policy		Time and one-half	Time and one-half	Time and one-half	Straight time
Leave policy		Liberal	Almost as liberal	Almost as liberal	Not so liberal

[a] Figures slightly altered to protect the anonymity of Center City. The relationship has not been distorted. Cities "A," "B," and "C" are at least as affluent as Center City. A "liberal" leave policy allows a leave of absence for military service. More important is an "injury leave" provision over and above normal sick leave.

larger and all of which are located in areas at least as prosperous economically, Center City fares rather well in terms of salaries and fringe benefits. While it is somewhat below the national average on city employee benefits, Center City is well below the national average in per capita income.

Table 2 shows that in the matter of police and fire chief salaries Center City is at or above the average in the other three communities — far above it in the case of the fire chief. The entrance salary is higher in Center City for both firemen and policemen, and the average annual salary is higher in all cases for firemen and higher for policemen in every case except one — City "B." Furthermore, Manager Hill's salary was well above the national mean for city managers of cities of comparable size — $16,535.

In the light of these data, the city employees in Center City seem to have used their political power to their profit in matters of wages, working conditions, and maintenance of the existing civil service system which gives them maximum job security. They have done this by using the machinery of the civil service system as an effective political instrument.

Manager Spencer Hill served as the top administrative officer in

Table 2

Salaries in Fire and Police Departments of Center City and Other Florida Cities

	Pop. about 62,000 Center City	Pop. about 90,000 City "A"	Pop. about 60,000 City "B"	Pop. about 90,000 City "C"
POLICE: Chief's salary	about $9,600	$9,841	$9,000	$9,500
Entrance salary	about $4,200	$3,874	$3,780	$3,840
Average annual salary	$4,585	$4,100	$4,606	$4,404
FIRE: Chief's salary	about $9,600	$7,917	$7,920	$8,800
Entrance salary	about $4,200	$3,692	$3,780	$3,720
Average annual salary	$4,964	$4,723	$4,709	$4,461

Center City for almost the entire study period (1947–1960). On the other hand, our data substantiate the notion that managers rise and fall with political factions — that is, when a power exchange takes place, a new city manager is likely to follow soon thereafter. The fact that Manager Hill escaped (at least until 1961) paying the price for the inevitable involvement of managers in the political process can be largely explained by his success in building an independent political power base. His power base was the city employee organization. While the possession of this power base gave Hill stability in a competitive political setting, that stability was not without its price. Dependence on the city employees limited his power to push for changes in the civil service system, especially provisions regarding promotion by strict seniority — a system he believed needed changing. In short, his inability to bring about reforms in the police department brought yet another scandal that precipitated a crisis in the politics of Center City and in the career of Manager Hill. This political explosion, a set of events that occurred just after the end of the field study, will be described later in this chapter.

A widespread consensus has existed in Center City that Hill's stability in the midst of change stemmed from his relations with the city employees' political organization. When asked why he had lasted so long, one ex-councilman and long-time resident replied: "His employees. He kow-tows to them; people like the Superintendents of Water, Gas, Streets, Fire, Police — all of those department heads are Hill men." He went on to remark that "Hill can damn near beat you running at large if he wants to." This comment referred to the distribution of city employees throughout the city that made them an important factor both in within-ward elections and in at-large contests. When asked how Hill built up such loyalty, the reply was, "I can't answer it, and I've been right under it all the time."

Another councilman noted that Hill had especially strong support from the heads of the fire, police, and public works departments. "He has their full support, and anybody running on a 'beat Hill' platform would surely lose. There is a lot of slack in the system, and anybody who opposes Hill would really bring out the city employees' vote in support of Hill." This particular councilman, a veteran Center City politician, summed up his view of Hill's ability to last by bestowing what was obviously one of the highest compliments he could imagine, "He lasts because he is one of the smoothest politicians that this city has ever known."

One councilman who subscribed fully to the power of the city employee's idea felt that it would be very unlikely for the city employees' bloc of votes to go to a candidate or slate of candidates pledged to the ousting of Hill. He stated, "If a new manager were recommended and the city employees could weigh what they could get from him as opposed to Hill, they might go along against him, but I doubt it. Just an anti-Hill platform would get nothing out of the city employees." When asked whether Hill ever entered the political fray himself by supporting or opposing candidates, the reply was, "Yes, he supports candidates. He just passes the word down." Hill himself noted that while he never took any *identifiable* interest in a candidate's election or defeat, on a few occasions he had passed the word to "trusted city employees in regard to a councilman considered very bad." Hill went on to say that he felt he had achieved stability because he stayed out of politics, knew the city "backwards and forwards," and took the "moderate approach."

It may well be that Hill could not have survived Center City's factional political battles if he had incurred the strong disapproval of any one of the three ingredients in the political pot — liberals, conservatives, and city employees. The fact that he did not and still managed to push with vigor a widespread program of public improvements for Center City is eloquent testimony to his political skill.

Hill's temperament was to seek always the middle way; he was an eager student of the political writings of Aristotle. He took defeat of even his most cherished programs with good humor, and did not consider it his obligation to continue to agitate in order to win council approval for a program. He displayed a fine sense of political timing. When a liberal faction was in control, he pushed hard for the improvements that he felt were needed by the city. Most of the major improvement programs he launched were started during such periods. If the liberal council members insisted on petty rakeoffs from bids or "kickbacks" on contracts, however distasteful he found the practice, Hill simply looked the other way. He always made what he considered the correct recommendation based on what everyone agreed to be high administrative competence and absolute integrity. If the council did not accept the recommendation, he did not pursue the matter further.

Control of Center City politics by the liberal faction during eleven of the fifteen years of the study period gave Hill considerable support for the programs he wished to push, and he took full advantage of the opportunities by launching broad-scale improvements in streets, sanitary sewers, storm drains, recreational facilities, and many other such programs. At the same time, the liberal council was willing to go along with the demands made by the city employees through Hill.

When the conservatives were in power, Hill simply modified his program aspirations to conform with the new economy atmosphere, and tended to concentrate his attention on improving the quality of the administration. His widely recognized honesty and efficiency made him quite acceptable to the conservatives, as did his membership in one of the "best" and oldest families in the community. His ability to control the various department heads and through them the city's administration is again more a tribute to his political skill than to any "textbook" knowledge of public administration. The *quid pro quo* of Hill's support for city employees' aspirations in such matters as salary and working conditions seems to have been an acceptance of his administrative leadership in building an effective administrative force. The only obvious exception was the police force, and the consequences of the failure to make any satisfactory adjustment of the problem were to have far-reaching effects.

Center City's politics, therefore, normally featured a blend of "spenders," "penny-pinchers," political civil servants, and a manager highly skilled in the art and science of politics and administration. The ingredients were blended in such a way as to produce manager stability in a politically competitive situation. Hill's possession of an independent base of political power must be listed as the major reason for his job stability in the midst of a competitive political environment.

Suddenly in late 1960 the care and skill of Manager Hill in balancing the various elements of Center City's politics were negated by an unforeseen set of circumstances. The series of events that occurred within the course of six months produced a "reform" vote that swept out of office eight of ten incumbent councilmen, including individuals from each of the two factions. Not the least significant event in the entire upheaval was the resignation of Spencer Hill as manager and the recruitment from another state of a young professional manager.

In late 1960 National Investigations, Inc. disclosed the results of an inquiry into the activities of a gambling ring which involved "kickbacks" to several members of the Center City police force. The local newspaper gave the story widespread publicity, and the State's Attorney undertook a thorough investigation of the matter, followed by a grand jury probe which confirmed the existence of rather widespread graft in the police department. The grand jury investigation and report of the affair aired in the press and through other news media, affected the council election in the late spring of 1961. The highlight of the revelations was the report of the State's Attorney, which not only confirmed the alleged dishonesty in the police department but went on to criticize sharply city government officials and the civil service system.

The appearance of the State's Attorney's report initiated a series of political maneuverings that was climaxed by the elections several months later. The report placed much of the blame for the "sorry mess" in the police department on the civil service system in general and, in particular, on the strict seniority basis of promotions. However, it also criticized City Manager Spencer Hill rather sharply for not seeing that the police department was cleaned up long before, more or less ignoring both the legal and political factors that bound his hands. The council and the Civil Service Board also came in for adverse comment. Hill, stung by the criticism of him in the report, immediately submitted his resignation to the council, "to take effect at such time as you may determine." It seems clear that Hill initially submitted his resignation mainly as a means of getting a vote of confidence from the council. In this he was successful because the council did not act on his resignation, but, in fact, praised him for his work in the city.

The State's Attorney's report contained a number of specific suggestions for reform, one of which struck at the heart of the strict seniority basis of promotion. It suggested that top echelon personnel be removed from the civil service system and be made responsible to the city manager, presumably both as to their appointment and removal. It suggested that the Civil Service Board be increased from three to five, that Board tenure be restricted to one term, and that no city, county, state, or federal employee be allowed to serve. Furthermore, the report recommended that promotions in the several departments be made through competitive examination, tempered somewhat by tenure. These proposals immediately gained widespread support in the press and other news media. Public sentiment seemed, at least for the moment, strongly in favor of the suggested changes.

In these circumstances, given the political structure of Center City, the council, especially the liberal majority, found itself in a difficult predicament. Any change would have to come through a charter amendment by the state legislature, then in session. The pressures to accept the reforms were strong; yet the perils of supporting them were all too obvious to veterans of Center City politics. The council delayed for a time, but they were more or less forced into action when Manager Hill resubmitted his resignation, to be effective just after the upcoming municipal election. Hill then urged strongly that the civil service system be modified at least to the extent of giving the city manager power to substitute an examination for seniority should he deem it necessary.

Hill tried to strengthen his hand by pointing out that he had recommended virtually all the changes contained in the report of the State's Attorney almost a decade earlier, but that his recommendations had "been thrown into the waste basket." He also stated flatly that no manager could hope to clean up the scandals in the police department unless the strict seniority system were modified to place wider powers in the hands of the manager and the council. To those city employees and council members who grumbled that the changes might put too much power into the manager's (Hill's) hands, he pointed out that his impending retirement removed him from the picture. Hill's strong advocacy of changes in the civil service system, coupled with the clamor in the press and other news media, made it impossible for the commission to delay action any longer. The council resolved to ask the county's legislative delegation to get a local bill enacted for a charter change that would modify the civil service system by giving the manager the option of making promotions by seniority or through examinations. Three council members, two conservatives and one liberal, gave especially strong support to the change. The reason for the action of the liberal member was the cause of considerable amazed comment, and no really plausible explanation could be found. One newspaper reporter voiced the opinion that he had given the reform proposals support in the beginning because of heavy pressure from the newspapers and radio stations, thinking that he would be able to back out of it when things died down. However, "things did not die down, and he found himself out on a limb, committed to a position he really didn't want to support, with no way out."

Reform-oriented elections in Center City, as was noted above, tend to upset the normal strength of the competing factions in the political structure. More specifically, the increased registration and voting that come with a wave of reform agitation usually bring about a defeat for the city employees and liberals, who yield control temporarily to the conservatives. The 1961 election in Center City was no exception to this rule, but it was also complicated by a number of other significant variables. The scandal in the police department was accompanied by other forms of petty graft (rumored or actual) practiced by all the liberal members of the council, and even by one or two of the conservatives. "Many councilmen," one nonoffending conservative remarked, "are in the thing for what they can get out of it. They don't do what is good for the city." Such things as expense-account abuse, "kickbacks" on city purchases, and a generally irresponsible attitude toward spending were pin-pointed publicly.

A second factor of major importance, though impossible to assess with any precision, involved a basic change in the Center City electoral system approved by the 1959 legislature and put into practice for the first time in the 1961 election. The old system of electing half the council from wards was changed to one in which the same five wards were kept, but all candidates were required to run at large, two from each ward. Our impression was that the new system would hurt the favor-dispensing style of politics more characteristic of liberal candidates than it would harm the good government, "let's do what is best for the whole community" approach of the conservatives.[4]

A third factor that produced considerable heat during the 1961 campaign involved a rezoning proposal in which a large motel and high-rise apartments would have been approved on the fringe of an upper middle-class residential area. One conservative incumbent declared, "The three plumbers and the two electrical contractors on the council supported the deal, and it looked like voting their selfish interests." The indignation of opponents to the rezoning was increased when, after voting seven to three for the rezoning, the council spent a sizeable sum of money in trying to promote its acceptance. The rezoning deal activitated the "old guard" wing of the conservative group to the most vigorous action it had shown since it opposed the threat of an out-of-town bank in 1951. A prominent attorney, long a leader in old guard circles, headed up an anti-rezoning group that put up sizeable sums of money in support of candidates opposing incumbents who favored the change. One incumbent council member remarked, "The anti-rezoning people really organized, and they did back candidates. Every person who had supported the rezoning thing was badly beaten in the general vicinity of the land in controversy, not just in the immediately surrounding area."

A fourth ingredient in Center City politics, the anti-liquor group, the "drys," were encouraged to become active by the general moral tone of the campaign induced by the police and council scandals. The drys took a vigorous part in the campaign and actively supported at least two candidates. A questionnaire was sent to each candidate seeking his stand on such questions as closing hours for bars and the nearness of bars and package stores to churches. At least one conservative candidate for re-election was caught in the dry crossfire when he supported a liquor license for a motel located within 500 feet of a Jewish synagogue. Because the synagogue offered no objection to the license, the conservative in question publicly lectured his fellow Baptists for insisting that it not be granted. He was badly beaten in the primary by a candidate supported by the "drys."

The political upheaval that enlivened Center City's politics in 1961 started with scandals in the police department, broadened to include specific charges — mostly against liberal councilmen — of misuse of

---

[4] Both liberals and conservatives seem to have supported the change out of a fear that a Negro would be elected to the council from within a predominantly Negro ward.

office, and was complicated by vigorous political activity by "drys" and anti-rezoning groups. In all of this, what happened to the original proposals for reform that came out of the report by the State's Attorney involving changes in the civil service system? One might assume that public indignation over inadequacies that had been widely blamed on the rigid system of promotion would force any alleged reform candidate to take a clear stand for at least the changes involving the restriction of the seniority rule for promotion that had been accepted, however reluctantly, by the council.

The final results of the elections did, indeed, produce a sweeping change in the composition of the council. All incumbents ran again — eight were defeated. The two survivors included one highly respected conservative whose long record of support for "clean" government and wide circle of acquaintance in all walks of life in Center City gave him an uncommonly strong political base from which to operate. The lone liberal survivor can only be explained as a "fluke." A typical response to the question of why he survived was, "It was luck in that he had a weak opponent who was not smart enough to take advantage of the reform atmosphere."

A sweeping change, then, did occur. Did it, as one might expect, produce a clear-cut majority in favor of civil service reform? The question might best be answered by identifying the stand taken on the question by the winners. Of the eight new councilmen, three opposed in their campaign any change in the civil service system, two held that the matter should be given more study, and three favored some change, at least a modification of the seniority system of promotion. The voter's choice was not always clear-cut on the issue, but in at least one instance an incumbent liberal campaigning vigorously for a change in the seniority system was beaten in the primary by a conservative status quo man. Of the two incumbents who survived, the conservative supported change in the civil service system, and the liberal opposed it. A whole range of questions remains unanswered as to just what did happen in the election and why. The follow-up appraisal we made was, of necessity, hasty and superficial. Taking the election results as the dependent variable, we are not able to assess with any precision the relative weight of such independent variables as the new election system, the rezoning issue, the police scandal, the petty graft on the part of the council, the importance of an all-out "get-out-the-vote" drive by the Junior Chamber of Commerce, the relative importance of the city employees, etc. Yet a number of things can be said about the outcome.

Politics in Center City during the period 1945–1961 divided along conservative and liberal lines, with the city employees playing an important part in determining the winner of the factional struggles. The liberals, supported by the city employees, were the majority faction, and held power during much of the period. The conservatives depended on scandals in government to arouse a generally apathetic public and produce registration and voting figures large enough to overcome liberal support by city employees. However, victory by the conservatives did not produce, during the study period, any strong move to alter the civil service system in a way designed to reduce the power of the employee group. The 1961 election continued the pattern of former "scandal-oriented" elections, with some added variations of its own. Nobody came forward to organize a slate dedicated to support of the changes in the civil service system recommended by the State's Attorney report. The only slates that appeared were put forward by groups interested in other matters. The issue of civil service reform, judging from the results, did not loom as decisive in the election. The best generalization that can be made from the data available, still largely impressionistic, is that the election was a "throw the rascals out" operation in which, in several cases, proponents of reform were also removed indiscriminately. The new council did not contain a majority favoring civil service changes, but most of those who proposed further study ultimately swung over to the side of change, after the new manager took over.

Was the election, then, essentially meaningless within the framework of Center City political factions? The answer is no. A liberal majority was replaced by a conservative majority, with the best estimate being that the new council was divided about 7–3. This means, we would speculate, that for the next two years, a more frugal attitude will prevail in the use of public funds, petty graft will decline, and the city employees will not get as much in the way of salary and fringe benefit improvements as they would like. Should no new scandals break out, and no new base of political power be created, one might expect that in 1963 the liberals will return to power behind the solid support of the city employee group, helped by a reduced registration and voting turnout. The conservatives will then fall back to their traditional minority position.

The election had meaning for Center City in one other important way. City Manager Spencer Hill had laid his position as manager "on the line" in giving strong support to civil service reform. If a majority favoring such changes had prevailed, it seems clear that he would have stayed. When it did not, Hill carried through with his previously announced intention of resigning. William S. Blackwell, a professional manager with a good record, replaced him. Within a year of his accession to the manager post, Blackwell has expressed concern over the political cohesiveness of the city employees. He took advantage of his initial popularity with the new council by establishing a system of promotion on the basis of competitive examination, firing the police chief, and appointing a much younger chief from the ranks. Naturally the city employees resent these moves. Whether Blackwell can survive the political structure of Center City, particularly if the electorate relapses into its usual apathy, is an open question.

VI

A number of groups and issues in addition to those already examined were of sufficient moment in Center City politics to deserve some analysis. Those interviewed agreed that the Negro vote is of sufficient importance to cause any candidate to seek Negro support and that there is a rather well-defined group of Negro leaders through whom candidates make the effort. There is a wide difference of opinion as to just how large the Negro vote is in relation to the total vote, and to what degree it is a bloc vote. Certainly there are several wards in which the Negro vote is in the majority, although no Negro has ever run for the council. One veteran observer of the political scene held that Negroes in Center City are split into conservative and progressive factions. He felt that this split helps keep them from being a significant factor in Center City politics. Conservatives are defined as those willing to settle for any favors the white power structure is willing to hand out. The progressives are said to be interested in using Negro political power to seek better services in the Negro sections. The few Negroes interested in the integration problem do not seem to have widespread support.

An incumbent councilman in 1960 described the Negro vote as "definitely a minor factor," but he went on to say: "They do vote as a bloc, and they have strong leadership. Winning the Negro vote involves spending a great deal of money. First of all, you have to have girls at the polling places to check Negroes in, to give them voting instructions. Secondly you have to pay taxicab drivers, mostly for gasoline, to take Negroes to the polls." He concluded that all candidates try to woo the Negro vote.

Manager Hill reported that Negroes had been registering and voting for a long while, and that it "just gradually built up" to what he felt was about 25 per cent of the total vote. After describing the "radical" (interested in integration), and "moderate" Negro leaders, he noted that candidates did try to get a bloc vote from the Negroes but without much success. The vote, in Hill's eyes, was usually obtained through promises of better services. Because the liberals were freer spenders, he felt they were more likely to win Negro support, especially from the younger group. Hill said that while the race issue had not been injected into city politics, the problem lurked below the surface and could boil to the top at any time. He noted that the city paid for a membership in the National Association for the Advancement of Colored People in order to have reliable information on what that group was planning — in other words, they had an "informer" planted in the group. In this way the city learned of an NAACP plan to stage a bus sit-in to force mixed seating on Center City's buses. Hill promptly called all bus drivers together, told them what would happen, and gave instructions that they were to let Negroes sit anywhere they wished. The NAACP representative came to town, but "she finally got tired of riding in the front of buses," her money ran out, and she left town with no incident having occurred, and with the great majority of people in Center City unaware of what had taken place.

The handling of another incident involving race illustrates Hill's skill in dealing with a potentially "ticklish" situation. A large church conference held in the municipal auditorium involved "six or eight" Negroes, who thus created an "integrated dinner" at the meeting's banquet. A group of white men, presumably representing such groups as the Ku Klux Klan and/or the White Citizens Council, moved among all the delegates' cars in the parking area and placed "hate" literature on all windshields. Hill had the police quietly follow and remove all the literature, and the incident never came to light.

Political participation by Negroes in Center City is not yet complicated by overt agitation on integration questions. The city's golf course was integrated at the request of a Negro group (after court action had been initiated) although separate club house facilities were constructed. Hill reported with some pride that the course was used considerably more than it had been before integration. His only problem was that many Negroes from a nearby city (in another state) which did not allow Negroes to play on the municipal golf course came to Center City to play.

An ex-councilman, in commenting on the Negro vote, said, "It's not a bloc vote any more. You just get it by knowing them." The fullest account of an effort to win the Negro vote came from a veteran of many Center City political battles. After estimating that Negroes constituted about 20 per cent of the total vote, he first held that they did not vote in a bloc, then decided they voted as a bloc in "a couple of wards," and finally concluded that they did vote as a bloc if somebody mobilized them to do it. He went on to describe his Negro vote-getting tactics as follows:

I get it touch with the undertaker, a gambler, a tourist court owner, and four or five others. My Negroes are on the lower east side and

I give a big blow-out for them with a little beer and that kind of thing and then I take a list of the colored people who get registered and I send around a car with a man in it, a Negro man in it, with a list. He goes around and takes all the people he can to the polls to vote and he comes back with the list with the names of the people checked who voted.

The same man went on to say that almost any candidate could win if he could mobilize both the city employees and the Negro vote in his favor. He noted finally that he was the only one who made such an elaborate attempt to organize the Negro vote.

Labor seems to exercise little political power in Center City despite the considerable amount of industrialization in the area. Most of the local unions are A.F.L. craft unions, and no effective central committee has been established. Their few ventures into politics have been ill-planned, poorly executed, and unsuccessful. One limiting factor has been the failure to unionize the largest industrial employer in the area. In addition, because much of the new post-World War II industry is located in the metropolitan area outside the city limits, many of the workers also live outside the city.

Church groups have become active from time to time, especially a militant "dry" faction that occasionally organizes behind a candidate. The surrounding county allows the sale of alcoholic beverages, and "dry" forces have not been able to marshal a serious drive in favor of adopting local-option prohibition. However, they do wage bitter battles over such matters as the regulation and location of bars and package stores. Religious bigotry has occasionally been evident in campaigns, especially on one occasion when a council candidate supported by the "drys" used "hate literature" tactics in defeating an incumbent Jewish councilman. Such techniques seem to have been rare in Center City politics, and the same Jew was later re-elected to the council.

Center City, in summary, is a town in which rival political factions are in continuous competition for control of the council. The competition centers around the liberal clique, the conservative clique, and the city employees. The Negroes are a minor force in this competition. According to our model, such a situation should have produced an unstable setting for the city manager, yet Center City's manager served from 1947 until 1961. A number of factors help explain the manager's survival amidst political turbulence, but the most important by far was his success in building an independent base of political power from which to operate as a participant, and a major one, in Center City's political process. The rather unusual effect of all this was to produce manager stability in the midst of sharp political competition.

5

Eastbourne

Eastbourne is an island of rural culture in the midst of one of the South's most densely populated counties. One of twenty-two municipalities in Jordan County, it has remained resistant to the modernization, urbanization, and industrialization going on around it as it has limped along in a poverty foreign even to towns in the heart of agricultural areas. In this respect Eastbourne is not unlike other towns of rural antecedents and stubbornly rural outlook around which a metropolis has grown up.

Eastbourne is, however, not just rural in outlook. It is a mean town, devoid of any cultural facilities of its own and of the slightest desire to understand the various faces of modern culture. Its leaders are immersed in petty personalities and pointless and issueless bickering for insignificant "place." This town is referred to by its more prosperous and citified neighbors as the "slum of Jordan County." The level of politics of Eastbourne will become apparent as the story of events in 1960 unfolds.

The principal impression one receives of Eastbourne on entering the town is that of a planless mixture of second-rate motels, trailer parks, small business concerns of all kinds, poor looking lunch counters, beer parlors and seedy restaurants, a number of churches, ordinary inexpensive homes, some of which are fairly old, and several rather large modern shopping centers. The centers were annexed during the late 1950's to provide the town with state cigarette tax money, which is still its largest single source of revenue. One sees along the federal highway that runs through the center of the town a very high proportion of aged retirees, many of whom look poverty-stricken and desolate as they sit among the trailers or on the porches of small cottages along the side streets. Eastbourne's population is made up primarily of working-class people and retirees from this class. Citizens of other towns in the same county describe Eastbourne as "a place to be from, not a place to go to."

Yet obviously the retirees have come to Eastbourne, for unattractive as it may seem to the academic observer, it offers an inexpensive place where a person may spend his declining years on Social Security. The 1960 census shows that 24.9 per cent of Eastbourne's population consists of persons sixty-five years of age or older. This fact alone makes it distinctly a retirement town. Also the town has 23.7 per cent of its population in the under eighteen group, another fact which fits in with the retirement characteristics of the town, as this is a very low percentage in the school age group.

Eastbourne grew from 1,031 in 1940 to 1,547 in 1950 and to 5,302 in 1960. Some of this growth came through annexation of the areas adjacent to the shopping centers already mentioned. However, a major part of the growth undoubtedly came from the influx of retirees.

Interestingly enough, the city council members and local newspaper editor do not like to convey the impression that Eastbourne is essentially a working class community. They all refer in a completely misleading way to middle-class subdivisions to the west of the town as parts of Eastbourne itself although in fact these subdivisions are *not* within the city limits of Eastbourne, and their residents want no part of the thought of annexation by Eastbourne. A number of Eastbourne businessmen live in these subdivisions along with some retired military personnel, most of whom seem to be of the rank of colonel, comander, or brigadier general, at the highest.

Younger people, described by Eastbourne councilmen as "technicians" in local factories, but actually factory workers in these electronics and electrical parts plants, are natives of Eastbourne. There are no Negroes, a fact which will be explained later, but their lack is no particular hardship, as there is little need for domestic labor.

Eastbourne is an old town, settled shortly after the Civil War as a fruit growing and processing center. Many of the orchards were planted during the 1880's and were long the center of Jordan County's prosperity. Today, however, there are few orchards left in the county, and most of the few remaining may be found in Eastbourne where they are proudly pointed out by local people in explaining the origin of the town as a crossroads marketing and processing center. Jordan County was founded by seven brothers Bray, most of whom seem to have settled in Eastbourne, for today all openly acclaim the Bray family in all its numerous ramifications as "running" the city. Eastbourne, then, differs from most rural towns in having *one* family, not several families, that dominates it.

During the twenties Eastbourne had a "boom" psychology, and it annexed a larger area. To service this area it went heavily into debt on a general obligation bond issue. Most of the improvements were not built, and the city defaulted on debt payment in the thirties. In fact, it tried to repudiate this debt, a gambit not permitted by the bond-holders or the courts. Several years passed, however, before the repudiationist sentiment in the town subsided sufficiently so that a refunding agreement could be made with the bondholders. Such an agreement was not made until 1951. In the thirties, most of the territory annexed the previous decade was de-annexed, and the town receded to its limited boundaries of the World War I period, at which it remained until the late fifties.

II

Eastbourne municipal government has two peculiar provisions: a recall election may be invoked at any time against elected officers, and the city manager is removable by the process of impeachment. These peculiarities may be explained by the fact that Eastbourne was the first city in the state to adopt council-manager government, and, indeed, was one of the first in the nation to do so. The concepts now attached to this form of government had not been well defined at that time. The original Eastbourne charter preceded the first draft of the Model City Charter of the National Municipal League by several years.

The town charter provides for a board of five commissioners who serve as councilmen, one of whom was elected by the council annually until 1960 to serve as mayor. In 1960 the charter was amended to provide for a popularly elected mayor, chosen for a two-year term. Terms of councilmen are for two years, with two elected in even-numbered and two and the mayor in odd-numbered years. Elections are held the first Tuesday in June. Vacancies in the office of mayor due to death, resignation, or inability to act are filled by the remainder of the council. The mayor is vested with general supervisory powers over all town officers except his colleagues on the council. The council elects one of its members as town treasurer. By a three-fifth vote the council may expel any of their numbers from office for nonattendance or "other improper conduct while in office" and by majority vote may remove the mayor. Councilmen were unpaid until 1961, but since 1961 they have received a salary of $50 per month, and the mayor receives $65 per month.

The city manager is appointed by the council, presumably by majority vote, and despite the impeachment provision the "common law" of town practice permits simple firing of the manager by majority vote of the council, as is customary in other council-manager towns. According to the charter the manager also serves as town clerk, town tax assessor, town tax collector, chief of police, chief of the fire department, sanitary inspector, superintendent of public service, supervisor of registration, building inspector, and anything else the commissioners wish to make of him. Actually the charter is completely out of date in these provisions, for most of these duties have either devolved on separate department heads as the years have passed or have been taken over by the county from the various municipalities, as in the case of sanitary inspection, tax assessment, and voter registration. The charter gives the manager power to appoint subordinates with the "advice and approval" of the council, but it fails to mention power of removal. It may be assumed that this power is either vested in the council in the form of the impeachment power given them, or that it is a simple derivative of the appointing power and belongs to the manager. It is unclear which interpretation should apply and, therefore, a fertile area for controversy is opened up.

The unique recall provision mentioned has no time limit on instituting recall petitions against local government officers. It is customary in other jurisdictions which use the system of recall to exempt officers from liability to this procedure during the first six months so as to enable them to formulate and at least start execution of a program. Not so in Eastbourne. At any time after taking office, any holder of an elective office may be subjected to recall by the process of a petition signed by a number of registered voters equal to at least 50 per cent of the total number who voted in the last preceding municipal election. The 50 per cent requirement is an extraordinarily high number of signatures for recall petitions. A special recall election must be called within twenty days of the filing of the recall petitions. Removal from office is immediate if a majority of the voters cast an affirmative vote for recall. Within three days after the canvass of the recall election the clerk must issue a call for a new election, to be held within thirty days from the date of canvass of the recall election. *If less than a majority of the board of commissioners remains in office after the recall election, the town clerk is vested with authority to appoint persons to fill the vacancies until the special election can be held.* Vesting such power in the clerk, who is an appointive officer, is an extraordinary charter provision, since this means giving a subordinate officer the power to make temporary appointments of those to whom he is responsible. This very power of temporary appointment may influence the outcome of the special election. It would seem that the normal set of relationships and lines of responsibility are completely inverted by this provision of the Eastbourne charter.

Eastbourne has had one of the highest turnover rates for city managers in the state, but much of this turnover among managers took place between the end of World War II and 1951. Not again until

1959 did any dramatic events occur in connection with a manager dismissal, and dismissal in that year is tied in with the bitter recall fight to be discussed later.

Mayor's role. The role of the mayor in policy-making and in administration has varied from one administration to another according to personalities. It is clear from a description of the brief regime of the Clay faction that Robert Clay took seriously the provision of the charter that the mayor is to supervise all officers and examine into the conduct of their offices and to make recommendations "of measures touching public service." Certainly he assumed policy initiative and administrative direction, for better or worse. In two respects he failed in exercising administrative powers. One — failure to appoint a town director of civil defense — was an oversight on his part, and through this lapse a political crisis of considerable magnitude developed for him. The other failure involved interference with the rights and responsibilities of the town manager over the police department. Although the charter clearly gives the mayor the right to investigate the conduct of town business by any official, it is silent on the disciplining or removal of town officials or employees by him. At the very least, this latter power is not specifically given to the mayor. Presumably it can be fairly implied as belonging to the city manager, one of whose charter duties is to act as police chief. However, Clay as mayor seized the inititative in getting the council to remove the police chief and disregard the impeachment process in the charter. The question of whether Clay as mayor could exercise the initiative in a removal does not appear to have occurred to the "old guard" fighting Clay. Instead they raised the issue of an open hearing versus a closed hearing for the chief before the council rather than the very existence of a power to effect ordinary removal through simple resolution. Simply judging by the way he handled the dismissal of the police chief, it is highly doubtful that Robert Clay ever actually understood the proper operations of council-manager government and of his role as mayor in this type of government.

The present manager was mayor for eight years during the fifties. Clay views this man, John Morse, as a mere tie-breaker who presided over meetings but allowed his brother-in-law, who was then manager, to run the council as well as the administrative side. In other words, during the Morse mayoralty it was the manager rather than the mayor who ran the city. The manager arranged for Clay to be appointed to a vacant council seat, and then the next year for the Bray "clique" to withdraw support from Clay in the election. Actually, the manager did not "invite" Clay to run for council.

The present mayor, a member of the Bray "clique," exercises considerable power over policy and administration. In fact, his interference in administration now is routine and is supported by at least two other members of the council. One of the present councilmen is a Bray brother-in-law, and another councilman has had a long history of political activity in the town. These two councilmen appear to allow the mayor to be the "strong mayor" type he wishes to be.

It would be futile to discuss with Morse, the present manager, how department heads are selected. For one thing, there have been no vacancies to test his influence with that of the commission over appointments. Second, most of the present council, including Morse as an interim councilman, voted as a body to rehire the police chief ousted by Clay. They were as clearly in violation of the charter as was Clay when he induced the council to fire the chief. It occurred to them no more than to Clay to limit council action to a recommendation to the *manager* to rehire the chief. Not a one of the "old guard," including Morse, seems to have conceived of the selection of the police chief as the *manager's* prerogative. If this episode is truly indicative of Morse's methods of operating, then Morse will never take the initiative in filling any post but will expect the council to make actual personnel selections and dismissals. This also means the present mayor, the manager, and the present majority do not understand the operation of council-manager government and do not have any notion — regardless of charter provisions — of the boundaries of administrative powers and responsibilities of the manager. This is a "no man's land" in Eastbourne that the council can invade at will. Indeed, one councilman told quite innocently of how he had called up the garbage supervisor directly without going to Morse, the manager, about some garbage left at his home, but stated that he called as a "private citizen."

Despite the closeness of the present council and the manager, bound by ties of marriage as well as of politics, all have denied holding pre-meeting conferences, informal or agenda sessions, or caucuses to debate issues frankly and arrive at preliminary decisions. The history of the Clay regime shows many closed door sessions, sometimes of the Clay bloc only, to arrive at council decisions. Indeed, this practice permitted a serious press criticism of the Clay bloc. But on this point the "old guarders" are contradictory and less than accurate. For example, they indicated that the manager had prepared a tentative budget which he "discussed with them privately." They failed to indicate that they hired Morse as manager at an "unscheduled" meeting of which the press was not notified and did not even announce his appointment at the next public meeting. The very day after the manager and council denied having private sessions, a local reporter trailed Morse and the council to a private luncheon meeting at the airport, where they went over a feasibility report of engineers on some public works projects under consideration that later became their major program.

Morse is not expected to take the policy initiative and does not, in fact, do so. In fact, he gives the impression of being very unsure of himself, an understandable impression in the light of his career and the secondary role he played as mayor. Although he has an M.B.A. degree from a leading graduate school of business administration, he was from 1945 to 1960 cashier-bookkeeper in a local Eastbourne appliance shop. He accepted the managership of Eastbourne, which pays $8,000 per year, because it offered him more money.

Manager turnover in Eastbourne. Looking at the list of managers Eastbourne has had since the war, it is readily apparent that the town had frequent changes from 1945 to 1951 and then one manager from 1951 to 1958, with marked turnover once again in 1958 and 1959. In 1945 John Morse, present manager and a Bray son-in-law, had been serving as manager for some time and resigned to accept private employment. He was followed by a manager who resigned in 1947 to accept a bank position. In 1948 Mason Blue served as manager, to be followed in 1949 by Ben Redd, but in late 1949 Blue was back again. Blue, an engineer who was considered a professional manager in Eastbourne, was intensely disliked and was forced to resign in 1951. He was escorted to the town limits by a jeering crowd to speed him on his way. Redd was actually a city employee used as a stop-gap manager. The council majority, representing even more explicitly than heretofore the interests of the Bray clan with two Bray sons-in-law now on the council, made another Bray son-in-law, Edgar White, the manager in 1951. Morse of the Bray clan was elected mayor by the council that year and served in that capacity until the June 1959 election when he chose not to run. The selection of brothers-in-law as mayor and manager is a "chummy" arrangement that is unusual, to say the least.

The rise of Clay's influence in the town and his defiance of White and the Bray clan, particularly in the recount he demanded for one of the council seats in the 1958 election, sent White into a decline, and he resigned as manager shortly after the June 1958 election. He was followed by Henry Frothingham, a professional city manager recruited from outside and an engineer by profession, who served from September 15, 1958, to October 8, 1959, when he was compelled to resign in a "power play" made by the Clay faction to try to save themselves from impending defeat in the recall maneuver precipitated by the Bray clique. The fire chief who was also public works head served as acting manager from October, 1959, to February, 1960, when John Morse, Bray son-in-law, was brought back as manager by the clique.

During a fifteen-year period there were therefore, two forced resignations and one, that of Edgar White, which anticipated possible forced resignation, two voluntary resignations, and two stop-gap manager appointments which were really temporary in nature, one of which was brought to an end in a way not clear to present informants. The forced resignations in each instance are explained by present Eastbourne councilmen, in recounting the history of these years, as due to personality deficiencies. Issues, they said, were never related in any way to manager terminations. The last two involuntary terminations of Eastbourne managers are clearly attributable to a "power play," that is, an attempt to forestall a change in factional control.

III

The big event in Eastbourne politics in recent years was the recall election in the fall of 1959, and much that developed in that affray explains the town. It is necessary to trace the rise of the mayor who was recalled in order to understand the 1959 sequence.

The origin of the Clay faction. Robert Clay, contractor and retailer in Eastbourne, became the focal point for the effort to challenge the "old guard" of Eastbourne in the fifties and the sixties. Immediately upon coming to Eastbourne after the war, Clay ran into headlong competition with Link, longtime councilman, who was engaged in the same business as Clay and did not fancy competition. In fact, the way of this town, as is so often true of rural centers, is not that of competitive business but of well-recognized historic monopolies. Clay, therefore, was a business interloper, and he did not endear himself to the dominant business group of the town by his outspoken and aggressive ways. Actually, therefore, it was something of a surprise when Edgar White, the city manager, suggested to the council in 1952 that it appoint Clay to a vacant council seat. Possibly this appointment was made with the thought of co-opting Clay into the ruling group at least temporarily and rendering him harmless.

Long-standing practice of councilmen in Eastbourne has been for them to ask each other to run before each election. Manager White and the "old guard" majority on the council in 1953 did not "invite" Robert Clay to run for a council seat. But Clay ran and won without their blessing and made himself a dissident minority voice on the council. The next year he was joined by another contractor, Leary, who regularly voted with him, and a real tug-of-war developed within the council; there were many tie votes which John Morse, then mayor, had to break in favor of the "old guard." In June, 1958, a Clay ally lost in a close election, and he and Clay demanded a recount. Although the council seat was not gained by the recount, because the court threw the case out on a technicality, Edgar White was so upset at the recount maneuver and unfavorable publicity regarding the election practices he countenanced, that he became ill and used that excuse to resign as manager before he could be fired.

Clay's articulated complaints against the Bray clique rule during this period are that the "old timers" gave favors to their friends and city jobs to members of the clan. "Practices were not equitable, and people were not being treated the same way," Clay declares in explanation of his opposition. He also opposed the way White as manager "ran" the council in the sense of determining who should be appointed to vacancies and who should get group support in elections. It is interesting, however, that Clay does not recall his own appointment to the council vacancy as an instance of this very type of interference by White. But more important in Clay's eyes was the opposition the "old timers" had to the growth of the town because of what Clay believed to be their fear that they would lose control. Clay had, and still has, the firm conviction that Link, his rival in business who has long been on the council, and the editor of the local newspaper both have a marked personal profit in keeping the town under their control, Link through supplying the city with certain goods and the editor through receiving lucrative legal advertising by the city. These are not inconsiderable items in a small town.

Clay and his ally Barnes, who was involved in the recount attempt, made an all-out attack on the Bray clique rule in the 1958 campaign and criticized family control of the town. They made it clear that they wanted to change city managers and charged that Manager White did not distribute city business fairly among local businessmen and had spent, in violation of the charter, sums in excess of $200. Just after Barnes' recount suit was filed, White became upset, had a "heart attack" (later admitted to be a digestive difficulty), and claimed that he must resign for health reasons. The council then proceeded to recruit an outside manager. The advice of a local retiree who seemed to have acquired considerable status with the council was sought and taken with respect to manager recruitment, especially as to both the need for a professional manager, particularly an engineer, and also as to the recommendation of Henry Frothingham. The latter was appointed in September, 1958.

Clay got together a regular ticket to contest for all three council seats open in the June, 1959, regular election, and his group campaigned vigorously from house to house, which aroused "old guard" ire, for such campaigning was not done in Eastbourne. Peters, a Bray ally and a small town Ohio retiree who ran a trailer park and who had beaten Barnes the year before in the recount fight, ran for re-election to a full two-year term. Barnes, also a migrant from Ohio and the operator of a small motel, ran again on the Clay slate along with Camp, a native of Eastbourne. Contrary to the usual practice in council elections, Clay had a platform, and Barnes was his principal exponent of it. Annexation of surrounding areas "with caution," an improved sewer system, paving standards, better street lights, and support of the city manager, with the council restricting itself to policy and leaving the town manager to carry out its decisions, and "a government for the people and by the people" were all planks in the Clay platform. Barnes, Camp, and Peters all won seats on the council, and since Clay was holding over from the previous year, this gave him control of the council. The council promptly elected him mayor. He was now in the saddle.

Early Clay faction moves. Sometimes the most minor and unexpected events precipitate crises. So it was in Eastbourne. About a month before Clay became mayor, Ben Abner, councilman and Bray son-in-law, resigned as civil defense chief of the town, and the post remained for Clay to fill. Clay neglected to fill this position and created his first real crisis: early in September the entire civil defense unit resigned in a body with the charge of lack of cooperation on the part of Mayor Clay, particularly important during the season of storms and natural disasters. It must be said in Clay's defense, however, that he looked upon civil defense as a part of national defense rather than in connection with local disaster relief and that in leisurely fashion he had been looking over local retired military officers with the thought of asking one with the proper background to head the local unit.

During the summer of 1959 there were other moves by the majority bloc that stirred some controversy, but nothing like the September gale which blew up and ultimately reached hurricane velocity to sweep Clay, Barnes, and Camp out of office by the end of October. A surprise move to annex two shopping centers by a strip annexation of rights-of-way to and beyond the centers had to be dropped when it was fought by the shopping center property owners, who threatened to sue the city. The councilmen who had voted unanimously to annex in late July also voted unanimously in early September to repeal the annexation ordinance. This made the Clay faction appear to be rash and precipitate in its actions, trying to "bull through" a move not sufficiently thought out. Editorially the local paper had applauded the annexation of the centers. At the end of July and well before the reversal of the shopping center annexations the editor praised the smoothness, thoroughness, and speed with which business of the town was being transacted by the council and Manager Frothingham. The harmony in the council was noted with approval. This was truly the lull before the storm.

The first budget presented by Manager Frothingham in early August, 1959, set a record for Eastbourne, exceeding the half million dollar mark. The increased expenditures were postulated upon expected increased revenues from annexation of the two shopping centers, a measure which collapsed in September. Budget increases provided for extension of water mains to all areas of the town, a sewer lift station and sewers for the east side of Eastbourne, three firemen to be employed to establish a full-time fire department, expansion of the sewage treatment plant, remodeling of the fire station, extension of street lighting on the main highway through the town, continuation of alterations of the city auditorium, widening and repaving of a major street, and many new equipment items. Actually the three full-time fire department employees were controversial not merely because of cost but also because of the kind of interest and club feeling of possessiveness developed by volunteer firemen in a small town. Ben Abner especially voiced doubts in council about a paid full-time fire department and opposed the item for a specific salary for the fire chief on the ground that this implied that the long-time fire chief would not remain in that capacity. This was really an unconscious admission by Abner that his friend, the chief, was unqualified for a paid job. Despite Abner's criticism, the budget was finally adopted as presented by Frothingham in late August, 1959.

The firing of the manager. The first major thunderclaps of the storm broke out on September 22, 1959, when Manager Frothingham turned in his "resignation," ostensibly to accept other employment, the plans for which were "not complete." His resignation was originally to take effect on October 17, but with the police "crisis" that developed in early October, he was forced to make it effective immediately on October 8, more than a week before the original date set. Actually, there is no question about the fact that Frothingham was fired by the council, but the reasons for the firing and Frothingham's precipitate withdrawal from Eastbourne are in dispute and by their nature impossible to establish factually.

On the one side may be placed the allegations by the Bray clan that Clay and Frothingham formed a working team to consolidate Clay's political hold on the town by firing the police chief, to be followed later, they claim, by a "cleaning out" of city employees. They allege that the two conspired to "frame" the police chief for inefficiency in handling police records by deliberately hiding missing police summonses in the desk of Frothingham's secretary. The label of "morally bad man" that Peters and Abner pinned on Frothingham is derived from two sets of innuendoes. The first is that Clay was trying to institute a 10 to 15 per cent "kick back" scheme from those who wanted to do business with the city and they imputed acquiescence in this scheme to Frothingham. They still repeat, "You must be able to trust the manager; he must be honest." The second set of innuendoes attributes to Frothingham "indiscretions" with the opposite sex. Peters and Abner claim that they forced Frothingham's resignation by threat of exposure (the subject of "exposure" remains vague) and induced Camp to join them in going to Frothingham with a draft of a letter of resignation, and that Frothingham agreed immediately to resign.

On the other side, Barnes and Clay deny the confrontation episode. A reporter from a major daily of the area confirms their description of the hostility displayed toward Frothingham by both Peters and Abner from the date of his appointment and their resentment against his refusal to allow them to interfere in petty details of administration. Barnes agreed that the Peters-Abner hints of "indiscretions" were a "factor" in dismissing Frothingham. But Barnes stressed as very important in the decision to fire Frothingham the latter's "bad public relations," which seem to consist of "rubbing people the wrong way," "driving like mad," "scratching off," "roaring to a stop," and generally offending the old people of the town. Also Barnes stated that Peters and Abner had caught Frothingham in "little white lies," which they exaggerated. Barnes does admit that the council members went to Frothingham with a letter of resignation written by Peters in his own handwriting, asking Frothingham to resign immediately because of lack of police protection in the town. (This was immediately after the *second* firing of the police chief and merely explains the reason, as Barnes remembers it, for compelling Frothingham to leave immediately). Barnes agreed that the council had voted unanimously to fire Frothingham, the Clay faction agreeing that he was "too much of a liability to defend." Both the newspaper reporter and Clay scoff at the "indiscretions" charge. Barnes and Clay both denounce the "kickback" innuendoes as "typical Bray smear tactics." Clay agrees with Barnes that the police "crisis" was back of the firing of Frothingham, and in his version of the story he was working on a contract some distance from town and could not be present when the other four council members demanded Frothingham's immediate resignation. He claims that he found it impossible to reverse this action when he returned although he persuaded Camp to reverse himself on the firing of the police chief after Peters and Abner had indeed induced Camp to defect to their side.

The editor of the local weekly considered Frothingham politically inept and blames him for making a bad political error in trying to annex the shopping centers. (At the time of the attempted annexation the editor praised this move). He considered Frothingham a personable man who made a good initial impression, but he accused Frothingham of falsifying the extent and level of his prior managerial experience in order to get the Eastbourne job.

The reporter from one of the dailies, already cited, praised Frothingham as a good administrator who had "cleaned up" city hall, reorganized the departments, started new procedures, etc. She attributed his downfall in large part to the sabotaging he received from the long-time town clerk, "Miss Mary," who "had her knife out" for him the moment he arrived at the Eastbourne city hall, as his way of doing things was not hers, and she obviously feared that her position with the council would be undermined. Frothingham, according to this reporter, moved too fast for Eastbourne, which had never heard of some of his ideas.

It is interesting to reflect that Frothingham had been hired as manager by the "old guard" group in 1958 in what was undoubtedly a "power play," an attempt to win public favor by employment of a professional city manager and thus to forestall the defeat they feared in the next election. They had advertised nationally and had found Frothingham's letters of recommendation and employment record superior to the rest but apparently had never called back to the town where he had been employed to converse directly with councilmen there about his weaknesses and strengths. Actually Frothingham had been fired twice, once as a department superintendent, in that town, but the written recommendations from that city to Eastbourne had been glowing. The retiree previously mentioned who acted as consultant to the council on the hiring of a manager was a so-called "consultant economist" but actually served as a right-wing propagandist for one of the country's largest corporations, and he claimed to the council that he knew of Frothingham in some fashion never made quite clear. The retiree recommended Frothingham highly; he also insisted that the vote of the council should be unanimous. A claim by Peters and Abner is quite unfounded that Clay had fobbed off in the person of Frothingham a former classmate despite a "gentleman's agreement" among the council not to push a friend of any of them. The employment record independently furnished by Frothingham to the study team shows that he grew up and attended public schools in an entirely different state from Clay and attended a different university.

Why was Frothingham fired in the first instance and the date of effectiveness of his resignation speeded up in the second place? Probably Barnes has given as accurate a set of reasons for the initial vote to fire as anyone — that because of bad public relations Frothingham had become a political liability. The way in which the shopping center annexations turned sour, the attack by the volunteer firemen, aided and abetted by Abner, on the Frothingham budget item for a full-time fire department, Frothingham's unfortunate manner with the public, his tactless behavior, the explosion over civil defense (which was not his fault at all), and the resignation en masse of civil defense workers by early September, 1959, all built up a belief that he was expendable and must be eliminated quickly to save the majority faction. Therefore, his firing was a "power play" by this faction in the same way that his hiring had been a power play by the other clique.

Why, therefore, was Frothingham's departure hastened when the police "crisis" broke? Why did Peters and Abner intervene to hasten his leaving when he would have left well before the end of the month anyway? Why did Barnes and Camp go along on this? It is at this point that one can believe that the "indiscretions" were used effectively with Barnes against Frothingham, as Barnes still believes it. As a regular Sunday school attendant who describes himself as a "good Christian man with a good Christian family," Barnes was especially susceptible to a story of this kind. Peters and Abner were intent at this point on destroying Clay and would brook no possibility of failure. According to several local informants, Peters masterminded the police walkout. Frothingham had a fair amount of administrative ability in the handling of routine problems and might have kept a police department in operation. Clay, in contrast, had no administrative ability whatsoever and was politically inept. Therefore, Clay without Frothingham was assuredly a doomed man, and it was imperative from the standpoint of Peters and Abner to get rid of Frothingham immediately. Hence, their use of vague allegations or the demand of the policemen as a condition for their return to their jobs to convince Barnes and Camp. Clay found these two had gone along with the minority faction, and it was all he could do to reconvince them to refire the chief and the policemen. The metropolitan newspaper of the area carried a story at the time of the second resignation quoting Abner that Frothingham had been definitely asked to leave by the council, a decision in which the majority bloc was compelled to acquiesce because of "the nature of the charge against Frothingham."

The police "crisis." The real undoing of the Clay faction, as well as of Frothingham as manager, came as a result of the police "crisis." This began with an investigation started September 29, 1959, by Mayor Clay into the records of the police department kept by Chief

Nick Gordon. The council met in closed session a number of times, but not until October 7, 1959, did the council finally act to fire Chief Gordon. Gordon's attorney at the first closed hearing, from which he was barred, threatened a recall petition if Gordon were fired.

Immediately upon the news of Gordon's firing because of missing and inadequate records, townspeople started a display of emotion for Gordon and indignation against the council that was not to abate for nearly a month. They shouted and pounded on the windows of the town hall that night.

Several local businessmen joined Don Bray and the local chamber of commerce vice-president in denouncing the Clay faction. One of these men called the dismissal of Gordon a dastardly act and attributed the instigation of it to resigned manager Frothingham. Frothingham had to leave by one police car still available driven by the lone "loyal" policeman, amid cries of "Send Henry back to Ohio," "We're 100 per cent behind Gordon," and "I hope your next job is outside the state." The recall petitions were started.

With the firing of Gordon, all members of the police force except one resigned. Manager Frothingham, on the job, called upon the sheriff for police protection of Eastbourne, and this was immediately provided. The news of the mass police walkout must have travelled fast, as semiprofessional safecrackers broke into two stores in an Eastbourne shopping center the next night and opened one safe, stealing $800 from it.

Clay and Barnes both declare that the town was without a police force, except for the one loyal man who did not resign, for only thirty-six hours. As a matter of fact, it was never totally without protection from an organized law enforcement unit because of the county sheriff's cooperation in patrolling. By the time, however, that Clay had hired policemen to replace those who had walked out, irreparable political damage had been done to him. For example, the Huntley-Brinkley television news report on NBC had publicized Eastbourne as the "town without a police force." News of the shopping center break-in frightened local business men. Following this break-in, Camp temporarily shifted to join Peters and Abner to vote to re-hire Chief Gordon and the resigned police force. Clay called an emergency town meeting that night as soon as he had pulled Camp back on his side, and he induced the council to vote once again to fire Gordon and rehire the "loyal" policemen. Actually no specific charges were made as yet against the chief. Peters and Abner walked out of this meeting. So Gordon stayed fired.

A packed city auditorium to which the town meeting was moved on October 13 was the scene of another noisy demonstration against the majority bloc. Don Bray of the "clan" denounced an injunction filed by the majority bloc against the recall petitions. The vice-president of the local chamber of commerce, not a resident or voter in Eastbourne, seized a microphone and made an impassioned speech to the crowd praising the ousted police chief and denouncing Councilman Camp for changing sides.

These speeches criticizing the majority bloc were a move in a planned campaign by the newly formed Civic Action Committee against the Clay faction.

Another move was a unanimous resolution of censure of Clay, Barnes, and Camp on October 10 by the board of directors of the chamber of commerce. Such a political stand is almost unheard of for a local chamber, as normal operating procedure is to eschew overt politics. The Eastbourne chamber resolution also asked immediate reinstatement of Gordon. The chamber vice-president, Clay alleges, had called the wives of businessmen and told them their husbands would be liable for any losses sustained in Eastbourne as a result of lack of police protection.

By October 15 Mayor Clay assembled specific charges against Chief Gordon. These were proof of missing court fine receipts and other police records in the police department, failure to report accidents, thereby creating difficulties for those trying to establish insurance claims, failure to investigate complaints of crimes, and use of insulting language against those charged with offenses. To the Bray faction these reasons were and still are inconsequential. Clay's charges against the chief were offset by the discovery that one of the policemen he had hired had been convicted of auto theft in Ohio years before. The sheriff had warned him of the need for a check into the records of police applicants and had offered to do this for Eastbourne, but Clay was no administrator and failed to see the need for such a detail or, perhaps the charitable explanation would be, had forgotten this advice in the press of activities. The storm increased around him.

The police "crisis" gave the Bray clique exactly the reason needed to oust the Clay faction from office: danger of breakdown of law and order in Eastbourne when the citizens were left without police protection. As a matter of fact, the people of Eastbourne were given a very distinct impression that they had been continuously without police protection from the time of the "strike" by the force when Gordon was fired. Although at the end of thirty-six hours a full complement of policemen was back on duty and the acting city manager was also acting police chief, the new policemen had no uniforms. The "striking" policemen had refused to turn in their uniforms, and it was easy for townspeople, not seeing uniformed policemen, to be led to believe that they were unprotected.

Furthermore, the local daily newspapers and the Eastbourne weekly played up the story of the police walkout and the contemporaneous theft at the shopping center — which may not have been connected — and by this act showed their bias in favor of the "old guard." It is easy to understand the Eastbourne editor's bias as he is one of the Bray clique, but what of that of the chief of the bureau for the metropolitan daily? The latter's answer is simple. He saw only one issue — freedom of access for the press. The Clay faction had barred the press from its more and more frequent closed council meetings or caucuses of its bloc. Therefore, Clay was understood by this journalist to be a dictator who must go, and the police walkout and the shopping center theft became banner stories with "scare" leads. However, closed meetings by the Bray faction have been fairly frequent but have not been similarly played up by this daily. One can only infer, therefore, that the news bureau chief had a personal hostility toward Clay and used the freedom-of-access reason to cover an animosity he could ill afford to admit as a newsman.

The recall election of 1959. A week before the actual firing of Gordon took place, and while the investigation of Gordon was still being conducted behind closed doors, Gordon's attorney had announced that a recall petition would be circulated almost immediately against the Clay bloc in the event of an actual firing. When Gordon was actually fired the second time on October 7, 1959, and Councilman Peters and Abner walked out of the council meeting, they announced that their only recourse was the petition already in circulation to recall Mayor Clay and Councilmen Barnes and Camp. They predicted the success of the recall effort. The petition began "blanketing the town," as the local weekly paper put it, within a few hours of the refiring of Gordon.

A Civic Action Committee was immediately organized, with Joe Thorn, a director of the local chamber of commerce as chairman, Mrs. Myra Wilson, a local merchant and also a chamber director, as secretary, and a Bray as treasurer. The principal task of this group was to obtain the necessary signatures on the recall petition — a number equal to 50 per cent of those voting in the last election (half of 914). In a matter of a few days 767 signatures were obtained. The headquarters for the Civic Action Committee was located in Mrs. Wilson's shop near the city hall. The chamber directorate clearly played a major role in getting the recall movement going, and the chamber president thanked Thorn and Mrs. Wilson for their services in this movement. Mrs. Wilson's role was a personal as well as a political one, as she was described by some as especially friendly to Chief Gordon and others on the police force.

The chamber of commerce board of directors followed circulation of the recall petition with its vote of censure and an open membership meeting calling for support of the recall petitions. At this meeting Thorn as chairman of the Civic Action Committee insisted on selection of candidates for the special election following the recall election — assuming success of recall — who would be sure to defeat the Clay slate. The chamber secretary praised the directors for the action they had taken against the Clay faction despite the tradition of the chamber in holding aloof from politics. Along this same line, the chamber president explained to the board of directors that the chamber had always "avoided politics," but that the "community was suffering and being injured and that it was well to discuss the matter and see whether the chamber might take some step to straighten out the police problem." The chamber passed a resolution expressing confidence in Chief Gordon and calling for his reinstatement or the resignation of Clay, Barnes, and Camp. The chamber vice-president at the town meeting declared: "The Eastbourne Chamber departed from its established policy of seven years to join with other citizens' groups to restore law and order to our town." This statement scarcely told the whole story about the chamber. It did not report, for instance, that the chamber set in motion and helped create the other group — Civic Action Committee — working for recall in order that it could publicly join an existing organization and not be compelled to circulate recall petitions under its own name. This is an old political device and really amounts to the use of a "front" organization.

The answer by the Clay faction was the only one legally feasible, that is, an injunction suit in circuit court to try to stop the recall election. This was filed within a week. The basis of the suit was a charge that the charter provisions on recall are illegal and unconstitutional by reason of failure to provide for notification to those whose recall is sought. The petition for an injunction added that the "grounds for the recall amounted to nothing more than ideas, opinions, and conclusions of its instigators, and contains no facts or grounds for which removal from office is sought." The Clay faction alleged that they were without means of defending themselves if they could not determine the charges made against them in the petition.

Within a matter of several days the circuit judge before whom the case was heard dismissed the action of the Clay faction, and at almost the same time the petition for recall was certified by the acting town manager and clerk. Reasons for dismissal by the judge were: (1) petitioners need not specify in any but general terms the reasons for seeking recall; (2) Clay, Barnes, and Camp took office knowing the terms of the charter, and, therefore, could not plead ignorance or lack of notification; (3) because the three seeking injunctive relief were not paid for their service on the town council, they could not argue loss of property rights or irreparable damage by reasons of recall. Therefore, the recall movement continued, and the election was set for November 2.

Bray clique leaders have said that the reason the townspeople became so anti-Clay in the recall movement was the widespread feeling that all the old-time city employees would be fired once Gordon was disposed of as police chief. The city employees contained more than a few Bray relatives and in-laws, and it is fair to say that the Bray family felt as the Bray leaders ascribed to the townspeople. In addition, the civil defense unit which contained many post office employees had become quite exercised about Clay's failure with respect to civil defense. It is fair to say that fear for position and status in a small town dominated by one family, now under threat, spread like wildfire very quickly. Undoubtedly Peters and Abner were not aloof from spreading this impression of wholesale dismissals.

Was there any real foundation for believing that the Clay faction would "get out the hatchet" for the rest of the city employees if they succeeded in making the Gordon dismissal stick? Clay and Barnes have vigorously denied any intention to remove others. But the fact is on the record that Camp moved in council to fire the public works director and fire chief at the height of the fight over the second firing of Gordon. Although this motion died for want of a second, the damage was done insofar as public opinion was concerned once the item appeared as a news story. The chairman of the Civic Action Committee picked up this point of Camp's motion and drummed on it publicly to develop fright among city employees. Furthermore, the editor of the Eastbourne weekly editorialized on the subject in the October 8, 1959, issue:

> It is only natural that other employees of the town should be worried and and fearful for their own jobs after witnessing the dismissal of the Chief. The charge, which one may hear voiced on the streets, that vindictiveness on the part of Mayor Clay or Manager Frothingham is the reason for the Chief's dismissal, may well be without fact, but the failure to issue sound and strong reasons for the action tends to lend credence to such gossip, especially when one other commissioner refers to it as "hatchet politics."

The weekly paper, both in its reporting and its editorials, took a strong pro-Gordon, pro-"old guard" position, expressing not only sympathy for Gordon and his policemen but also deploring the "wreckage" of Eastbourne's "smoothly functioning Civil Defense organization" and the bad reputation the town was suffering. The paper also defended the Eastbourne chamber of commerce for its censure action.

Right on the eve of the recall election Mayor Clay raised another issue which was manipulated against him. He asked where were the civil defense uniforms that belonged to the town. One of the former members of the civil defense unit answered that he had turned in all uniforms to Clay himself at his place of business. Clay also demanded return of a county-owned radio that was in the car of a former member of the unit, but that man replied that he had paid $100 to have the radio installed, and he demanded the services of a skilled mechanic to remove it. Clearly Clay was getting nowhere.

In its last pre-election issue the local weekly carried a front page editorial calling for the recall of Clay, Barnes, and Camp on the ground that "a dictatorship is in the making." More significantly, the paper carried a full page advertisement by the Civic Action Committee urging a "yes" vote for recall and containing many questions "loaded" with innuendo as to the basic honesty and character of Clay and former manager Frothingham. The advertisement shouted its condemnation in big block letters: EASTBOURNE IS IN A MESS! AND THE CLAY BLOC MADE IT! THE JOB OF MAYOR IS TOO BIG FOR CLAY. THE JOB OF COUNCILMAN IS TOO BIG FOR CAMP AND BARNES. The "old guard" also paid for spot announcements every fifteen minutes for several days before the election. Mailed statements were also sent to all voters by Clay, Barnes, and Camp, and by Abner.

The evening of November 2, 1959, was as packed with emotion as an old-fashioned "whing-ding" revival meeting. Eastbournians not only voted to recall Clay, Barnes, and Camp; it was by a vote of 820 to 417 out of a total of 1,310 cast. By 2 to 1, therefore, the Clay bloc lost office and the "old guard" marched back in. The acting town manager, one of the "old guard" himself, was empowered by the charter, since there was no majority left on the council, to appoint three new interim councilmen. These were former mayor and manager John Morse, a Bray son-in-law, Link, the bitter business rival of Clay's, and Thorn, the leader of the recall movement who had served as chairman of the Civic Action Committee. Immediately that night this group reappointed Gordon as police chief and elected Peters as mayor pro tem. Peters had supposedly masterminded the police "strike." Also all "striking" policemen were rehired and the "loyal" policeman resigned, as the temporary patrolmen hired after the walk-out of early October all lost their jobs forthwith. People came to the town hall by the hundreds to witness the return to the seats of power of the "old guard," and some wept while others were noisily jubilant or joyously embraced Gordon.

The Clay group felt they had to run someone in the special election of November 30, 1959, and they turned to Leary, Clay's old colleague on the commission who had been the first recruit to his faction and who had dropped out in the 1959 regular election. The "old guard" continued the Civic Action Committee as a vehicle to run a slate which consisted of Joe Thorn, Link, and an inconspicuous minor member of the Bray clique who had formerly worked for one of the Brays. Morse, it can be observed, decided to drop out. Two of the Bray slate were past masters of the local Masonic lodge. The "old guard" won overwhelmingly. In February, 1960, at a closed meeting they appointed their old colleague, John Morse, also a past master of the Masonic lodge, as town manager. In the regular June election Abner and Joe Thorn beat a Clay candidate.

Clay tried to make a real issue of the method of financing a new public works program put forward in the fall of 1960 by the Bray group. He organized a taxpayers' group and even took the issue to court unsuccessfully, as will be explained in the discussion of town issues. In June, 1961, he fielded a full slate for mayor and two council posts to contest with the Bray faction, but his efforts came to nothing. Out of a total of 1,104 votes cast, the Bray slate received 713, 750, and 723 against 372, 279, and 276 for the Clay slate. In 1962 Clay refused to put together a slate, publicly declaring his "disgust" with politics. The Bray clique remained firmly in control of Eastbourne city hall.

IV

The tense political events of 1959 may quite correctly be considered "issues" of Eastbourne politics. One may also correctly note that these "issues" center around personalities. One may well ask whether there are any issues in Eastbourne that center around public policy in the same sense that most other municipalities debate differences over public programs. As a crude classification device, one can say that the Clay bloc was interested in providing those basic municipal services such as streets, sewers, full-time paid fire protection, minimal police record-keeping, and criminal investigations that elsewhere would incite no debate but are taken for granted as requisites of urban living. The "old guard" group, on the other hand, was interested merely in keeping Eastbourne as it was — a country town — without taxes insofar as possible and with little or no urban services until the fall of 1960. By then they felt impelled to have a program of public improvements, most of which had been talked of by the Clay bloc, as a means of preventing the opposition from raising any issues that might appeal to the voters. A pitifully shabby and ill-equipped town hall and lack of modern recreational facilities had not worried the Bray clique until 1960, as they expected little or nothing from urban living. A run-down of the list of common municipal issues is instructive to illustrate Eastbourne attitudes.

On land use and planning neither the "old guard" nor Clay has any conception of what would be involved were a rational approach adopted for Eastbourne. Clay's sole notion is that of zoning. The "old guard" has had no real respect for zoning controls, even though a zoning ordinance was adopted in 1950 under their regime, and "spot zoning" has characterized the town. Even the editor of the weekly newspaper, who is a part of the "old guard," admits this attitude toward zoning. No one in Eastbourne has ever conceived of urban renewal or public housing projects.

As indicated above, a public works program became a real issue because Clay stressed such projects as a new water supply, a new city hall from the proceeds of the sale of city property for $40,000, extension of street lighting (a white way) on the federal highway through the town, more sanitary and storm sewer construction to serve the entire town, which is covered only in small part now, and revamped sewer and water rates to provide for the construction. Until 1960 the "old guard" dwelt in great detail on the settlement of the bond issue of the twenties, a settlement not achieved until 1951 because of local "repudiationist" sentiment. The town had been forced to contract its boundaries drastically after the debacle of the real estate "bust" in the twenties and the depression years. Because the "old guard" has a strong nostalgia for the simpler rural life of the old days and fought so long against settlement of the debt through refunding, they long refused to become interested in incurring new debt through public works. Furthermore, their belief that they have developed a taxless paradise led them to reject any extensive public works program, as that would surely end this idyllic state of affairs.

But the fear of Clay's return to power was apparently greater than fear of spending money in 1960, and the "old guard" voted to employ an engineering firm to make a feasibility report on a whole portfolio of public works projects. This report, given in July, 1960, and approved by the council, was adopted for financing in the fall of 1960. It included the following construction: (1) a new town hall, (2) a new library, (3) a new police station, (4) a fire house, (5) a recreation building, (6) an expanded water system, and (7) a modern expanded sanitary sewer and drainage system. The price tag on this public works program was $2,325,000. A metropolitan daily of the area, in describing Eastbourne's town improvement program labeled its story " 'Rip Van Winkle' Awakened."

An interesting addition to the Clay agenda of public improvements that the "old guard" made was in recreation. Clay had never mentioned the need for any expanded facilities of this nature. Abner of the "old guard" became interested in this activity through his Junior Chamber of Commerce activity, and he headed a council committee working on proposals for expanded facilities. His committee proposed a recreation building and debated but shelved a public swimming pool. Fear of racial integration at such a pool was openly expressed despite the lack of Negroes in the town.

Tax and revenue sources became highly controversial in 1960–61 as a result of the new public works program. All elements in Eastbourne have long been proud of the fact that there is no ad valorem real property tax in the town except that required by law to retire the old debt left from the twenties. Also up to 1960 there was no utility tax. The state remission of cigarette taxes was the principal source of local revenue, and this was cited approvingly. However, the new public works program required new sources of revenue, and the council came up with a proposal for issuing forty-year revenue certificates against proposed income from the improvements in the form of water and sewer rentals, a 2 per cent utilities tax, and the state-remitted cigarette tax. Actually the council voted the utilities tax in advance of the adoption of the public works program. The method of financing immediately came under attack from Clay, who quickly formed an organization to oppose the fiscal proposals. His organization was called Eastbourne Freeholders. This organization took a stand for a separation of projects for fiscal purposes. They agreed on the use of the revenue certificates to finance all except the expanded water and sewer program, and these they wanted to see financed on a front foot assessment basis instead of by monthly water and sewer rental fees. They not only held the latter system to be inequitable in affecting all property owners alike but they pointed out that several areas in the town had recently installed water and sewer systems at their own cost and would be paying the same charges as those areas that would be getting complete new facilities. It is to be noted that they had reversed their stand on water and sewer fees in the course of a year.

The first tactic of the Clay group in opposing the method of financing was to employ a lawyer, raise money for a suit, and to go to court. Interestingly enough, the answer in court by the town council to the criticism of the use of the 2 per cent utilities tax was that if it were inadequate, it could be raised to 10 per cent to meet costs, and sewer and water charges could be correspondingly raised. The Freeholders lost their suit and also an effort to force the whole program to a referendum. (An important point about the use of revenue certificates is that they obviate the need for a referendum which is required for approval of a general obligation bond issue.)

The second tactic resorted to by Clay and his Freeholders group was to put up a slate of candidates in the regular June, 1961, council and mayoral election. As pointed out above, their slate was easily beaten. Therefore, the method of financing adopted by the council became a settled thing.

However, in July 1961, the council took two significant steps on taxes. It reduced the ad valorem on real property by two mills because it claimed additional revenues sufficient to offset this reduction would result from a county reassessment of real property. The council continued to use the real property tax solely for reduction of the old debt. The second major tax decision was to instruct the manager and mayor to investigate the need for raising the utility tax to 4 per cent to finance construction of the city hall, recreation building, and other facilities. Incidentally the council at the same time passed an ordinance requiring all buildings within 200 feet of sewer lines to hook up to them within a year after service becomes available and prohibiting the repair of private sewerage facilities after the city's new facilities are operating. This was the "old guard's" answer to Clay's allegation that he would have to pay for facilities he did not need and could not use. He would be compelled to use the city sewer lines.

On the matter of property assessment, the "old guarders" have expressed a deep resentment against the centralization of this function in the county assessor's office. Most informed citizens of Jordan County approve this centralization as productive of office efficiency and preventive of duplication and overlapping. Not so the "old guard," who launch into tirades on the virtues of home rule on this matter, meaning home rule at the lowest possible level and not home rule for county government. But despite their tirades, they were eager to seize the benefit from county assessment and reduce their millage.

Annexation as an issue has been manipulated for clique advantage in Eastbourne. Clay seemed eager for growth of the town, especially through annexation of shopping centers and adjacent new subdivisions of somewhat higher valued homes than those now within Eastbourne. He showed this not only by pushing through too fast the attempt to annex two shopping centers in 1959 while he was mayor but also by pushing hard while only a councilman for the annexation of another area by special act of the legislature. In this he succeeded, and thereby the size of the town was doubled. He also worked assiduously at that time for the annexation of the entire shopping center area in another district, an annexation opposed by Morse, then mayor, and the "old guard," who wanted to take care of one supermarket only, as the annexation of the entire shopping center cost the city $10,000. Clay declares that the city could have obtained $40,000 had it been aggressive enough to annex the whole area adjacent to the shopping center. The local newspaper editor explains the longtime reluctance of the city to annex any but shopping centers because of the city policy in allowing developers to recover from the city the cost of installing water and sewer connections by a refund for every "cut in" of a new property. This policy made annexation of residential property quite costly to the city.

In 1961, the "old guard" started a move to annex the same two shopping centers that the Clay bloc had tried to push through in 1960. Again the property owners objected. In 1962, the city council introduced an annexation ordinance and even talked of annexing a wide residential area. But they met two major obstacles: the shopping center property owners threatened a court suit, and the neighborhood associations of homeowners threatened possible incorporation to head off being swallowed by Eastbourne. Unquestionably the homeowners associations, which represent a higher economic and social class than the vast majority of townspeople, do not wish to identify with Eastbourne and will put themselves out of pocket to head this off.

Industrialization is the usual "will o' the wisp" to Eastbournians as to other small town people despite the extolling of the rural background and rural virtues in Eastbourne. The local chamber has sent out literature and has also emphasized the town's lack of an ad valorem real property tax for anything except debt retirement. Nevertheless Eastbourne has failed to attract any significant new industry despite the fact that some major national industrial firms located sizeable new plants elsewhere in Jordan County. Eastbourne even failed to obtain the location of a branch of the county junior college in 1961. It is doubtful that Eastbourne would actually welcome a sizeable industry which would demand high quality services from the city.

Prejudices of various kinds are important and alive in Eastbourne and must be reckoned with in the politics of the town. Most important of all is religion. It is clear that the Masonic lodge plays an important political role in this town, and this is one more factor that gives it a nineteenth-century flavor. The fact that no Catholic has ever been elected to the council does reveal something of town biases, but even more specific is the fact that none of the Clay bloc belonged to the local Masonic lodge. (Barnes had never transferred his Masonic membership from another lodge of which he was a member and was never really considered a "brother" by the Bray clique who were all important figures in local Masonry.) One of the "old guard" council members referred sneeringly to President Kennedy's religion, and the council in 1960 denied rental of the town auditorium to the local Catholic church for temporary school purposes, but a Protestant group was soon thereafter allowed to rent the space for church purposes. One point that is sometimes baffling in trying to assess the ties that hold the Bray clique together politically is whether those of blood are stronger than those of Masonry, so significant is the latter in the lives of all its members. Furthermore, a number of observers of town politics have described the local lodge as being "active" in town politics.

Prejudices that might be expected of Southerners against Northerners operate against all outsiders who demand more than the minimal services Eastbournians are prepared to give. Eastbourne is really xenophobic. It wants no invaders in its business circles. Acceptance of the status quo appears to be the price of local acceptability, regardless of section of origin.

Although the "old guard" denies that race is an issue in the town, it is a curious fact that no Negroes live in Eastbourne. They retreated some six or seven years ago, with encouragement from the town, to two local crossroads settlements some distance away. This retreat occurred when a street widening was undertaken and most of their houses had to be moved. Also of significance, however, is the fact that the town several years ago zoned an area near a Negro church (which remained in the town when its parishioners left) for "business" when the council discovered that the church owned a considerable surrounding acreage that might be used for a Negro development project. The council also raised the possibility of Negro use of a public swimming pool if the town were to build one despite the fact that the town has not a single Negro resident and public beaches in the county are open to Negroes. This would appear to be looking for trouble.

"Sin" is really no issue in the town, since there is no activity to provide either behavior problems or possible corruption of the police force. The "old guard" proudly describes Eastbourne as a "church town," as they make clear their own opposition to liquor stores, although the town is not dry. Indeed, the time-honored tactic of the "old guard" on the council when the state awards a new liquor license in the town is to stall off selling an occupational license, although actually this is not something which may be refused once the state has given the permit. Most of the churches appear to be of the fundamentalist variety which take their opposition to liquor and gambling very seriously, a fact which accounts for council attitudes.

V

Eastbourne at the beginning of the decade of the fifties was a town in which a family political clique held a tight grip over city government and made the city manager their chosen instrument for execution of clique decisions. At the end of the decade the clique had firmly re-established its tight grip and, in addition, had learned a lesson. They had learned that a public works program would make them look good and help their continued grip on control of the city. Such a program could be financed without hurting them as small businessmen and it would give the city a more modern look — as though it were really moving ahead. Most important of all, it would rob the opposition of the one set of issues it had tried to build up against them.

But what was the clique founded on and what is the cement that holds it together outside of sheer enjoyment of the feeling of importance and lift to the *amour-propre* that comes from ruling? As is made clear in the foregoing account, there are family ties, lodge ties, religious biases, and mutual profit from longstanding business arrangements. The family is not hard to find in Eastbourne; in fact, it is ubiquitous. The marriages of the Bray clan, through which political power has been retained, are reminiscent of the dynastic alliances forged by Queen Victoria for her children in the nineteenth century to cement British hegemony across Europe. Among Bray sons-in-law who have been local officeholders are Edgar White, former city manager, John Morse, present city manager, Ben Abner, present councilman. Another long-time councilman who went off the council several years ago is married to a Bray woman, as is the long-time former town attorney. In addition, there are many somewhat more distant relatives who may be found among the city employees.

In more sophisticated and citified areas lodge membership has been falling off both in sheer numbers and in status implications for either political or other advancement. Not so in Eastbourne. Four of the present five councilmen are Masons, and furthermore, Police Chief Gordon, the center of the 1959 "cause célèbre," is a Mason. In fact, Ben Abner stated publicly in a council meeting to Barnes in the midst of the police "crisis" that the latter shouldn't vote to fire a brother Mason. A number of observers of town politics have testified to the fact that the Eastbourne Masonic lodge channels campaigning for public office by the "old guard" through the Masonic lodge. The non-Mason is as much an "outsider" as the person from another community; in fact, even more so as the migrant from another community who is a Mason and would take the trouble to transfer his membership might ultimately be accepted by the "old guard."

But cronyism takes the form also of "closed corporation" business arrangements. This was evident in the 1959 censure of Clay and his bloc by the directors of the Eastbourne Chamber of Commerce. Of twelve directors, one rented his business quarters from Link, Clay's business rival and long-time councilman. Another was the editor of the local weekly newspaper, who was indebted to the "old guard" for the years of legal advertising it had placed in his paper and also for their suppression of a throw-away weekly advertising paper that had threatened to reduce his income from advertising. Another director was a local insurance agent who had long benefitted from the "old guard" practice of allotting insurance without resort to open bidding. Still another director was Thorn, who became chairman of the Civic Action Committee and was soon to be picked to go to the council. Another was president of the local bank (the newspaper editor was a director of this bank) and through that institution closely tied in with virtually all the local businessmen. In addition, there was the amiable woman merchant who was friendly to the police department and did so much to promote the recall petitions that would restore Chief Gordon to his job.

Any group founded on family ties, lodge bonds, and cronyism in business dealings will not take kindly to attempts to talk about issues in the form of town needs, to demands for rational business procedures in the handling of city business, or to "outsiders" challenging their control. Possibly more infuriating than anything else to the "old guard" was simply the fact that they were supplanted by strangers who had dared to campaign for office by house-to-house canvass of voters and by suggesting that their close-knit little world could be improved upon. Much of the behavior of the clique in 1959 can be explained by sheer outrage at these things. There is no other explanation for all that happened in 1959 or for the fact that the "old guard," once restored to the power they loved so well, adopted the very program that had been anathema to them only a few months before.

Eastbourne presents the picture of a town that makes sense to the observer only on the basis of emotional — that is, irrational — reaction to politics. Unquestionably the questions, approaches, tactics, and types of personalities that might operate acceptably in the politics of many another community cannot be expected to work satisfactorily in Eastbourne. The rural orientation of its thinking places Eastbourne in rebellion against much that has been going on around it, as it is in almost the geographic center of one of the most urbanized areas in the state. Eastbourne doesn't fit into the pattern of the rest of Jordan County, and it will have none of it. In addition, Eastbourne more and more is made up of low economic status retirees from other parts of the country who cannot be very well satisfied with their lot, whose thinking is that of a bygone age just as the thinking of the "old guard" that rules Eastbourne harks back to an earlier period, and who can be appealed to by the "old guard" to reject all the costly, newfangled ideas of the city "slickers" outside their boundaries.

The "old guard" will unquestionably continue to rule Eastbourne for some time to come. They will get votes from the retirees. Clay is inept politically and makes as many enemies as he makes friends. Peters and Abner, on the other hand, have a kind of peasant cunning that enables them to flourish in Eastbourne. The town can continue to be an island politically as well as culturally for a long time to come.

6

Westbourne

There are many kinds of isolation sought by different types of towns. One of the commonest is through zoning, which Robert C. Wood has described as "the sharp cutting edge" of local politics.[1] Surely one of the main motivating forces for the incorporation of so many suburban communities has been the elitism of the middle and upper income classes searching for status. The desire for status leads to a search for legal weapons to protect the "character" as well as the economic values of their residential neighborhoods. Strict zoning has been the one surest legal weapon on which the separate municipality may count. Through this established device the economic law of the private market place gives way to a public control of land use and land value based upon local consensus. To put the problem in social-psychological terms, search behavior leads to success when it is consummated in suburban zoning.

Recent events in Los Angeles County in connection with the growth of the "Lakewood Plan" support this thesis. Since 1954, there have been over twenty-eight municipal incorporations, with virtually all municipal services supplied to almost all these new cities by the county government on a contract basis.[2] These cities, therefore, are a hollow shell created as a receptacle for state tax rebates to municipalities, to be sure, but more importantly as zoning districts. Let no one be deceived about the increasing interest of "Suburbia" in zoning as a major public issue or as the cement which can hold people together politically in such areas.

---

[1] In a lecture to a conference on urban politics called by the Florida Citizenship Clearing House, at Winter Park, Florida, March 2, 1962.

[2] Winston W. Crouch, "The California Way," *National Civic Review* LI (1962), 139–144, 154 and "The Urban County: A Study of New Approaches to Local Government in Metropolitan Areas," *Harvard Law Review* LXXIII (1960), 526–582.

Westbourne is an example of a suburban city centered almost exclusively around zoning. It could well serve as a model for the middle-class dormitory suburb in one of the nation's larger metropolitan counties. It is a developers' town in the sense that it was their creation and not the product of any natural or spontaneous economic development or population movement. Its business district consists of a four-block area for small local merchants along one street. Not only does it have no "economy" in the usual sense, but it has effectively halted the economic exploitation of land along a main federal highway into the large central core city in its own scheme of protection of residential property values. Because its residents are above average in educational background, they are articulate in their opposition to the metropolitan county government which they fear for its broad planning powers and authority to set *minimum* zoning standards for the county. These latter they do not wish to see become maximum and supersede their own much stricter standards.

First incorporated in the late twenties, Westbourne became a council-manager city in the early thirties. The town increased its population from 2,000 in 1940 to nearly 10,000 in 1960, a growth rate twice that of the central city and slightly above that of the county. It is now virtually completely "developed."

Westbourne is a white-collar city made up of business and professional people who work in the central core city. Their homes are single-family residences, well landscaped on lots larger than those in neighboring suburban towns, and well above those of adjacent areas in assessed value. These white-collar workers do not include Westbourne city employees, as only three can afford to live within the city limits, and only a handful of Negroes, who are domestic servants, live in the community. One ex-city councilman commented on this latter point, "If a Negro family came into this community, it would blow the town apart."

Nearly one-fourth of Westbourne's population twenty-five years of age or older has completed four or more years of college, and an equal proportion has completed one to three years of college work. For the county as a whole only a little better than 10 per cent of the twenty-five or older category has completed four or more years of college and about 11 per cent one to three years of college. Just to show the contrast to Eastbourne, described in the previous chapter, we can point to 5 per cent who have completed four or more years of college and less than 10 per cent who have completed one to three years of college in Eastbourne's population.

Westbourne has a larger concentration of Catholics than neighboring towns, which stems in part from the presence of a Catholic college in the vicinity. Actually the proportion of Catholics in Westbourne has decreased in recent years as more Jews have moved in. Protestants constitute the largest religious group, with Catholics second, and Jews third, the latter group representing perhaps 10 per cent of the total population. The homogeneity of the population in terms of income and occupation creates a sensitivity to any influx of "different" people. The coming of an Oriental family at first caused a great stir, but it finally died down, and the family was more or less accepted.

I

Westbourne follows the most common form of council-manager government. Its five-man council is elected for four-year staggered terms. The mayor is elected by the council from among its own members. Traditionally the councilman polling the highest number of votes is named mayor for a two-year term, followed by a new mayor after the next councilmanic election. As is customary under this form of government, the manager is named by the council for an indefinite period. All department heads except the police chief are named by the manager after some informal consultation with council members. The police chief is named by the council and theoretically is responsible to it. As far as informal administration is concerned, however, the police chief is controlled by the manager as fully as the other department heads. The manager is charged with preparing and submitting the budget to the council, and he does so after some informal prior consultation with selected council members and/or the mayor on items that seem potentially controversial.

The relationship between the council, the mayor, and the manager is a simple one, at least on the surface. The almost total absence of any controversial issues that divide the town (detailed below) results in a smooth working relationship that shows little evidence of disharmonies. The same manager, Harold Daniels, has held office since 1935. Daniels describes his relationship with the mayor as somewhat closer on matters of policy than his dealings with the other council members. To some extent the mayor is his contact man with the rest of the council on policy matters. One ex-mayor declared that the mayor was much more active in policy matters than the rest of the council, working closely with the manager in developing policy proposals. Another ex-mayor who served for several terms noted that the mayor provided a line of communication between the manager and the council, often reporting to them his conversations with the manager on policy matters. In a town with so great a consensus on matters of internal moment as Westbourne, there has been, in any event, little of major consequence to discuss. In addition, the consensus on relations with the metropolitan county government is equally great.

No department heads have been able to develop direct council-department head relationships, and neither mayor nor council meddles in the day-to-day administrative affairs of the city. This is particularly noteworthy in view of the "semiretired" status of some council members and their availability for such meddling. Their spare time is used in other activity than interfering with the manager's administrative duties.

II

Many towns across the country, especially those which have grown as rapidly as Westbourne, find themselves torn by controversy over the kind of community they should try to become. The choices are many for some towns — industrial or retirement center, white-collar business or market area, dormitory suburb, tourist center, and many others. Westbourne suffers from no uncertainty as to its destiny. There is an amazing consensus on what it has been, what it is, and what it wants to be — an upper middle-class residential area tightly controlled through uncommonly strict zoning regulations. Zoning has been the only community problem, as well as the only issue, of any significance in the town, and it is not an issue in the usual meaning of that term. There is virtually no internal disagreement on the single, overriding objective of Westbourne — to use strict zoning regulations and building codes to maintain the serene, comfortable, upper middle-class sameness in an otherwise hectic, varied, and disordered metropolitan area.

A remarkable consensus exists that zoning has been the most significant factor in making Westbourne a "good place to live" and that it must be maintained to keep the town a good place to live. As one newspaperman put it, "The Constitution of the United States will crumble before the Westbourne zoning ordinance goes down." The only sharp political skirmishes that could be identified have involved zoning, and the only major groups seeking access to the political machinery of the community have been motivated by the same problem. Westbourne has spent a great deal of time and money in the courts fighting efforts by outsiders to break the strict zoning regulations. A nationally known expert was employed on a consultant basis to assist in preparing the cases, and the town has had remarkable success in achieving court victories.

From time to time, a request for a zoning variance involving some minor change has won the approval of the council. Invariably, however reasonable the change might appear, a storm of protest from the community's more militant "zoners" has ensued. On occasion the council has stood its ground and granted a variance involving, usually, some minor adjustments in the business district. Only one instance could be discovered in which a clash of major proportions between the community and the council took place over the question of zoning. In the 1940's, a proposal was made for a civic group to build a meeting and general recreation hall. Land donated for the building required rezoning because it fell just beyond the existing business district, with a residential area between the business district and the proposed clubhouse. Careful measures were taken to provide for buffer zones, and the public was assured that the action represented no general slackening of the strict zoning regulations. In spite of these precautions a citizens' group quickly formed to oppose the variance granted by the commission.

Westbourne found itself divided on the issue. The council and one group favored the variance, while another group opposed it with bitterness and vigor. The council held its ground and granted the variance, but before the hall was completed, an election was held. An "anti-civic club hall" slate was formed to oppose the incumbent councilmen, and in every case except one the "anti's" were successful. The new council obtained an injunction to stop work on the hall, and the project died. This was the only case in which councilmen were defeated after granting a zoning variance. Those who favored the club supported the general strict approach to zoning but felt that in this case the opposition had gone too far.

During the 1950's, increasing pressure was brought on Westbourne to rezone Royal Palm Avenue, the main east-west arterial highway, for business. Much of the land along the highway was undeveloped, and out-of-town owners pressed their claim that refusal to rezone was an unreasonable restriction on the use of the property. The key argument of those who wanted the rezoning was that the land along the busy thoroughfare would not, in fact, be used for residences. When the city officials despaired of being able to hold the line, a vigorous and well organized citizens' group moved into the picture to wage the battle. Over a thousand persons contributed to a "war chest" with which to wage the fight. Donations came largely from persons who would not have been affected directly by the zoning change. The fight was carried through to the state supreme court, and somewhat to everyone's surprise the citizens' group opposing rezoning won. The city then resumed responsibility to fight any additional skirmishes, and the citizens' group disbanded. Its leader ran successfully for council shortly after. The question of rezoning Royal Palm Avenue is now virtually moot, because most of the land has been used for residences. The city encouraged this by building parallel roads to serve as a buffer zone between the houses and the busy arterial highway. Zoning reigns supreme, then, as the magic thread that binds Westbourne together.

The supremacy strict zoning enjoys today may be illustrated by the successful informal opposition to construction of a church on a principal street of the city actually zoned for such a building. In other words, not even that type of structure was desired because it would bring crowds of people together. Clearly, it is only at the city-owned country club that "togetherness" is encouraged.

A number of other questions might be classed as problems, but they are relatively minor. Questions of annexation and relationship to the county government in the area have stirred some interest from time to time, but they have not divided the community in any serious way. Westbourne is one of the municipalities of Columbus County with the strongest antipathy toward the county government, as presently re-organized under a metropolitan charter. This antipathy is well illustrated by the description given by a long time Westbourne councilman of the consequences suffered by an ex-mayor who bucked the anti-Metro trend and fought hard for the Metro plan at the time of its adoption. The former mayor did not run for council again, lost his job, and lost a bid for the Metro county commission from the Westbourne district, supposedly all because of his support for Metro. Westbourne mayors and manager have played a leading part in the county league of municipalities' attacks on Metro. Certainly Westbourne has been one of the "hard core" areas of opposition to Metro, with the prime motivating force being a fear that something like county-wide zoning would crumble the legal wall that now guards the exclusiveness of the town. There is every indication that anti-Metro sentiment is stronger than it was when Metro was established some five years ago.

Westbourne has no utilities under town control as it buys its water from another city, a privately owned utility provides electrical service, and the county government now operates public transportation. Like much of the remainder of the county, Westbourne has no sewerage facilities, as it is a septic tank town. Few seem interested in providing sewers, and consequently this idea never becomes an "issue."

The elitism dominant in Westbourne gives a different twist to annexation. A number of neighboring communities, some incorporated, some not, yearn to be taken into Westbourne's fold. One area has formally petitioned to be annexed, but after careful consideration, the Westbourne council rejected the request of this town. The official reason was the excessive cost of bringing the standards of service in the area up to existing Westbourne levels. An added unspoken reason was the feeling that the petitioning areas would not be socially compatible. There has been no division within Westbourne over the issue, and it is unlikely that any annexation will take place.

A number of other issues that trouble many communities in other parts of the country are of no moment in Westbourne. Industry is no problem; there is no tourism; Westbourne is united in wanting neither. The retired people are virtually all in the upper income bracket and make no special demands on the town. Race is no problem; Westbourne has no Negroes, other than domestic servants who "live in," and does not intend to have any. "Togetherness" is the rule, and zoning is its protector.

III

The existence or absence of factional rivalry determines, in our scheme of analysis, whether a town's politics can be classified as monopolistic or competitive. Westbourne is an almost perfect example of a consensus community. No significant areas of disagreement over problems of any moment could be discovered. The lack of issues seems to lead to an absence of organized groups operating in politics. The political leadership structure, therefore, is monopolistic, in that there are no identifiable competing factions. In fact, there are no factions of any significance. The entire town can be described as a single, united faction that is in strong agreement on all questions of any moment. Councilmen are drawn from no particular social segments of Westbourne, because there is no fragmentation of the community into segments. The stability of town politics is correlated with the long tenure of the present manager, dating from 1935.

The one issue of overriding importance in the community centers around the question of zoning. The economic and social unity on which Westbourne's stability rests was produced by the strict zoning that was instituted when the area was developed as a town. There are no identifiable groups in the community who desert the "line" on zoning. Westbourne realtors and builders join the rest of the community in erecting a strong protective shield against the clutter and disorderly development that surround it in the metropolitan area. The various outside pressures that have been brought to bear from time to time to break the strict regulations have been uniformly unsuccessful. The closest thing to a defector is the Westbourne Bank, the sole bank in the community, but this would-be defection is quickly explained by the ownership pattern of the bank: non-Westbournians are principal stockholders. The bank group controlled a rather large amount of land on Royal Palm Avenue and sought to get the land on this street rezoned for commercial use.

The bank group made a serious effort to enter the political life of the community by running an employee as a candidate for council in order to bring favorable action on its rezoning aspirations. The community, unaware of this objective, elected the bank candidate to office, and, in fact, gave him the highest number of votes, which in turn led to his selection as mayor. After all, to middle-class types, who could be more trustworthy than one backed by a bank? The bank group promptly began issuing orders to the new mayor regarding what it wanted done through his office. For instance, council members received letters from the mayor on bank stationary telling them who the mayor (i.e., the bank) thought should be put on the zoning board.

The consensus in the community is well illustrated by the ensuing events. The mayor became more and more uncomfortable in his role of bank advocate and, in any event, failed to get support on the council for the things the bank wanted. As an employee of the bank, he found his loyalties subjected to an impossible pull which he rectified by resigning from the bank, giving up the mayor's post, and moving to a town across the state. The bank tried on one other occasion during the fifties to elect a man to the council. They did not run a bank employee, but the candidate had his campaign headquarters in the bank, and a vice-president of the institution served as his campaign manager. The bank candidate violated the rules of the game for Westbourne in another way in that a large amount of money (by Westbourne's very modest standards) was spent in his campaign. The "good" bank in local business and political affairs, located just outside Westbourne but controlled by residents, ran its own candidates, who won handily. The "bad" bank's candidate came in last.

Although the Westbourne Bank's efforts to seek political power in order to gain support for rezoning its land on Royal Palm Avenue caused some stir in the community, it did not divide the town in any significant way. Westbourne was united in opposing the rezoning and fought the battle on this and every other front until victory was assured.

The only other identifiable group in the community has been the "recreation group." The issues of concern to this group can hardly be described as other than trivial. Dispute did not revolve around adequate facilities; Westbourne's recreational facilities are superior in quality and quantity. Westbourne owns its own country club, and occasionally the golfers have become exercised about such weighty matters as the times assigned for starting play, the location of tees or greens, the operation of the golf carts, and the like. In the essentially issueless atmosphere of Westbourne, such matters can take on considerable significance, and the golfers have on occasion put up a candidate for the city council in order to bring speedy action on the problems involved. They have not been successful in electing a man to the council, nor have they had any better success in attempting to act as a social acceptability panel for council candidates. The golfers rather pointedly excluded the only Jew in one council race from their list of acceptable candidates, but the candidate in question won anyway.

The Westbourne political structure, therefore, consists of a "dominant" leadership clique that includes practically anybody in town who wants to participate. The prerequisites are simple — status and a belief in tight zoning. The Westbourne Bank group cannot be classified as a rival faction to the controlling clique but only as a "one-shot" success in electing a mayor.

Westbourne's political status during the entire period of analysis (1945–1960) was monopolistic. There were no power exchanges during this time, and political stability was the rule. City Manager Harold Daniels served for the entire period and seems likely to remain until retirement at a ripe old age.

A considerable number of respondents, when asked who ran the town, replied that "the manager runs things" or words to that effect. A number of councilmen agreed that the popular image in Westbourne was that the manager did indeed run things. They were quick to point out, however, that the town was run through a joint effort of the manager and the council. We concluded that the "joint effort" analysis was accurate. The manager ran the town because he was essentially a part of it, a long-time permanent resident, and he and any given council found themselves in almost complete agreement about what needed to be done in the present and for the future. Manager Daniels belonged to civic clubs, the chamber of commerce, and similar groups, and took a leadership role in them from time to time. Neither he nor Westbourne's councilmen believed that a manager should move from job to job but all agreed that it was preferable to stay in one community as long as possible and identify completely with the values of that community.

In Westbourne there seems to be almost unanimous agreement that policy initiation comes from the council and the manager, with both proposing major policy jointly or alternatively. One council member described the council and the mayor as playing a dominant role in policy initiation. The manager saw himself as initiating most policy recommendations, usually in the form of a memorandum to the council. In most instances his proposals were accepted. It would be an error, however, to attribute this agreement to any rubber stamp attitude in the council. Rather it grows from the delicate political sensitivity of the manager and the universal consensus in the town. Daniels knows the town, he knows the council, and thus he can judge when a particular proposal will be accepted. However, the manager does not propose merely those things which he believes to be acceptable to the council. If he sees a need, he makes the proposal even if he does not anticipate majority support. The best example was a proposal for a sanitary sewer system for Westbourne. Daniels proposed such a system twenty years ago, but there was never a majority of the council with him. In such a situation, he would not continually agitate the issue. It was simply dropped indefinitely, with occasional "feelers" as to whether sentiment might have changed.

Westbourne is a nearly perfect example of the politically stable community described by an earlier study of council-manager government.[3] No major issues divide the town. The manager is integrated fully into the community, and has no plans to leave. There is little possibility that he will be forced to do so. No power exchanges or power plays are in prospect for Westbourne.

Manager Daniels takes no overt role in selecting and electing candidates, but one has the feeling that his informal, privately expressed views might be important in such matters. One losing candidate for council did accuse him of opposing her. Occasional surface ripples mar Westbourne's tranquil waters, but no tidal wave threatens to produce a political upheaval that would threaten the stability of the community's politics, and thus the manager's security. The council-manager plan certainly "works" in Westbourne, but then one might argue that any form of local government would work well in an environment of such complete consensus as to the kind of community desired.

[3] Harold A. Stone, Don K. Price, and Kathryn H. Stone, *City Manager Government: A Review After Twenty-Five Years* (Chicago: Public Administration Service, 1940), pp. 224–235.

7

Dorado

Change — whether of substance or of outward form — can be painful to a community, especially when it is forced by internal pressures and conflicts. Dorado, an attractive coastal city, is now experiencing the pangs of a metamorphosis of many dimensions. Most obvious is its transformation from a millionaires' retreat to a retirement city for all classes. With respect to its government, Dorado is being converted from a closed corporation of cosy private "deals" among a small ruling clique to a more efficiently and openly directed administration based on competitive politics. Into its economy, soporific a few years ago except for the limited "season" from January to April, have moved development "hustlers," eyes firmly fixed on a fast profit, casting their nets widely and unselectively for a mass housing market. The day of the "estate" millionaire is nearing its end in Dorado, as, indeed, it may possibly be in our nation as a whole. Dorado's political and economic story may, therefore, be read as typical of many of our "restricted," upper-income, "estate" suburbs on which large-scale developers have laid their hands, pocking or fringing them with popular-priced homes and sprawling shopping centers.

Change goes fast in most of South Florida, and into sixteen years have gone transformations for Dorado that took decades elsewhere — from slow-moving fishing village to millionaires' hideaway to developers' paradise. In its first two phases Dorado basked in the warm glow of a remarkable consensus on virtually all governmental questions. A few years ago differences began to emerge, and both rich and poor were forced to choose sides when one of the millionaire "estate" owners decided to become a real estate developer and put some new propositions to the town. Dorado's story is the story of quarrels that have ranged from the "grand issue" of the destiny of the town down to the matter of who socializes with whom.

Dorado may be viewed within other frames of reference than that of the political scientist. The economist would view it as a community struggling to achieve a viable economy. The sociologist would see the associational patterns, the changing class structure, and the clashing role perceptions among and within these classes and their leaders. The fashion commentator interested in matters of taste and entertainment would be intrigued by the local snobberies, feuds, whims, and pretensions. Yet, interestingly enough, analysis within each frame of reference yields the same results: a little world that moved from consensus to conflict.

I

Taking what most people would agree is the most trivial basis for analysis first — fashion comment — we find Dorado was characterized by a writer in this field as the answer of the *nouveau riche* to the *haut monde* of Palm Beach. Described by everyone as a town dominated by millionaires — there were sixty to seventy in Dorado in 1950, and no one knows the exact count in 1962 — Dorado does not have the gay scions of the Woolworth, Widener, Dodge, or Flagler fortunes, and Dorado millionaires do not cavort regularly among the fleshpots of the Gold Coast or commute to the Riviera. Dorado's wealthy people are not considered Society with a capital "S," and would not be included in a guest list that embraced the Duke and Duchess of Windsor, the literary lions, or other ornaments of either the "international set" or the "horsey set." By the same token, they are not the aristocratic "old wealth" types of Boston or Philadelphia, where distinguished ancestry counts for much. The Dorado millionaires are, by contrast, primarily midwesterners and include a number of solid managerial types who have engineered large industrial corporations and advertising firms into the "Big Money" and have benefited handsomely themselves. Others have merely inherited or married their money. They converted Dorado into their town, with the idea of making it a strictly zoned, small-scale showplace like Palm Beach — a resort rather than a sportsman's retreat. Spacious lawns ring their estates along Ocean Drive. One millionaire vies with another in the importation of almost anything considered decorative, ranging all the way from exotic plants to, in one case, thousands of pieces of mother-of-pearl for adornment of an outsize barbecue pit, swimming pool, and al fresco dance floor. This latter type of décor represents a quaint Indiana notion of "living it up."

Across Ocean Drive on the bay side one of the nabobs has promoted an upper-class subdivision on a series of finger fills created by dredging sand out of the bay and building up lot areas (a typical Florida way to maximize the number of water-front lots for real estate exploitation). In this subdivision known as Aurelio Point he has forbidden such architectural "oddities" as flat roofs, and he even dictates the color of paint to be used. Every would-be purchaser of property in this subdivision must be scrutinized by a board of examiners to pass upon his suitability for membership in the Aurelio Point Beach Club. Only when accepted into the beach club may he become a purchaser.

Physically, whatever is beautiful in Dorado is man-made, such as the gardens of the estates on Ocean Drive, the "millionaires' row," or the generous plantings of palm trees, shrubs, and flowering plants by the city. Added to such man-made beauty are such man-made "gimmicks" for high real estate profits as the finger fills, described above, which are to be found in a new low-priced subdivision as well as in those of considerably higher cost. Even the less affluent areas of the town are kept clean and spotless and attractively landscaped by the lot owners. An attempt at Palm Beach type patio-style architecture for at least one commercial building lends an air of distinction to the small business area. Few visitors would not look with approval on Dorado as it now appears.

Dorado's ocean location failed to stimulate spectacular growth until after 1950, as the town grew from about 1,200 to only 1,465 between 1940 and 1950. The 1960 census showed a jump to 4,655. Unfortunately for certain real estate promoters in Dorado, this increase was insufficient to meet their economic needs, as they had been building their hopes on a total in excess of 5,000. This latter figure is the statistical cut-off point at which large holders of mortgage capital compile data for loan purposes on various communities. Even its estimated 6,000 in 1962 is still insufficient to satisfy insurance company investors.

An economic analysis of Dorado shows that 40 per cent of the census population is employed, with 13.5 per cent in the professions, 17.7 per cent in the managerial or business proprietor group, and only 4.0 per cent in the "operative" category. Of all persons over fourteen years of age, 45.9 per cent are *not* in the labor force, a somewhat higher proportion than is to be found in small Florida cities that have a little industry. This proportion would, no doubt, be much higher if all retirees would allow themselves to be counted in Dorado's population, but the common practice of this group is to consider for census purposes the city of origin as still the place of permanent residence. Hence, the census figures for a town like Dorado do not reflect in full the economic distribution of the population. Similarly, the income figures are not properly reflective of the large number of upper income residents although over one-third of all families are shown in the highest category of $10,000 or more per year family income. This contrasts with Westbourne where 43 per cent of all families fall into the top income group. But Westbourne has a higher proportion of employed persons who obviously consider that city their home and are counted in the census.

Chamber of Commerce members parrot the usual "line" about getting light industry to the town, but most admit the "line" is unrealistic. Actually the town boasts only a limited amount of mercantile activity except during the winter months when the "exclusive" shops catering to wealthy winter residents reopen. Today, however, a town cannot exist on the trade and patronage of winter millionaires. Judged from an economic standpoint, the increase in population from 1950 to 1960 is insufficient to produce adequate income for the merchants who are forced to supply high quality goods and services to the winter millionaires and for the professional people who have come to Dorado to work in a semiretired rather than a retired status. In other words, the business and professional contingent of the town needs a solid base of ordinary citizenry and year-round tourists to enable merchants and others to afford to serve the millionaires on a quality basis during the winter months.

The "boiler plate" master plan produced in the late forties for Dorado by one of the large national planning consultant firms failed to produce anything but a tight zoning system tailored to the desires of the millionaires, and it failed to contain any economic study of the town. Consequently now that the town has grown in population, the pressures have accumulated to bring in year-round population at whatever the cost to the original plan and to the tight zoning system.

Sociologically, the age groups in Dorado show that it is truly a retirement town, with 20.3 per cent in the age group of sixty years old or over. In contrast, a typical small city with some industrial employment and few retirees shows only 13 per cent in this age group. When one remembers the tendency of retirees to report permanent residence as the city of origin, then it is clear that Dorado has a much larger proportion of older persons than the census data would indicate.

The proportion of Negroes in Dorado has declined, standing in 1960 at 14.5 per cent. Actually, many Negroes originally in the town have moved in the last decade to lower cost communities nearby. Only now are plans being made for decent low-cost housing that they may purchase, although there has been a limited amount of good quality rental housing constructed for them by the development corporation sponsored as a philanthropic enterprise by Dorado millionaires.

Persons who have completed four or more years of college constitute 17.9 per cent of the adult population twenty-five years of age or older, and an additional 12.9 per cent have completed one to three years of college. High as these percentages are, they also would be even higher if the retirees were all counted, for the proportion of college graduates in Dorado must certainly be as high as in Westbourne, but again, the point must be made that Westbourne has a larger proportion of employed persons who report that city as their permanent residence. Also Westbourne has very few nonwhites.

The social and economic make-up of Dorado changed in the decade of the fifties, especially in the last four or five years. In 1950 the city was made up almost entirely of very wealthy absentees and the working-class people who took care of their estates, served as domestic help, and ran various local service shops. Before the millionaires came, the few year-round residents had been commercial fishermen, but now there is little commercial fishing left. Today, Dorado's population ranges from the earlier settlers — the multi-millionaires — through millionaires, less than millionaires, comfortable upper middle-class, and ordinary laborers. The latter include a number of the original "Crackers." Some of the upper middle-class are retired professional people or industrial managers, and some are retired military officers. The less prosperous retirees for the most part live outside the city limits. Dorado is described as having about sixteen physicians and as many attorneys, an excessive number for a town of this size, but this figure, which would represent extreme competition, is mitigated by the fact that many of the physicians are semiretired.

What of the working class in Dorado? Primarily dependent upon the millionaires for their livelihood, they have remained loyal to their patrons, as attested by the glowing words of praise for the rich sung by several persons interviewed, including a former councilman who is an ex-landscape gardener for one of the millionaires and also including a present councilman who has been general factotum for another millionaire. These people enjoy the paternalism of their relationship with the estate owners. Such councilmen were placidly accepted by Doradans for a number of years as "agents" of particular millionaires.

The working class has not increased as the town has increased, but rather it has disfranchised itself by moving to cheaper areas outside the city limits. Therein lies a part of the tale of the political downfall of the "old guard" absentee estate owners and their political agents, especially the long-time mayor, Miles Alden, and city manager, Henry Blank. The politics of Dorado changed as its social and economic make-up has altered, and the dwindling of the working class eroded away the "old guard's" strength all the while the "old guard" was building up a retirees' bloc.

II

A description of the form of government and the way in which the peculiar features evolved in Dorado is necessary at this point. In this section the development of the structural-institutional features of government will be set forth, and in the next the political history of the town will be analyzed. This section necessarily overlaps the next one.

Dorado owes both its form of government and many of its civic improvements to the millionaire estate owners of Ocean Drive. Dorado was long their "pet charity" and the officials of Dorado their trustees, in a true paternalistic system reminiscent of the Middle Ages. For example, the Dorado Foundation allows wealthy donors to give money to the city in tax-deductible gifts with no strings attached and to receive in return from the city improvements on their own property, such as groins at their beach to prevent beach erosion, a street paving job, a storm sewer, etc. Thereby, private improvements have been deemed public improvements and worth-while federal tax relief successfully obtained at the same time. Of course, some of the millionaires' beneficence has been truly public, such as a swimming pool for the Negroes of Dorado, a community hospital, a low rent housing project for Negroes, and a municipal pier. Cynics, of course, say that the pool for Negroes assuredly kept Negroes off the beach and the housing for them kept a supply of domestics available for the millionaires.

The Dorado Citizens Association was formed in the immediate postwar period by the absentee millionaires to keep watch on local government officials during the long months of their absences from Dorado. There was even a "study arm," the Rio Grande County Research Association, created to furnish factual studies for the Dorado Citizens Association. Both organizations had high dues and originally restricted their membership to the social elite of Ocean Drive.

Council-manager government was recommended by the Dorado Citizens Association and adopted in the late forties. Manager applicants were screened by the Association, and Henry Blank, the long-time manager of Dorado, was appointed in 1948. Indeed, the Citizens Association for years paid half of Blank's salary. Blank had held a minor supervisory post in the State Road Department and then had been manager of a tourist attraction in a nearby town. Neither by training nor experience was he a professional manager.

Under the original city-manager charter the mayor was elected separately by the voters for a two-year term at the same time as two council seats were filled for four-year terms. Two other council seats were filled in the succeeding biennial election. The mayor and the council appointed the city manager but with the unique feature in Dorado that the manager was under contract for a fixed term during the entire tenure of Henry Blank. When Blank's contract was not renewed in 1960, this procedure was abandoned.

Blank really acted like a "straw boss" for work crews and was devoid of any concept of management. His ineptitude as an administrator was compensated for by Mayor Alden's creation of a large number of committees that exercised actual administrative powers over many jurisdictional areas of city government. Blank's obsession with construction projects led him to avoid paper work assiduously. Whether his inability to furnish fiscal reports was deliberate obfuscation of "hanky-panky" or the result of inability to cope with figures is not too clear at this point. But the point that is clear is that Blank's professed inability to render an accounting exactly suited the purposes of the "Cracker" clique in power until 1960 as surrogates of the absentee millionaires.

The membership of the Citizens Association was broadened and dues lowered in the mid-fifties in an effort to interest the local businessmen and the upper middle-class professional persons coming to Dorado as retirees. One of the chief mental characteristics of retirees is a "set" or attitude produced by the realization that they will never again earn more income. No matter how high a pension or rentier income may be, the retiree becomes acutely tax and government cost conscious. Consequently, the more popularly based Citizens Association began to demand an accounting of Dorado city officials and to work toward reduction of costs through a more efficient organization of government. Some younger businessmen in the Citizens Association worked with them towards these goals.

The Citizens Association soon became interested in charter revision. A council committee had been appointed in 1958 to undertake this task, but it soon became apparent to Evan West, a young accountant active in the Citizens Association, that Mayor Alden and his council were only going through motions and did not really want charter revision, as they did not want their power curtailed. West induced the Citizens Association and the Rio Grande County Research Association to vote funds to employ accountants to work on the fiscal sections of the charter, and the city council was maneuvered into matching their funds. West further succeeded in getting the city council to expand its small council committee into one of fifteen prominent citizens, called the Charter Drafting Committee, which

became a real working committee. Another larger committee consisting of fifty leading citizens was also created to lend prestige to the
work and was called the Charter Review Committee. Although the
Research Association fell apart and disbanded because of the pique
of its president in not getting on the Charter Drafting Committee, the
Citizens Association continued to flourish and the charter drafting
proceeded.

Although Mayor Alden was visibly unhappy over the trend of
events toward charter revision, he was outmaneuvered and boxed in
by West and the Citizens Association. West was active in the Chamber
of Commerce, which was drawn into endorsement of charter revision,
and Alden grew afraid of resistance to charter change.

The next problem was to get the state representative behind the
charter revision, which was easy. The state senator at first, however,
refused to sponsor the requisite special legislation incorporating the
charter change unless the city council requested him to introduce the
bill. West turned this idea around, with the senator finally agreeing
that he would introduce the bill if there were no opposition to it by
the city. The council was maneuvered into taking no stand on the
charter. Jay Standish, then a councilman and later mayor, moved that
the council go on record in support of the charter changes. West, on
behalf of the Charter Drafting Committee, opposed this and argued
that the council should merely go on record as not opposed to the
changes on the ground that if the changes did not work well, council
members would not have endorsement on their consciences. Actually
Standish could not have carried a majority of the 1958 council for
charter revision, and West's tactics forestalled defeat of Standish's
idea. Therefore, the charter revision in essentially the form originally
proposed by the Rio Grande County Research Association was duly
enacted into special legislation in 1959. Because no opposition to the
proposed charter was ever voiced at hearings held in early 1959, no
referendum was provided.

The charter changes of 1959 were several. One limited the mayor
to two terms and, in effect, was intended to reduce him to *primus
inter pares* on the council. The council itself was enlarged to seven
with three members elected every two years. Under the old charter
the police and fire departments had been independent of the city
manager with their chiefs reporting to the council directly. Because of
Blank's weakness in administration the finance department was also
made independent of the manager.

It is hard to comprehend why Henry Blank was chosen for the
managerial post aside from the fact that he had had experience in
supervision in the state highway department. In addition to his lack

of sense of organization, he was hopelessly uninformed on fiscal procedures, unwilling to learn, and found it impossible to delegate. At first, his "straw boss" supervision of construction and garbage and refuse collection was all the millionaires expected in their little town. Despite the confusion resulting from administration by committees created to offset Blank's ineptitude, nevertheless, this system of administration was still carried forward and made official under the new charter. A combined Parks and Recreation Board was set up that quickly got into some disputes with Blank over development of a new park.

Unhappy over confused administration and difficulty in determining costs of government, the Dorado Citizens Association in 1960 paid a firm of outside accountants to make an analysis of Dorado city government. The accountants' report, dated June 15, 1960, made a great many proposals for tightening Dorado municipal administration. These recommendations reveal something of Blank's and Alden's haphazard and rather extravagant approach to administration. They are:

1. *Council:* Abolish the committee system of operation.
2. *City Manager:* Employ an experienced city manager if and when the services of the present city manager are terminated.
3. *City Charter:* Amend charter to place finance, police, and fire departments under the jurisdiction of the city manager.
4. *City Clerk:* Establish an accounting department separate from the office of city clerk; reduce the staff of the existing operation to two employees.
5. *Tax Department:* Make assessments of partially completed buildings. Do not fill the position of draftsman when it is vacated by the present incumbent. Eliminate the department and transfer functions to County Tax Assessor and Collector.
6. *Engineering Department:* Abolish the department, and arrange with private engineers to handle work from time to time, as needed.
7. *Building Inspection and Zoning:* Discontinue radio communication system. Eliminate full-time position of permit clerk, part-time position of draftsman. Revise permit fees if necessary to make department self-supporting.
8. *Police Department:* Do not increase staff of department. Do not add additional patrol cars. Continue system of one man in each patrol car. Use county jail and radio facilities when new courthouse is built in Dorado.
9. *Fire Department:* Complete negotiations with county for equitable sharing of expenses.

10. *Garbage Department:* Do not include a new garbage truck in the 1960–1961 budget. Conduct sanitary land fill operations with the city employees and equipment. Eliminate telephone service at garbage dump. Eliminate sanitary inspectors. Place operation under Public Works Department.

11. *Trash Department:* Use mechanical equipment for loading large accumulation of trash. Reduce trash service to once every two weeks. Eliminate one trash truck and personnel. Place operation under Public Works Department.

12. *Parkways Department:* Discontinue department and assign employees to Public Works Department. Pass ordinance providing minimum requirements for maintaining vacant property and reimbursement for city service in performing work.

13. *Sidney Park:* Abolish department and assign employees to Parkway crews. Charge maintenance and utility costs to Recreation Department.

14. *Recreation Department:* Eliminate assistant recreation director position and employ part-time help as needed. Eliminate maintenance employee. Eliminate part-time secretary. Defer consideration of new recreation building.

15. *Street Repair and Maintenance:* Council should require work performance budgets. Place operation under Public Works Department.

16. *Municipal Pier:* Consider admission charges if pier is reconditioned or rebuilt.

17. *Bay Dock:* No expansion of facilities. Try to fill facilities or rent on net basis with lessee paying all expenses.

18. *Water and Sewer:* A number of recommendations are made about billing and elimination of clerks, transfering accounting records to the City Clerk and office personnel to the city hall and water plant No. 2, trying to sell equipment in plant No. 1 and related well field pumps, etc., effect economies in operation of maintenance shops, and direct all departments to use shop facilities.

19. *Public Works Department:* Establish this department with personnel of the present service departments. Employ superintendent and cost clerk. Accurate cost records and works standards should be used. Delay street servicing until sewer plant has been established. Reassign straw bosses to working assignments. Evaluate level of service to be rendered.

20. *Time Records:* Install time clocks for service personnel. Make department heads responsible for accuracy of salaried employees' time records.

21. *Public Works Construction:* Perform future public works construction with private contractors.

22. *Capital Improvements:* Provide current contributions to a capital improvement trust fund.

These recommendations would indicate first of all that the city of Dorado was very poorly organized, considering the large number of departments of city government. Second, it would appear that some activities were overstaffed, although, on the other hand, the accountants appeared to be unrealistic on the idea of cutting back some functions. In some instances there was rather "plush" equipment for a city the size of Dorado, such as radio communication equipment to the building inspectors out on a job, which is typical only of large metropolitan building inspection departments where personnel must be deployed over wide areas of a city. It would appear, on the other hand, that modern methods of accounting and record keeping had not been introduced into city government in Dorado. The accountants stated in discussing their recommendations:

Lines of authority are not clear. Various department heads did not know whether they were responsible to a committee, the city manager, or the council.

Existence of the committees tended to confuse the city manager as to his responsibility. When problems arose, he did not know if they should be handled by him or the committees, and he was at times reluctant to act.

Sometimes it was difficult to get committees to meet and, as a result, no action on problems was taken. Or one member of a committee would make decisions for which the committee as a whole was responsible.

The accountants also said:

It is difficult for the city manager and department heads to become adjusted to committees, now trying to act only in an advisory capacity to the manager and/or the council. As a result, most of the conditions resulting from past committees still exist.

There was a clear implication here that, in the past, committees were really running the departments in the sense of giving orders and that the department heads and the manager could not become adjusted to any other condition or way of operating.

The accountants also said:

We feel that the council can best function by dealing directly with the city manager. Therefore, we recommend that committees be limited to special committees appointed to perform a specific function and which cease to exist after their particular duty has been performed.

In other words, they meant *ad hoc* committees were the only kind that could be justified, rather than standing committees such as had been used in the past and were still being used for administrative purposes. The report stated that most of the city manager's time had been spent in public works away from his office, and it alluded to the fact that half his salary was paid as director of public works. The accountants stated, "As a result, the administrative functions of the city manager's office are somewhat neglected."

Blank believed that the accountants wanted to convert him into a "paper-shuffler," which was his interpretation of their recommendation that he should become an administrator. Certainly their notion of contracting construction would have cut him out of much of his work. The accountants recommended that when a new city manager might be employed (but they did not indicate that the incumbent should be dismissed), a trained administrator be selected, and that the city also employ a qualified public works director.

The accountants, in referring to the matter of transferring accounting functions to bring them all together, pointed out that this work was scattered around in a number of departments, particularly in the Department of Water and Sewers and in the City Clerk's office. In addition, they wanted special state legislation to transfer the city tax assessment and tax collection functions to the Couny Tax Assessor and County Tax Collector under special requirements which would reduce the present state fee.

The accountants, moreover, criticized the program and management of the Parks Department. Half the employees of that department, the accountants alleged, were unnecessary. Furthermore, they criticized the Recreation Department for the limited participation of the people of Dorado in local programs, in spite of the fact that the department had a full-time director and a number of part-time assistants, plus a full-time assistant director. Only 1,450 people took part in 1959 in all types of recreation offered. The accountants claimed more people would have participated had activities not been limited to spectator sports. They urged more playgrounds and equipment. Parenthetically, it is interesting to observe that several Doradans accused Henry Blank of using the overstaffed Parks Department as a political machine to "clobber" opponents of the "Cracker clique."

Finally, the accountants made a significant charter recommendation. They referred to the fact that the 1959 legislature had passed a new charter for the City of Dorado which became effective in May, 1959, and that this charter provided that the city manager was to be responsible for the administration of all departments of the city except finance, police, and fire. The accountants stated:

> We feel that these departments should also be responsible to the city manager, and we recommend that the 1961 legislature be requested to amend the charter so that the finance, police, and fire departments will be under the jurisdiction of the city manager. The city has now had approximately one year of experience in operating under the new charter. Therefore, we recommend that the city manager, city attorney, city council, and other interested parties carefully review the charter to determine what changes, if any, should be requested of the 1961 legislature.

Henry Blank's shortcomings as a manager had been of little interest to the millionaires who ruled Dorado. Blank was faithful to their interests, especially on inflexibily strict zoning, and he, along with his immediate patron, Miles Alden, was an effective surrogate for the real rulers of the town. Uninterested in the details of municipal costs in an operation that was "peanuts" to them, the millionaires asked no accounting of Blank, and he gave none. At first Blank arrogantly refused to answer questions on finance raised by the retirees; later he proved to be incapable of answering had he even wanted to do so. The town simply changed, and Blank could not change with it; he had to go, and his going will be described later.

The elimination of Henry Blank and Miles Alden did not end the matter of charter revision but rather precipitated Dorado's bitterest political fight. Although Alden had been a strong and ruthless mayor, Jay Standish, his successor, also reached eagerly for power. But Standish's motives seemed to spring more from a need to satisfy his ego — he is a rich man — than the need to add to his resources. Consequently a move that started innocently enough in the council in 1960, to carry out the accountants' recommendation for centering administrative responsibility in the manager and making the mayor appointive instead of elective, was converted by Standish into a restructuring of his control over the manager.

The amendment, as originally drafted, put all departments under the manager and gave to the mayor the additional powers of serving as the sole channel from the council to the manager, the right to act in the absence of the manager, and authority to issue orders to the manager that could be countermanded only by the council. But since it also provided for the council to select the mayor and for abolition of the system of popular election of the mayor, the drafters argued that the council was, in effect, using its mayoral appointee as its agent. It should be noted, however, that the concept of having the manager dealt with by the mayor alone violates council-manager theory. Standish opposed dropping popular election of the mayor. Later when the charter amendment emerged, carrying the additional powers for mayor without changing to his appointment by the council, he plausibly defended this proposal as merely making Dorado "more democratic as the mayor is the elected representative of all the people." Evan West, a member of the council at this time, bitterly opposed the amendment as a perversion of council-manager government, but Standish outmaneuvered the council in his propaganda and forced them to present this proposal to a referendum. The charter amendment fight in November, 1961, was characterized by personal accusations, exposés of favors granted under earlier administrations, social ostracism, and a confusion of issues by the Standish forces. Standish proved to be a surprisingly good political operator despite his earlier career as a dentist, and the result was a victory for his amendments. But having won and apparently having satisfied his ego by confounding his enemies, he has since failed to use his power. Nevertheless, it is there for a successor.

The mayor's role. The part played by Miles Alden during his long tenure as mayor in deciding what needed to be done by Dorado is not difficult to unravel. Alden was a strong man, and apparently what he wanted, he got. He, Blank, and Clem Hicks, a councilman, were very close to each other. They got the city to award a contract to one of Alden's business enterprises, and Alden's resources grew noticeably. He even founded the first bank in Dorado. One of their friends received a lucrative contract to run the airport, for which he never made an accounting to the city. Hicks was established at $12,000 per year as vice-president of a real estate company operated by "his" millionaire, and he handily took care of the interests of his patron before the city. Blank himself acquired considerable property.

Blank described the council as expecting the mayor to take the lead on all policy questions. At another point, however, he described himself as an "activist" on policy origination. Alden maintained an office in the city hall during his incumbency and came in daily to receive the public and dispense favors. Under the old charter the mayor had a free hand in signing documents and presumably, therefore, in making contracts. It is clear from testimony of others that Alden really did originate policy when he was mayor. Also the belief was general that his "inside" knowledge of investment opportunities in Dorado, through the office of mayor, was most profitable to him.

As to Jay Standish, present mayor, it is clear that he would like to be another Alden in the sense of playing the strong leader, has been imperious toward his council opposition, and has kept daily office hours. In fact, he has found that he enjoys politics, and his enthusiastic followers — mostly retirees — form a demonstrative claque for him at each council meeting. He is a loud, irascible, bulldozing type who literally drove two younger men off the council and discouraged two others from seeking re-election.

Mayor Standish has expressed the notion that policy determination should properly be in the hands of the council and that the manager should observe a decent humility toward the council and be subordinate to it and to the mayor. He stated that he was in favor of the manager making, in properly deferential fashion, appropriate recommendations to the council as to policy they might consider. All this indicated, as did some explicit remarks, that he believed the council during the Alden regime had left entirely too much to Manager Henry Blank, despite the latter's well-known inability as an administrator. Thereby, he believed Blank had the upper hand with respect to policy, particularly if one fits in with these descriptive remarks the fact that it was impossible to get fiscal information about the city from Blank. On the whole, Standish believed the council and mayor during the Alden regime had been insufficiently attentive to city business and had turned too much over to the city manager to decide. But Standish was reluctant to blame Alden for policies during the Alden regime, despite the fact that Blank was really Alden's agent and that insofar as Blank had real power, such power stemmed from Blank's membership in the "clique" and not from any innate strength of his own.

But what did Standish do as mayor? First of all, he came into open conflict with vice-mayor Evan West early in his administration over his own unilateral action in hand-picking the new director of public works and in conveying to him the understanding that he would move up from public works director to become city manager upon the expiration of Blank's contract. The council was presented with this action as a *fait accompli,* and although West did induce the council to insist on advertising the managership in the International City Managers' Association *Newsletter,* this advertisement was merely a gesture. Standish quickly got his way on his choice of manager immediately after the first *Newsletter* announcement.

Strong tendencies to interfere in the details of day-to-day administration were soon shown by Mayor Standish. For example, he insisted on dealing directly with department heads on trival details instead of going through the manager. In one such case, he physically attacked the public works director for "military arrogance" in refusing to carry out his orders. This assault resulted in a $35,000 suit for damages against Standish. Of the new manager, he demanded a daily report of his activities at 4 P.M., but this was successfully rejected by the manager.

The council's role. Council intervention in administration was, in effect, institutionalized through the committee system during the Alden-Blank regime. When Alden finally retired as mayor, the new council put in their own man as finance director during the last year of Blank's tenure. Actually one of the accountants employed by the firm under contract for the consultant study was utilized for this directorship although he was not really a city employee. The council administrative committees were continued until the new manager came into office. Thereupon they were either disbanded or converted into purely advisory committees for policy purposes.

Because Evan West was the most articulate member of the council majority in 1960, his views on council-manager relations are worth noting. Although he believed the manager should play little part in policy initiation but rather primarily execute the policies laid down by the council, he said paradoxically that a good manager would really be the principal policy originator. West also believed that once the manager received his "clearance" on policy from the council, he should proceed to carry it out and "discreetly" go before the public to defend his policy. Thus, he really wanted the manager to develop new policy ideas but not to make the ultimate policy decisions and to be skillful in public relations.

As to the mayor, West believed that he should be merely a ceremonial official and a presiding officer at council meetings, with no office in the city hall, no daily reception of callers there, and no more power to influence the council than any other member of it. He objected strenuously to Mayor Standish's assumption of priority of authority and leadership. "There is no room in a city for two executives," West declared, "and the manager is the executive under council-manager government." He denounced Standish as an egomaniac long before Standish forced him off the council by his own bitter onslaughts and the jeers of his claque. West's description of Standish as really following the crowd instead of leading it was confirmed by the veteran councilman Clem Hicks, the only really professional politician on the council. Others, too, such as the local editor and other councilmen, view Standish in the same light as does West, but to our research team it seemed clear that Standish did both lead and follow, with a fine sense of reciprocity between him and his retiree followers.

On the matter of budget-making, Blank claimed that he had always made the budget, and that the council did not look at it or know what was in it until he presented it to them. With an air of conspiracy, he averred that he was in 1960 putting some fat in the budget for council to trim down. One of the council members confirmed that in the past Blank had made the budget and that was "it."

For the council elected in 1960, however, according to one of the new councilmen, Blank merely prepared the outline of a budget. The basic budget, a minimal one of absolutely essential services, was prepared by the finance director. The council preferred taking the "basic budget" and adding to it where necessary to taking Blank's version and trying to lop off considerable amounts. But it is significant that the councilman reporting the "basic budget" procedure regarded this as a stop-gap procedure until Blank would leave his office. The ideal budget arrangement to this councilman would be placement of responsibility for budget preparation in the manager, requiring him to show clearly where money goes and where it will go, e.g., for how many miles of streets, where it is proposed to build them, type of streets, etc. The new manager did apparently make "his" budget, and it was this that was adopted in 1961 despite serious attacks on it by a newly formed taxpayers' league.

III

The politics of Dorado is complex, fascinating, and ruthless — a "no holds barred" kind of game. These tactics were used by the "Cracker" clique but have been practiced with consummate skill by one of the millionaires who would actually like to be boss of the town. The cast of characters needs to be listed. The millionaire "kingmakers" are Ian Watters, advertising man and developer of Aurelio Point, the luxury subdivision; Mason Perkins, who put together a motor manufacturing combine; and Albert Bickel, former large-city corporation lawyer and now well on the way to building a powerful real estate development-construction-finance empire. The major office-holders include Miles Alden, mayor for twelve years; Jay Standish, wealthy retired dentist, now in his second term as mayor; Henry Blank, city manager for twelve years; Clem Hicks, "Cracker" fisherman and long-time councilman skilled in determining which side is the winning one and affiliating with it; Evan West, leader of charter reform, manager of Watters' Aurelio Point subdivision, and as vice-mayor the chief antagonist of Jay Standish on the council in 1960 and 1961; and now Albert Bickel, elected to the council in 1962 and quickly identified as West's replacement in opposing Standish. Bickel is not actually allied with West, but both merely oppose Mayor Standish.

Miles Alden, a "Cracker" with an eye to opportunities for profit, was able to maintain undisputed sway as mayor and leader of the "Cracker" clique for twelve years, 1948–1960. He and his close allies, Henry Blank and Clem Hicks, were consistently faithful to their rich absentee patrons in maintaining tight zoning, the overriding interest of the nabobs. Determined to keep Miami Beach "honky-tonk" type of hotel-motel-night club facilities away from their town and particularly from the beach, the millionaires were and still are deeply concerned that only the "right" kind of people get on the beach. This concern they have passed on to the upper middle-class retirees who live at or near the waterfront. On the other hand, the absentee millionaires cared little about the quality of politics and administration carried on by the "clique." This indifference allowed Miles Alden to take full advantage of his opportunities and to become a rich man himself, even helping to open the first bank in Dorado and serve as its president. One of Alden's deals involved a contract between the city and a business he owned, without benefit of advertising for competitive bids. The very notion of conflict of interest never crossed the minds of members of the "Cracker" clique, a lack of perception quite characteristic of this class all over Florida. In fact, these people believed there was little reason to hold public office unless you used your inside knowledge to personal advantage and "swung" public business your way.

The first real split occurred among the millionaire patrons over rezoning on Ocean Drive to permit the Aurelio Point Beach Club to be built. Although Ian Watters claimed to have filed plans for the beach club with his original subdivision plat, the Ocean Drive nabobs did not realize the nature of the plans until a permit to rezone for club use was requested. Watters had employed a respected architect and interior decorator for the club and had set standards of impeccable taste. But his neighbors grew excited over the possibility that at some future time the club might be converted into a Miami Beach "honky-tonk" if Watters or his heirs ever sold the place, and that this possibility could be made more real by the granting of a liquor license to the club. Mason Perkins led the group opposed to rezoning. This was no ordinary zoning fight but a real feud that has left Mason Perkins and Watters still not on speaking terms today, never both invited to the same parties. As far as the club itself was concerned, the city council finally voted to rezone it, but they forbade sale of liquor after 6 P.M. under the liquor license granted.

Shortly before the beach club issue split the millionaires, a rezoning issue of far more significance to the future of the town was decided with virtually no controversy. A variance to permit cooperative apartment houses at the then undeveloped north end of Ocean Drive brought into Dorado the first upper middle-class retirees, who are now a numerous and vocal political group. This was certainly an unanticipated consequence of bringing in a new social group. Coming as this move did about the time of the broadening of the base of the Dorado Citizens Association, it foreshadowed the change in control of that organization to dominance by the retirees.

In 1957 Albert Bickel, retired corporation lawyer, came to Dorado and purchased an apartment in the first of these cooperatives and shortly thereafter decided to construct such a building himself. He was soon drawn into a major business venture in the town and began to conclude that he should look into the way the community was run. Of key importance to him and the future of Dorado was the fact that he was rejected by Ian Watters for membership in the Aurelio Point Beach Club.

Bickel was born to wealth that was lost in the stock market crash of 1929, at the time he was graduated from law school. He is an intelligent man, extremely hard working, single-minded in his persistence, and driven by the desire to dominate all he touches. Within two decades after he graduated from law school he had become a millionaire and decided to retire, but he is scarcely the kind of person who could retire with ease of mind. He defends creation of his real estate development ventures by stating that he believed it imperative to get his investments out of stocks and into real estate and that to execute this financial maneuver successfully, he had to direct his real estate operations himself. But, of course, Dorado offered unusual investment opportunities to a bold, persistent entrepreneur who was willing to try to change the focus and, indeed, the destiny of the town. Bickel was just bold enough to do this, particularly after his rebuff by Watters.

With an unerring instinct for reaching for the jugular, Bickel utilized all his big city lawyer's experience to unearth the details of all the conflict-of-interest operations of Mayor Miles Alden and Clem Hicks. If he could discredit the "Cracker" clique, he could "break" the hold of the beach front millionaires on the town. Virtually all of Bickel's friends warned him that he would face brutal pressures from the "Cracker" clique: intimidation, business harassment, and social ostracism by the millionaires. After all, the nabobs did not want their little world torn apart; they were quite satisfied with the way their agents in government were holding the line on zoning and providing a reasonable level of services. Too much efficiency and openness of administration would destroy the nabobs' own control of the destiny of Dorado. The Alden-Blank-Hicks axis growled angrily, but they were actually helpless to curb Bickel, who was far more sophisticated than they in the techniques of keeping an enemy on the defensive and was not afraid to do his own "homework" to support his accusations.

Verbal castigation of conflict of interest was followed by a taxpayer's suit against Mayor Alden to force repayment to the city of the profit he had made from his contract shortly before the 1960 mayoralty campaign. This suit forced him to change his mind about running for re-election. Although a minor real estate broker who later left town filed the suit, it seems clear that Bickel both masterminded it and provided the resources for it. Bickel virtually admits his part in promoting the suit by calling attention to the fact that it was he who ran Miles Alden out of politics and made an "honest man of him." Alden ultimately was ordered by the court to repay the city $5,000.

Having disposed of Alden, Bickel was instrumental in organizing support for a minority council member, Jay Standish, for mayor in 1960. Actually Watters also backed Standish for mayor, as West, Watters' vice-president and manager of the Aurelio Point development, was a successful candidate for a council seat on the slate with Standish. Mason Perkins half-heartedly backed Standish's opponent.[1] Standish won but refused to listen to any of the nabobs or Bickel on policy questions, turning instead to the large group of retirees who admired him. Bickel quickly grew disenchanted with Standish, let this fact be known, and had to suffer the social disapproval of Mrs. Standish, a wealthy woman in her own right, who exercises great influence over the "party circuit" of the Dorado millionaires. It was quite natural that Bickel would be drawn into the 1961 battle against Standish over ratification of the charter referendum to increase the mayor's power. The nature of the referendum issue was described in the preceding section.

Evan West, Watter's vice-president for the Aurelio Point subdivision and leader for the successful charter revision movement, was the leader in organizing a slate of young businessmen for the council in 1960. This slate included the manager of Harbor Haven, the subdivision created by another millionaire for upper middle-class retirees, the manager of a botanical garden owned by a millionaire, and a local contractor tied to the developers. All were elected.

Mayor Standish had not only refused to look to Bickel for ideas, but he had almost immediately upon his accession to office resented the ideas of Evan West who was chosen vice-mayor. Because of West's leadership of the charter revision movement and his representation of

---

[1] The Perkins "pet" charity in Dorado is the community hospital, and this institution is especially dear to Mrs. Perkins, chairman of its board. Standish had made disparaging remarks about the quality of the hospital, thereby permanently alienating the Perkinses.

the interests of Watters, admittedly a major power in the city, Evan West was looked to by other councilmen of the slate as their natural leader. This Standish bitterly resented, as he believed the council should look to him and to no other for policy leadership. The Evan West group came to be denounced by Standish as the "unholy four," but none of them was capable of replying publicly in kind. Instead, they feared Standish's irascible temper and sharp tongue. Also their own strategy could not be planned in advance as they found it more and more difficult to determine where Standish would be on any issue, for he would quickly retreat from any position that he found unpopular with his retiree admirers. Furthermore, those admirers attended council meetings in large numbers and constituted a rooting section for Standish, booing West and the "unholy four."

Standish's manipulation of his own change in stand on an issue can best be described by his initial advocacy of a utilities tax after a disastrous hurricane swept the town.[2] This measure was supported by West and his group to pay for rebuilding the large municipal pier on the ground that it would put everyone into the taxpayer group and that everyone should pay for the pier. When the retirees, however, began to denounce the utilities tax publicly, Standish quickly retreated from it. One of Standish's friends persuaded one of the millionaires to offer to pay for rebuilding the municipal pier if the council dropped the utilities tax measure. Naturally the council complied with this stipulation, but at considerable cost in popularity to West. Publicly, therefore, Standish became the defender of the common man against the developer interests that wished to pass off additional tax burdens upon him.

At the time the 1961 municipal budget was under consideration before the council, a newly formed taxpayer's league exposed the assessment favors granted four major developers by the council in 1954 during the heyday of Miles Alden. In brief, these concessions amounted to assessment of all developments on submerged lands, the areas on which dredge-and-fill finger fills are built, as *undeveloped* submerged lands until two-thirds of all property in such subdivisions was sold. Three of the four subdividers were still receiving this benefit in 1961 as only one subdivider had sold the required major fraction of his land.

Standish revealed again this skill in manipulation of issues by guiding his eager supporters during the charter amendment campaign to tie the submerged lands "deal" to opposition to the amendment.

[2] Utilities taxes are permitted to Florida cities by state law and are a common source of local revenue.

Just before the election a "Committee of Taxpayers for Jay" ran a
large advertisement to this effect:

BIG against LITTLE
4 against 4,000 PEOPLE
CLIQUE against VOTERS
(4)   (4)
Managers and Councilmen
SO
WHO gets the tax reduction?
WHO sweats out $3,000,000 difference?

	City Assessment	County Assessment
Aurelio Point	$50,340.00	$1,015,650.00
Harbor Haven	63,300.00	1,288,150.00
Del Oro	29,650.00	573,250.00

Needless to say, this issue was scarcely related to the mayor's control
over the city manager at stake in the referendum, and only one incumbent councilman, Clem Hicks, had been a party to the "deals."
But it apparently was a successful gambit, for Standish's amendment
won despite the advertised opposition of five out of six councilmen.

Standish's followers and their techniques, both in advertisements and
conduct of noisy, partisan demonstrations at council meetings, were
denounced by the newspaper as divisive of the city in a totally new
way. The old "Cracker" clique monopoly had not only broken down
and disappeared, but competitive politics had arrived in a boisterous,
rowdy way — despite the upper middle-class origin of the noise — and
this was disturbing to those accustomed to the quiet, backroom "deals"
so long characteristic of the town.

Evan West and another councilman aligned with him resigned shortly
after the charter referendum election; a third councilman in this group
of the "unholy four" announced that he would not seek re-election.
West issued a public statement: "A man trying to raise a family should
not be subjected to the vicious and slandering type of campaign conducted against me in the recent charter change referendum." He
expressed displeasure at the "recent inexcusable incident in our city
government," (referring to the assault by Standish on the public works
director) and declared, "I cannot participate in council meetings in
which the presiding officer permits raucous spectators to make scenes
and allows an elected official to be subjected to catcalls and obscene
remarks if he takes a position contrary to those of the citizens who
have time to come to the meetings." His colleague who resigned
attributed his resignation to the "impossible situation" he faced as a
councilman as a result of the increased powers granted the mayor.

Mayor Standish's physical assault on the public works director alluded to by Evan West was just an interim incident of no lasting significance during the post-referendum period while Standish was actually concentrating on forming a slate for the February, 1962, council election. His slate, as finally launched, consisted of a woman realtor, a photographer, the wife of the retired general who headed the "Taxpayers for Jay" group in the charter referendum election, and a retiree whose main claim to local recognition was his distinguished Virginia ancestry and ties to various notables in nineteenth-century American politics. In fact, this man, Randolph Cabell, was something of an enigma to Doradans of all classes, as they were never able to explain to themselves how or why he should cut the same kind of swath as the Ocean Drive nabobs when the kind and amount of his assets was so unclear. Despite the mystification of those who were less than enthusiastic about Cabell, he won finally in the second run-off. Dorado's 1959 charter required a clear majority of all votes cast for election to a council seat. Sixteen candidates filed in 1962, and two run-offs were required to decide the outcome of the race for the seat for which Cabell had filed.

By 1962 Bickel was much stronger politically as a result of his successful launching of his development-construction-finance corporations after the 1960 hurricane. Bickel tried to get some prominent local businessman to run for mayor against Standish, against whom he was completely alienated by 1962. Although he was unsuccessful in this endeavor, he was persuaded by those he was trying to convince to run for the council himself and agreed to do so. Actually this was not exactly what he desired for Dorado or himself. Bickel firmly believes that Dorado needs a political machine. Since machines normally have "bosses," the implication is clear that he should be boss as he at least has a clear notion of the direction in which the city should move. But as a "boss," Bickel would undoubtedly prefer to stay in the background. Aligned with Bickel in the council election was a woman realtor whose firm handles the business of one of the major developers, and a retired Air Force general. Both Bickel and the woman realtor were elected. In addition to Cabell, Clem Hicks, the "Cracker" fisherman, and a newcomer from Tennessee whose main appeal was a striking facial and verbal resemblance to "Tennessee Ernie" Ford, was also elected. This man was an ex-truck driver and building contractor who owned a small motel in Dorado.

The 1962 council consisted of three members who were clearly anti-Standish, one follower of Standish, and two straddlers who were waiting to see where the ultimate strength on the council would lie. One straddler was Clem Hicks, always essentially the professional politician like Councilman Walters in Hiberna, who could accommodate himself to any faction that came out on top. The other, the counterpart of "Tennessee Ernie," had no ideological orientation and would drift where power lies, a "potential seducee" of Standish, as Bickel described him.

But this description of the council in 1962 omits the monomania of Bickel to control Dorado and thereby to "show" such people as Watters, who blackballed him from his club, that he, Bickel, can take over the town and change its character completely. Bickel did his homework assiduously on the local airport contract held for thirteen years by one of Miles Alden's cronies without the benefit of a cent of income to the city. This Bickel exposed — as he intended to expose such favors and "deals." He drew up a list of needed reforms which included classification of city jobs by position, systematic assessment procedures, an established long-term policy for sewers, streets, and sidewalks, a review of municipal insurance coverage, investment of idle city funds, and similar management devices calculated to end the "favors to friends of the clique" approach. Bickel knew exactly what kind of town he wanted, with low-priced subdivisions for low-income retirees, middle-bracket homes for those a little better off, and a series of country-club subdivisions along the ocean front north of an existing major upper middle-class subdivision. He was reaching out to take over development firms in trouble in other populous South Florida counties and had entered into a gigantic scale land scheme in the Everglades for low income retirees sponsored by big city "hustlers." He was a rich man getting richer and reaching persistently, perseveringly, and ruthlessly for political power. Unquestionably he was unafraid of Standish's sharp tongue, violent temper, and socially discriminating wife. But he did not forget the latter's efforts to ban him from the "cocktail circuit." In fact, he was apparently "masterminding" a lawsuit against Standish for damages by the public works director who had been hit by Standish. He had unearthed some minor business dealings between Standish and Clem Hicks' patron. His obsession was clearly to "break" Standish.

Thinking ahead, Bickel voiced to the interviewers the possibility of Clem Hicks as the next mayor of Dorado and laughed to think of the incongruence of Hicks as mayor of the millionaires' town. But Clem had one key to power for Bickel that was indispensable. "Clem Hicks has a 'lock' on the 'Cracker' vote, and Standish has a 'lock' on the retirees' vote," was Bickel's way of stating the voting alignments. He needed Hicks, whom he had once fought and frightened with threats of lawsuits for conflict of interest violations, because the "Cracker" bloc was essential to his own mastery over the retirees, Watters, and the other millionaires. Bickel's thinking ahead is reflected in his commentary that, of course, the present city manager would probably have to go because Standish "had ruined his usefulness by cowing him," and that he himself was starting to think about how to get a good replacement.

Bickel's will to dominate Dorado is shown by his determination to bring the local newspaper into line with his business enterprises and his thinking. He believed that Clem Hicks' patron was getting far more publicity than he deserved, and exercising an excessive influence over the town. Therefore, he demanded "freedom of the press" of the local editor, meaning at least equal or better space than Hicks' patron received. To clarify his point, Bickel ordered all his contractors and subcontractors to withdraw their advertising from the local paper — $15,000 worth of advertising — and he made his point for what he calls "freedom of the press."

Although Bickel has studied the politics of Dorado as painstakingly and obsessively as he has analyzed its economy (and, it might be added, he is the only businessman apparently with a real understanding of the sources and uses of relevant data), still his political reach may exceed his grasp. In the long run, the greater the number of retirees who move into Dorado, whether to purchase a home in one of Bickel's country club subdivisions or in one of his more modest developments, the greater the negativism that will be expressed in elections against both the "Crackers" and the developers' interests. The long-run political future of Dorado, therefore, may be with the Standish-type of leader of retirees, who yields to the demands of his constituency at the same time that he manipulates his constituency against his political opponents. Even assuming that Bickel can become the "boss" of Dorado, pulling the strings for Hicks, he cannot rule for long if the retirees can produce someone with Standish's manipulative talents.

The Dorado Citizens Association is today entirely dominated by upper middle-class retirees and is no longer an arm of absentee millionaires. Consequently its major focus of interest is on taxes — keeping governmental costs down; it is also strongly pro-Standish but does not actually make any public endorsement in elections. Bickel has some contempt for the organization on the ground that it is timid and eager to avoid controversy. Others regard it as entirely negative at the present time and restrictive on city policies. But the city manager gave them credit for some positive actions and policies and attributed to the Citizens Association the credit for an excellent study of water supply and the moving of the city government toward resolution of the water supply problems for the whole area. It is clear that the Citizens Association is a power in city politics that is by no means pro-

Bickel and could actually slow down Bickel's advance to more power by strengthening Standish against Bickel. Standish may manipulate his retiree followers cleverly enough to prevent Bickel from extending his own following among this group.

On the other hand, it is entirely possible that in the foreseeable future Bickel's alliance in the exploitation of Everglades land for a vast retirement colony may so hem in Dorado that Dorado merchants become almost completely dependent upon him. He may then so influence the local Chamber of Commerce and the businessmen in the Citizens Association as to split the latter organization apart and have his own way, politically unhampered in the community. In the event that the projected low-income mass-retirement colony develops as he believes it will, then Dorado's political alternatives may be eliminated by reason of the elimination of economic alternatives.

IV

Issues in Dorado have been suggested in the recapitulation of its politics. Still, several recurring themes are worthy of some analysis. One of these is zoning because the town has largely misunderstood zoning and attributed to it virtues it does not have.

Zoning is regarded by Doradans as equivalent to community planning rather than as merely one tool in the implementation of community planning. The city's so-called "master plan" in 1948 was not a plan at all but merely a narrowly conceived set of zoning regulations. Had a comprehensive community plan been developed at that time, the question of the kinds of people to be attracted into Dorado and the kinds of housing to be developed to attract them would have been set forth. In addition, water-front public recreational facilities would have been sketched out and not left to the vagaries of those struggling for political power to propose and manipulate. Other public recreational facilities also would have been indicated. Last but not least, an analysis of the town's economic potentialities and problems would have been set forth. As a matter of fact, none of these matters was covered. Therefore, the town failed to recognize the long-run significance of one major zoning decision — the variance to permit beach-front cooperative apartment houses — which has had more to do with the change in the composition of the town and its style of politics than any other single decision. Instead, the town was bitterly divided over the Aurelio Point Beach Club, with the feud still not healed between the major protagonists. The beach club did nothing to change basic land use or style of life in the area and could only by the wildest of surmises be construed as changing land use in the future.

Serious consequences have flowed from the failure of the "boiler plate" master plan given to Dorado to clarify the economic problem involved in trying to run a town based almost entirely on winter season millionaires. The economic hardship caused the small businessmen who dominate the Chamber of Commerce has led them to embrace first, the chimera of attracting light industry and ultimately, the development of retiree subdivisions for lower income persons. The retirement colony of vast proportions being developed in the adjacent Everglades by Miami "hustlers" in cooperation with a Dorado financier, with lots marketed by mail order, will probably tie the retirement colony to Dorado economically, if not politically. The influx of retirees of middle-class status or less is in the process of changing the entire substance as well as the "face" of the town.

Although the agents of the millionaires are fond of reiterating the idea that Dorado was modeled on Palm Beach, they overlook one relevant fact: Palm Beach is a small community suburban to the much larger West Palm Beach, which has its economy geared to a far different and more numerous population than that of the winter season millionaires. Dorado is suburban to nothing else and has had to try to survive economically on its own resources, a next to impossible feat with only a millionaire clientele.

Mention was made of the failure of the master plan to sketch the kinds of recreational facilities needed, their desirable location, and types of facilities. Dorado has gradually acquired a few public facilities, primarily by action of former Mayor Alden in one case and by the munificence of various millionaires in other instances. Alden in the early days of development of Ocean Drive compelled the Dorado Land Company to deed to this city an area along the beach front equivalent to all street ends running to the ocean that were in their tract. Ultimately Manager Blank started improvement of the public beach area by landscaping and establishment of a parking lot, thereby precipitating a typical Dorado imbroglio. Adjacent beach property owners objected to improvement of the city property or construction of public conveniences or a bathhouse on the ground that Negroes, migratory farm laborers, or other "undesirables" would invade the beach. A few property owners, however, had been compelled by persons already using the beach to permit use of their lavatory facilities, and these beach-front residents were eager for city development of this water-front area as a park. It was not until 1961 that one of the millionaires gave about $15,000 to construct public conveniences, drinking fountains, etc., on the beach area that had been named Henry Blank Park just prior to the 1960 election. Now no one objects to this park because, ironically enough, very few people use it. Instead public interest has shifted to getting the city to purchase land at the beach end of the main crosstown thoroughfare for development of another small park and parking area. The same type of opposition is repeated, but in this case it may be more successful as the city would need to purchase the land involved. Some persons who support use of this area for a park do so in part on the ground that because the land is too valuable to remain idle and too expensive now for anything but an "estate," the property owner will soon be forced to request rezoning for commercial use of the property. For this to happen would represent the first breach in the solid front against commercial development on Dorado's beach front.

The "bread and butter" issue of taxes and property assessments has been a lively one for the last few years, growing hotter year by year. Costs of local government are a major concern to the upper middle-class pensioners in contrast to the indifference formerly manifested by the original millionaires' contingent. The fiscal practices of Dorado are of pressing importance to the retirees, and the fights over a utilities tax and the submerged land agreements previously described are understandable in the light of this fact.

The direct part that Ian Watters and the developer of Harbor Haven had been playing in Dorado city government by having their development managers serve on the council was abruptly curtailed by the exposure of the submerged land agreements in 1961. A newly formed taxpayers group, in which a local newspaperman was a leading figure, brought to public notice for the first time agreements made by the city under Mayor Alden in the early fifties to assess all finger-fill development properties held by four major developers as unimproved submerged lands until 60 per cent of all lots were sold. As of 1962, the three subdivisions still enjoying these favors ranged from 20 to 29 per cent sold. These agreements, of course, amounted to an enormous tax concession, as was indicated in the critical advertisement quoted above. The city had not, however, paid for the improvements, such as streets, sewers, water and utility lines, street lights, and signs, which had been installed at the developers' expense. Injection of this issue into the 1961 charter referendum fight, which was a bitter one, accomplished two things for Jay Standish. It settled the fate of his amendment favorably, and it knocked the developers' men off the council.

But Standish did not settle the issue itself, as his talents do not seem to run in the direction of rational analysis of a legal and fiscal problem. The question was raised by many persons and the newspaper in the 1962 council election, but was exploited in a deprecatory manner by an unsuccessful candidate who was an active leader in the taxpayer's league. The successful candidates either took the position that a searching examination be made of the submerged land agreements to determine legality or that recognition be given to all valid contracts made by the city. Bickel, an astute lawyer, is now the key to settlement of the conflict over submerged land assessment and is in the process of working out a proposal with attorneys for the developers. He expected in 1962 to establish a different basis for assessment fairly expeditiously, long before 60 per cent sales could be achieved.

Charter revision has, of course, been a continuing issue charged with increasing tension until it nearly tore the city apart in November 1961. Much of the lack of clarity in the charter could have been avoided had the charter drafters of 1958–59 relied more heavily upon the Model City Charter, of which they seemed unaware. They might have saved the city the bitter battle of 1961 and the continuing necessity to reform the council election process that forced two run-off elections in 1962.

Conflict of interest became a major public question in Dorado after Albert Bickel started taking an active interest in city government. No one concerned himself prior to that time with the matter of city officials using confidential or advance information to maximize their resources or to prejudice council decisions in favor of a patron or one's own business activity. Bickel made the council aware of Florida Supreme Court decisions against maintenance of conflict of interest and chastened the council by the suit against Alden. Even Standish, who was originally critical of Miles Alden's contract, now regards Bickel as a ruthless scourge of those he opposes. Standish might well fear this scourge, for his own business deal with one of the millionaires has been probed and is known, although everyone, including Bickel, stresses the innate honesty of Standish. In fact, Bickel declares that he backed Standish for mayor in 1960 because he believed Standish's wealth would make him immune to the temptations to which poor men like Alden and Hicks had succumbed.

The Dorado airport contract, not a conflict-of-interest issue but an issue of "favoritism" in awarding government contracts, was exposed by Albert Bickel in 1962. As a member of the council, he pointed to the failure of the merchant-banker who held this contract to post bond (as required by the contract), to render an accounting to the city for thirteen years, and to remit to the city its share of net profit from airport operation. Over the period involved, this amounted to one-half of $134,000 which the city had never received. Bickel set all this out at length to the council, but they rejected the notion of refusing to renew the contract and merely required actual posting of the bond, which they permitted to be a personal bond instead of a fidelity guarantee

bond. In effect, this council action was not atypical of governmental
actions in a small city, where all residents must live together in some
modicum of harmony. Politicians in a small city will try to avoid
"issue" politics which expose opponents to charges of graft, conflict of
interest, favoritism, and the like. Instead, they seek the "soft" way out,
minimizing the blow. Even Standish, who had not hesitated to "slam-
bang" into the developers in his charter referendum election, wanted
to ease off on the airport contract as to do otherwise would be "a
reflection on previous councilmen."

The city manager was a burning issue in the 1960 council election.
Standish. Even West, and the other members of the "developers' slate"
were pledged to get rid of old Henry Blank. Actually Blank had served
the developers well, as had Miles Alden, but Standish found it expedient to attack him, and Evan West had a personal grievance against
Blank for an obscure quarrel over installation of sewers and streets in
Aurelio Point. Blank interpreted this attack upon him as that of youth
against age. "I'm an old man," he said, "and they want to change me
into a paper-shuffler." Unquestionably there was a clash of youth vs.
age, but youth that insisted on adequate and full records, public
reporting, competitive bids, modern personnel procedures, etc. Blank
was hopelessly at odds with the performance standards youth had set
for his job. Thus, because he was inefficient, really a "straw boss"
rather than a manager, and a major member of a punitive tight little
clique, he had to go.

The city manager Mayor Standish hired to replace Blank is an
engineer by profession, receptive to professional ideas, and apparently
capable of keeping abreast of his job. But Standish interferes with
and harries him. The manager declares he is the only one who has
no quarrel with Standish. This may be the result of Standish's respect
for another "professional," the manager's submissiveness, or extreme
diplomacy on the manager's part. In any event, he is suspect in the
eyes of Bickel, who regards him as "ruined" by Standish and, therefore,
slated for removal, once Bickel gets the upper hand. Here again,
is a case of identification of a manager, willy-nilly, with the policies
of the clique that put him into office — especially with the mayor who
"hand-picked" him in this case — and when the mayor goes, he must
go.

The social patterns of Dorado may be considered something of an
"issue" closely related to and at times actually inspiring political actions. For example, the blackballing of Albert Bickel by Ian Watters
from his Aurelio Point Beach Club had a far deeper long-run effect
than Bickel himself will admit or may even be aware of. The fact that
he himself would refer to it and revert to it in conversation today re-

veals its rankling effect. The continuing feud between Watters and Mason Perkins resulting from the zoning battle over the Aurelio Point Beach Club led Perkins to back an unsuccessful candidate for mayor in 1960 because Watters then supported Standish. Perkins and his wife dislike Standish not merely because Watters once supported Standish but much more so because of Standish's criticism of the community hospital built by the Perkins family. On the other hand, Mrs. Standish and her husband are sufficiently dominant in the "cocktail circuit" to restrict invitations to those politically opposed to Standish or at least to raise unpleasant questions with hostesses who defy their ban. Because Doradans have much time for social life and the financial resources to enjoy it on a somewhat lavish scale, the question of who is acceptable in what homes takes on sharp significance. The "cocktail circuit" is important. The social cross currents of the city are an integral part of its politics.

Dorado is expected to have a year-round population of 10,000 and a winter increase up to 22,000 within the next five years. This fact alone will give it a different pace. The coming of the retirees has already given it a different style of politics, moving it from monopolistic to competitive. Within five years' time one astute retiree has risen to political popularity and another who aspires to political power is achieving financial power that extends far beyond the limits of Dorado. In this same period the beach-front millionaires have declined in both political and economic importance in the town. Dorado has in this period been compelled to adopt a new charter, more business-like methods of administration, open council meetings, exposure of "deals" and "steals," and, in short, to "go modern." Reputations have been blasted, people have been alienated from each other in all the struggles that these changes represent, and the social abrasion resulting from political competition has been severe. Or perhaps one should say that the social abrasion in the case of one leader at least triggered off a whole series of political maneuvers that fit into the economic changes in the city. A possible lesson from all this is that he who aspires to be a small town Ward McAllister should not also try to be its Boss Tweed.[3]

[3] Ward McAllister was the social arbiter of New York City society in the "gilded age" of the nineties and created the notion of a "Four Hundred" of socially acceptable people the nabobs of that city could safely invite to their lavish parties. He created his famous invitation list for Mrs. William Astor, leading hostess of the group.

8

Hiberna

Hiberna's setting among the limpid lakes of central Florida gives it a marked esthetic advantage over many of the other inland cities of the state. Added to the advantages of location on water are the gigantic live oaks and large old citrus trees lining its shady streets. The city nestles around four lakes all connected by canals to form a continuous waterway. The two striking man-made features of Hiberna are the expensively landscaped homes lining the lake shores and the neatness of its streets and houses. Indeed, the tidiness is reminiscent of an old New England village. The resemblance to the more attractive New England towns is carried one step further by the presence of many expensive shops along Main Street, filled with resort clothing, *objets d'art,* antiques, china, silver, lamps, and even decorative candles. These shops are in a number of instances arranged in arcades around fountained courtyards, adding a southern European (or perhaps just Palm Beach) touch to the overlay of New England atmosphere — a not unpleasant combination. The visitor immediately senses that this is no ordinary Florida town. Hiberna is something special.

Unquestionably non-Floridians consider Hiberna a low-voltage winter resort of sedate quality in sharp contrast to the flamboyance and fleshpots of many other resort areas. Today, however, for an increasing number of permanent residents, it is merely a suburb of a much larger central city in which they are employed. Yet it is older than that neighbor and, indeed, senior to most Florida towns, having been founded before the Civil War. It early became a center for higher education in Florida, as a fairly well-known college was established in Hiberna well before the end of the nineteenth century. Although its New England character was stamped upon it by a sizeable group of settlers from that region who laid out its central section at about the time the local college was established, the man who shaped its early destiny was a midwestern industrialist. Like so many later promoters of Florida towns, he created a land company for expeditious real estate development. His lineal descendant is today the major owner of the land company, which still holds title to a very large acreage within the city limits of Hiberna, much of this property either grove land or held as a large estate. Despite the land company's efforts, however, the town did not grow much until after World War I. It numbered only about 1,000 persons in 1920 but more than trebled in size during the next decade. The Depression slowed its rate of growth considerably. But with the end of World War II the real upsurge came, as it did to most of South and Central Florida. Hiberna almost doubled its population from 1940 to 1950 and more than doubled from 1950 to 1960. It stands today at close to 20,000.

The land company entrepreneurs envisaged Hiberna as an "estate" town, to be peopled, whether intermittently or permanently, by *rentiers* as well as by persons who wished to retire after having "made their pile." Some Hibernans still refer wistfully to the days of the "sixty-seven millionaires." The old elite of the town irrevocably stamped its mark on Hiberna, and the town still combines the comfortable to munificent elegance of semitropically landscaped lakeshore estates with the mercantile and service amenities of a New England village. There is a thriving university club of some seven hundred members, a Harvard Club, a dining and wining club popular with the upper middle class, and a lively artists' group. But the fact that the town boasts more inhabitants listed in *Who's Who* per thousand of its population than any other city in the nation suggests another type of latter-day migrant: retired university faculty and high-ranking military officers. Although less affluent than the earlier estate settlers, these latter-day retirees are welcomed as appropriate members of the elite.

As indicated above, Hiberna is popular as a winter resort with the more elderly, upper middle-class type of tourist who seeks a sedate hibernation in subdued surroundings. Consequently the town boasts a modern, well-landscaped, and tastefully decorated hotel as well as some old hostelries that have been frequented for years by the same antiquated winter clientele. The dignity and leisurely pace of Hiberna's winter colony are in sharp contrast to the usual frenetic noisy activities of the average winter tourist to Florida.

The end of World War II and the decade of the fifties brought other kinds of newcomers to Hiberna: the dormitory suburbanite and the locally employed white-collar worker. A large industrial plant was built near the central core city of the metropolitan area, and its younger professional and managerial groups found new subdivisions in Hiberna to be attractive living areas. A regional state office building and several regional insurance offices or locally-owned national offices provided white-collar payrolls. A new multi-millionaire who was also a newcomer to the town financed the establishment of a commercial bank and some savings and loan banks as well as other local business enterprises. More recently a type of living new to Hiberna has been constructed — the large cooperative apartment — financed by local capital but designed by outside promoters. As Hiberna filled up in the postwar years, it was clear that the sameness of its physical appearance was deceptive. The town had changed in subtle ways — in proportion of employed persons, in social origins of its inhabitants as well as in their present social classification, in age distribution, and in kinds of leisure time activity enjoyed. In short, Hiberna began to show a variation in life styles.

A population pyramid charted for its age distribution in 1940 takes the form of a rectangle instead of a pyramid for white residents. This form of graph means that an almost equal distribution exists for all ages plotted in five-year groups. This particular pattern of graph is common for retirement towns or for those growing through fast in-migration of adult workers beyond the years of greatest human fertility. But by 1960 the population graph had changed slightly toward a pyramid from a rectangle, thereby indicating more young families present in the population.

The influx of "new people," referred to variously by Hibernans as "new people," "people who work for a living," and "young people" (apparently any working adult under fifty for the last group) created political tensions of major proportions in Hiberna. The following aggregates seemed to be major elements in Hiberna politics:

1. The "old guard," comprised of the land company crowd, long-resident estate families, and local business and professional men who identify with them.
2. The retirees, who are a somewhat heterogeneous aggregate — some being *rentiers* and long resident — really belong with the "old guard." Others are relatively highly paid pensioners ($600 to $1,000 per month). For many members of this aggregate, local citizenship has become a full-time vocation. Some local politicians call them "sidewalk superintendents." "They don't have anything else to do but breathe down my neck," said one harassed local official. If this aggregate has any group foci, they are the University Club and the Harvard Club.
3. The "independent" (i.e., of the "old guard") business interests, who break down into two major sub-groups, and many of whom have migrated into Hiberna in the last ten to fifteen years. These business interests fall into a wealthy group of entrepreneurs looking for new investment opportunities and centered around

the commercial bank founded by their wealthiest member and spiritual leader and, on the other hand, a larger number of small businessmen engaged in modest mercantile and service activities. If the first group has any social focus, it is the local dining and wining club, which has a certain fashionable *cachet* in Hiberna.

4. The "new people," made up at the top of the payroll elites of Hiberna and the surrounding metropolitan area and largely consisting of younger managerial and professional types. This class is augmented by a similar age bracket of lower white-collar elements living in the $14,000 to $18,000 houses in Hiberna's newer subdivision developments. These people were a nullity as an active political force until 1960 because they had failed to register to vote in city elections.

Despite the several dozen millionaires resident in Hiberna, the average per capita personal income of Hibernans is low as compared with many other Florida towns ($1,955) and is below the figures shown for other towns of upper middle-class or wealthy character. This is due to several factors, the most obvious of which is the large percentage of nonwhites in the local population — 27.4 per cent. This is a larger percentage of Negro population than can be found in a number of other cities in the central tourist and citrus areas of Florida. Also, there is a sizeable proportion — no one knows exactly how large it may be — of the millionaires who are not legal residents of Florida at all and therefore are not counted in the local census figures. A third factor, too, is the fairly high proportion of retirees of very advanced age who retired to Hiberna when average pension payments were much smaller than is typical today for those of their former occupation and class.

An examination of the age and educational status of Hibernans, as revealed in the 1960 census, shows a high median age — 36.7 years — and 12.6 of school completed; 20.4 per cent have had four or more years of college. The average is almost two years higher than that for the surrounding county. The occupational spread is also revealing. Only 1 per cent of the labor force was engaged in manufacturing, 7.5 per cent in salaried managerial positions, and 14.8 per cent in professional and technical work, 9.6 per cent in clerical work, and 8.6 per cent in sales.

II

Hiberna today operates under a council-manager charter adopted in 1949. Hiberna's first municipal charter was received in the late nineteenth century, and other early charters were adopted in 1925 and 1933. The present council-manager charter, adopted in 1949, provides for a mayor who is elected separately by the voters to serve as the presiding officer of the council and the ceremonial officer of the city. Both mayor and council serve three-year terms, but elections are staggered so that the mayor is elected alone one year and two council seats are filled in each of the other two years of the cycle. Under this arrangement it is possible and probable that a candidate may be elected mayor on an issue contrary to the stand adopted by the majority of the council and be unable to persuade the council to help him fulfill his commitments to the electorate. If there has been any persistent tradition in Hiberna city government, it has been that of the strong mayor carried over from the days of the mayor-council form of government prior to the present charter.

Actually, the present charter did not initially establish council-manager government but rather that of the mayor-commission form. It provided that citizens might petition for a referendum option on adoption of council (commission)-manager government, which Hibernans did within the first six months after approval of the 1949 charter. By a two-thirds majority they voted for council-manager government, which went into effect with the date of effectiveness of the new charter, January 1, 1950.

Formal meetings of the council must be held at least once each month but are usualy held twice monthly. In addition, the council, until the spring of 1961, held numerous closed or executive sessions, euphemistically called "work sessions." Apparently most major issues were discussed at these informal, closed sessions and determined one way or the other, usually thereby converting the public meetings into *pro forma* affairs. Only the threat of state legislation in 1961, the purport of which would have attached criminal penalties to the violation of a state-wide requirement of public meetings for transaction of public business, induced the Hiberna council to vote to open all its meetings to the press and public.

Until 1960, Hiberna city government had become encrusted with a barnacle-like coating of council-appointed boards and committees of citizens to handle a variety of matters. Some of these committees created for a short-term need were not dissolved promptly when their work was completed and although inoperative, remained in existence because of sensitivity of the council or their members to the symbolic status-value of committee memberships. In 1960, a re-shuffling of a number of committees led to the abolition of three of a total of fourteen, a step viewed with hostility by some of the committee members. In 1959 the number of administrative departments under the manager had been reduced from twelve to nine.

Although the city manager is supposed to have authority over all administrative departments, the police chief is, in fact, independent of the city manager. Moreover, the police chief, who is an old "Cracker" type and relatively uneducated, had a strong friend in a long-time councilman and has a host of influential friends all over town with whom he has ingratiated himself by favors over many years. Reputedly a master of the art of obtaining favorable publicity for himself and his department, the police chief has been reported to have given orders to the manager and to have boasted of having rid the city of at least one manager. The chief is not a man to be defied.

Eleven years of operation under the present council-manager charter have been characterized by as much turnover among mayors and councilmen as among managers. The city has had eight managers and two short-term acting managers who will be shown later in relation to political cliques and factions. Only three of these managers were professional city managers, and only one of the eight who preceded the present manager left voluntarily. But in the same period there have also been nine mayors, two of whom were mayors pro tem until an election could be held. In the first two years under the present charter there were five mayors. The last two mayors before the present incumbent were the first to fill out the terms for which they were elected, and each was defeated for re-election at the time of replacement. Deep-seated political struggles and changes are represented by the coming into office of the present incumbent and his two predecessors.

Apparently Hiberna voters like to elect their mayor. Despite the opposition to the practice of an elected mayor as contrary to the principles of council-manager government that had been preached by Admiral March, Hiberna's recent civic hero, the voters in 1960, immediately following the death of the Admiral, defeated an advisory referendum on a charter amendment proposing to go over to a system of having the council select one of their number as mayor.

III

What kind of a town is Hiberna to be? This is the unresolved problem basic to all others that has faced this city for a decade. Up until the end of World War II this was no problem, for the kind of city Hiberna was to be — an estate and retirement town — appeared to have been well settled decades before. With that goal in mind, the "old guard" land company group ran the town unchallenged. But the coming of "new money," especially in the person of the aggressive William Caxton, a new multi-millionaire and president of one of the major manufacturing firms in the country, brought new ideas and new types of residents. Real estate developers and businessmen intent on investment outlets sought "clean" businesses, especially of the white collar variety, to locate in Hiberna. They also tried to boom tourism of a more lively variety than that hitherto characteristic of Hiberna. The new subdivisions opened by the developers attracted dormitory suburbanites. This latter group, younger itself and with young children, represented a new dimension of demands upon local government. The clash of interests over the destiny of Hiberna was real.

The problem of the town's destiny raised other problems long quiescent, such as modernization and extension of public works and a broader tax base and property reassessment, especially in taxing grove land within the city limits on the same basis as developed land. The city has experienced a somewhat more stringent financial pinch than a number of other neighboring communities by reason of its lack of a municipally-owned utility of any kind that might serve as a source of revenue. City streets need repaving, many old sewers need rebuilding, and extension of sewer lines to unsewered areas of the city has become more pressing. Additional means of disposing of garbage and trash have become more critical as the city has become more populous.

Ultimately the question of additional access to the lakes will emerge as a serious problem. The dormitory suburbanites, who are as addicted to boating and swimming as are their contemporaries all over Florida, have only one boat-launching ramp on all the lakes within the city limits and only one small swimming beach, the width of one lot. On the other hand, the estate owners and older residents clustered around the lakes object to the noise and speed of boats. Not to be ignored is the fear of Negro swimming in the lakes, particularly in view of Hiberna's failure to provide a Negro swimming pool.

In connection with what might be called the "grand issue" of Hiberna politics, the major alternatives on the question of the destiny of the town seem to be these:

1. An estate and retirement town; or
2. An expanding community with clean, non-industrial payrolls
   a. Developed with an emphasis upon rapid, boom-type growth and real estate speculation per se; or
   b. Developed with an emphasis upon updating the town's large deficiencies in the services needed to satisfy the new elements in its population.
3. Emphasis on tourism in combination with 2a.

In a general sense, the "old guard" and the longer resident retired people have chosen Alternative No. 1. Some business and commercial groups and many of the "young people" either have chosen or are believed to be about to choose Alternative 2b. A few businessmen favor Alternative No. 3.

Alternative 2a developed as the earliest alternative to the traditional policy of the "old guard." In 1952, James Roberts, candidate in a mayoralty election for an unexpired term of two years, defeated the "old guard's" candidate by a vote of 1331 to 970. Roberts' candidacy was sponsored by, and he was a member of, a so-called "bank group," which was made of such figures as these: William Caxton, the industrialist, who also had established Hiberna's first commercial bank, one Blaine, a local manufacturer of concrete building blocks, and some directors and officials of the commercial bank and of the local federal savings and loan association, also financed by Caxton. Roberts and the "bank group" were successful again in 1954, when Roberts was unopposed for a full, three-year term. In the meantime Roberts seemed to go "whole hog" for Alternative No. 3. In the mayoralty primary election of 1957, however, Roberts was beaten by Marvin Thomas, who was not affiliated with either the "bank group" or the "old guard" and who went on to win decisively in the general election. However, the "bank group" made a strong come-back with a former councilman of their faction in the mayoralty election of 1960. This man, Lester Morgan, immediately took steps as mayor early in 1961 to settle a long-standing issue in which the "bank group" was vitally interested: rezoning for construction of a large cooperative apartment. There is no indication to date that the "bank group" wishes to revive Alternative No. 3.

Although he is not legally a resident of Hiberna, Caxton, simply by virtue of his wealth and the respect for it that accompanies wealth, is the leader of the "bank group." If there is a "Mr. Big" in Hiberna at present, Caxton is it, according to Grace, the present city manager. Caxton appears to typify the "new money" (as distinct from the "old money" of the "sixty-seven millionaires") which has come into town since 1950. The "bank group" typically and secretly circulates nomination petitions for its candidates to the council and mayoralty and uses for this chore one particular former councilman to signal to others the slate which has "bank group" support.

Although at least two members elected to the council in 1958, Admiral March and George Billow, were elected with the "bank group's" endorsement, both men broke with that group shortly after that election. Similarly Edward Westerly, elected in 1959 as a "bank group" man, broke with that group on some important issues. Oddly enough, Mayor Thomas, who defeated Roberts in 1957 and was defeated himself by the "bank" candidate in 1960, was reported by the manager to be the council member most responsive to "bank group" pressure.

In 1959 and 1960 the council on occasion stood up sharply against Caxton, and the "bank group" appeared to be out of power during that period. The "bank group" retained control of the Economic Development Committee of the Chamber of Commerce, which it reputedly "packed" by tricky maneuvering, but it does not control the other major Chamber of Commerce Committee, that on Civic Affairs.

The council was apparently groping in 1959 and 1960 against the "old guard" and the "bank group," toward Alternative 2b. Most strongly committed to that viewpoint were Admiral March and Edward Westerly, who could usually count on carrying Billow, another councilman, with them. Veteran councilman Walters and Mayor Thomas, were in a somewhat volatile manner, in and out of the majority. The former was universally described as the council's sole true "politician," apparently in the sense of a coalition builder and skillful maneuverer. A newspaper reporter characterized that council as a "stabilizing and coordinating" one, dedicated to the establishment of an "organic community," informed by an indispensable system of central and lateral communication.

Then in November and December, 1960, the Republicans of Hiberna, elated over the large majority they had amassed in the presidential election, decided to work for the election of a Republican stalwart as mayor. This man was a former councilman and a strong member of the "bank group." The Young Republicans of Hiberna called themselves the "Friends of Morgan" and worked assiduously in a house-to-house canvass especially directed at the suburbanites who had not previously voted in city elections and who were overwhelmingly Republican in sentiment. Morgan was elected by a large majority. His platform had been explicitly to cut municipal expenditures and implicitly to fire the manager. However, once in office he turned his attention almost solely to a rezoning issue which involved an investment opportunity for the "bank group" and apparently lost interest in budget-cutting or firing of the manager. Belief that he wanted the office of mayor solely to build himself up as a Republican candidate for Congress was apparently confirmed by his successful candidacy in 1962. Most believe that he capitalized on Young Republicans and dormitory suburbanite Republicanism to serve the "bank group's" interests in the town as well as his own ambition for national office. It is interesting to note that Walters, the veteran councilman, ran unsuccessfully for Congress on the Democratic ticket. He resigned his seat to make his race; Mayor Morgan did not resign, but his attention to his own race had virtually disintegrated the council.

IV

Unravelling the politics of Hiberna can be done by looking at current issues to see what the divisive questions are in the town and how economic and political factions line up on these issues. Each aggregate in the Hiberna power structure has, *ex hypothese,* an actual or imputable position on the grand issue of Hiberna politics. A detailed examination of recent specific controversies will strongly suggest that much, if not all, of the variation in position on particular sub-issues is explicable in terms of grand issue position.

Two major issues in Hiberna in recent years which show how competing groups align and which have, indeed, as issues stirred prolonged and bitter controversy are zoning and land-use. As in so many zoning controversies, Hiberna's major zoning fight involved large stakes for investment by those interested in speculative financial opportunities in town. This fight was over rezoning an old hotel property on the shores of one of the largest lakes to permit construction of a large "luxury"-type cooperative apartment house of 310 units. The apartment house is to be built with local funds but has been planned and will be supervised in construction and administered in operation by a large West Coast firm which specializes in such enterprises. The present hotel, fringed by some of Hiberna's oldest estates, is itself a relic of the days of the *rentier* tourist in Hiberna and is inhabited each winter by a rapidly diminishing band of octogenarians. Opponents of the present hotel have contended that it has not had a new customer in ten years.

The hotel rezoning case originated in 1958, when the present mayor was a councilman and actually served on the zoning board, helping to rule in cases in which he was attorney for various petitioners. However, after he went off the council in 1959, the zoning board was composed entirely of non-council persons but significantly of some individuals who might have a stake in construction activities: a lumber company proprietor, an architect, the proprietor of an air-conditioning firm, a retired person, and an individual interested in flying and airport facilities. The board held the required public hearings on the rezoning of the hotel property, and the hearings were, as might be expected, packed by vociferous opponents of rezoning. This case was especially bitter, lining up as it did the old estate families against rezoning and the newer moneyed elements on the other side.

At one point Councilman Westerly, who lives next to the old hotel, held several meetings in his home to attempt to talk with outraged waterfront property owners around the lake. His account of their objections to the apartment house is revealing. One property owner across the lake objected that the new apartment house, by virtue of its height, would spoil his view. All neighbors were concerned that the apartment building might produce "honky-tonk" conditions approximating the alleged excesses of some Atlantic front hotels in Miami Beach, and a good deal of anti-Semitism was expressed in connection with these remarks. A major objection to the cooperative apartment building was that some of its one-room units would sell for as little as $5,000 to $10,000 and that, as the objectors put it, this would bring the wrong kind of person to Hiberna (or at least to their part of Hiberna). Those interested in promoting the apartment house countered with the argument that they had kept the one-room unit prices low in order to accomodate the survivors of the elderly clientele who had been coming to the old hotel and might want to continue in the same location. However, it was pointed out in rebutting the pro-apartment house group that the range of unit prices in a new cooperative apartment house under construction along another lake runs from $14,500 to $53,000. Pending completion of the apartment house rezoning case, the designers of the apartment house venture were reported to be contemplating redesigning the floor plans so as to produce units with a higher minimum sale price.

Ultimately the zoning board made its decision in favor of rezoning to permit construction of the new cooperative apartment house, and the battle arena then shifted to the city council. Mayor Thomas tried to escape this "hot potato" by proposing a referendum, but the council voted to sustain rezoning. Litigation by affected property owners was started, and the courts upheld the rezoning. By this time a new mayoralty election was held, and Mayor Morgan, who is a member of the "bank group," which was financially interested in construction of the new apartment house, brought the whole issue to a conclusion at the beginning of his administration. (It might be mentioned also that the mayor himself had been given a suite in the cooperative apartment house owned by the same company in payment for some of his legal fees). It certainly does not now appear that his connection with this rezoning case is unpopular with the majority of the voters in the town, nor a matter for consideration as to possible conflict of interest, nor does it appear that Hiberna ever disapproved in principle of cooperative apartment houses. As a matter of fact, in the council election of 1959 voters approved annexation of a subdivision around another lake, in which area the large cooperative apartment house referred to above was to be built. Therefore, it is possible that the heat and bitterness engendered over the hotel rezoning case were sparked by a sense of frustration among the old estate owners who had already seen control of the town slip from their hands to the "bank group" and who resented seeing the very symbol of the "bank group's" money power in their neighborhood.

Equally bitter and equally symbolic as an issue has been the general use of land. This issue especially centered around the city's purchase of a swamp as a recreational area. However, this issue spills over into another — that of property assessment — and also carries overtones of race antagonisms. A brief explanation of the land-use issue is in order.

Land use in Hiberna is affected by three very general sets of factors. One set is physiographic: Hiberna's location on a number of lakes maximizes the desirability and value of water front property, always valuable in any urban area. The second is demographic: the doubling of the city's population in the decade of the fifties, primarily as a result of in-migration. The third set of factors is economic: they relate to the extreme importance of real property in the economic system of the city, whether the land is public or private, since the salad days of the land company.

On the aspects of private ownership, it is obvious that during a period of rapid population increase and payroll development, not only does demographic pressure on the land become greater, but the opportunity to speculate increases as well. Many of our respondents were candid to admit that they knew hardly anyone who was not interested in some piece of real estate or another. Although we probed hard to find evidence that various mayors or members of the council were involved in speculative ventures connected with their offices, we could elicit only the expression of some respondents' opinions that many voters in 1957 apparently thought that Roberts and some of "his" councilmen were too heavily involved in real estate development.

As to public ownership, it is important to stress the major role that the ad valorem property tax plays in Hiberna's public fiscal policy. Although the city collects a tax on public utilities, it owns no utilities itself (not even the water plant), and thus has no utility profits. The principal revenue source is, therefore, the real estate tax. In addition, the city collects sanitary sewer rentals (although it is still largely a septic tank city) and garbage-trash collection fees. Purchase of public lands consequently puts a severe strain on city finances unless there is a real possibility for the city to convert the land to some effective income-producing use.

Land use as a major issue came to the fore during Mayor Roberts' term essentially as a result of Roberts' large-scale projects for long-term planning. Early in 1956, the council on his recommendation hired a nationally known planning firm to develop a long-range "arterial" plan for Hiberna. Two reports were produced by this firm which were on the face of things rejected by the council, although the major arterial street development recommended by the planning consultants has since taken place. But more significant of the dreams of Mayor Roberts for Hiberna was his attempt to step up tourism by the city's purchase for around $200,000 of a large swampy area back of the town's motel row, to be converted into an auditorium and recreation center. This land would have required extensive filling and the creation of an artificial lake for drainage purposes, to have become usable. These steps alone would have been expensive. Mayor Roberts proposed a swimming pool and an auditorium for historical drama along the lines of the Paul Green plays, as major tourist attractions. Here even more in the way of submerged issues and resentments against a proposed new way of life were involved than in the hotel rezoning case.

The "bank group" and the Chamber of Commerce boomed the civic auditorium and recreation center idea. The "old guard" naturally frowned on this project. Many affiliated with neither side considered these proposals costly "plunging" and idle dreaming, and, significantly, many who had remained neutral as between the two warring factions become vocal in their criticism of the project. During the mayoralty primary of 1957 Marvin Thomas attacked Mayor Roberts for squandering city funds on a swamp, and the public believed that Roberts was too involved in real estate "deals" for the city's welfare. He was resoundingly beaten by Thomas and did not even get into the run-off. Councilman Walters, always skillful at taking political soundings, estimated public opinion correctly as still hostile to the civic center idea in 1959 and criticized council purchase of the swamp when he ran for re-election that year, although he had voted for purchase. The candidate who nearly nosed him out was a "bank group" candidate who strongly supported the center. But when the latter soon broke with the "bank group," he lost interest in the civic center and like Mayor Thomas, Admiral March, and Walters, he expressed a desire to see the city liquidate its investment in the swamp if it could do so without loss.

To what extent the council's later antipathy to development of a recreational center at the swamp site was conditioned by the abutment of this area on the city's Negro district, it is hard to say. However, between 1956 and 1959 a number of court cases brought by the N.A.A.C.P. for equal access to public recreational facilities were won by Negroes, including Florida Negroes. Councilman Walters, the avowed segregationist on the council, frankly admits that these court decisions were a factor that could not be overlooked. Today the civic center is dead even with Mayor Morgan of the "bank group."

Closely tied to land use is property assessment, which largely determines the uses to which land may be put. Hiberna still has some fairly extensive old citrus groves within the city limits which had been taxed until 1962 on the basis of actual present use rather than on the basis of best alternative use value. (Obviously, the best alternative use would be as residential subdivisions). The interest of city councilmen in seeing the city develop its land at highest use is understandable, especially in view of the fact that most current extensions of municipal services must, apparently, be financed out of current revenue. Decisive opinion in favor of a general obligation bond issue is considered impossible to mobilize, as a bond issue must be approved under Florida law in a referendum of real property owners, especially registered for that purpose, with at least half such registered property owners casting a vote. Given these premises and the heavy reliance on the general property tax, the questions of assessment level and millage become crucial.

One form that the property assessment issue took was the need for more efficiency in the tax assessor's office. This official is appointed by the manager, but the general understanding seems to be that his low salary militates against employment of anyone but a kind of super-clerk, who at best can only hope to keep track of most of the major value-producing changes in the use of Hiberna real estate. For major re-assessments the city periodically hires an outside firm of professional assessors. In the last general reassessment, that of 1954, the total assessed valuation, exclusive of homestead exemptions, jumped from $26,000,000 to $40,000,000, and a number of previously submarginal homesteads came on the tax rolls. (Submarginal homesteads would be those valued at $5,000 or less and owner-occupied, which in Florida are tax exempt).

In connection with promoting different use of land, the council has on occasion used the assessment and equalization processes under the best use doctrine to force the commercializing of old residential properties adjacent to expanding business areas. But the most critical test of this doctrine rests upon the attempt of the council to tax as subdivision land the grove land owned by the land company heiress. This extensive grove area encircles half the shores of one of the lakes and is also used as a park, complete with peacocks, bougainvillea, and winding roads. The land company heiress refused to discuss the matter directly with the former mayor but threatened through her attorney to end use of another part of land company property as a public golf course. However, the present mayor, although affiliated with the "bank group" and not essentially sympathetic with current use of the land, is very deferential to wealth in any form and has had preliminary success in broaching the matter of property reassessment at best use and winning consent at least to start this move.

The real estate tax rate has also been controversial in Hiberna. Again the owners of substantial properties, "old guard" and some retirees, take issue against the new people in Hiberna's dormitory residential subdivisions, whose demands for services have created the need for substantial capital outlays. As earlier indicated, local senti- ment in Hiberna has made it extremely difficult to finance such outlays by means of general obligation bond issues. As a result, the city government has been forced into a pay-as-you-go policy, which, of course, postpones many capital improvements. The long-term effect on the millage of a cash payment policy may approximate the long- term effect of a bond issue on the millage. Since the reassessment of 1954, the trend of millages has been steadily upward, and the trend seems to be approved, if feared, by most present members of the council, even when, as on occasion, they have manipulated proposed millage increases so as to facilitate the electoral success of some of their colleagues seeking re-election. The size of the present budget was the grand issue of the 1960 mayoral campaign as it was played up in an attack by the present mayor who promised to cut the budget, and thus the millage. However, once he took office, he lost interest im- mediately in the budget. One of his colleagues on the council has remarked, "This was good politics. Always attack the 'ins.' Even attack your own vote as an 'in' in order to get back in. But once in, the mayor couldn't do much about the budget. It was our budget, and we were not going to undo it, and he knew that."

Another major issue in Hiberna politics appears to be recreation — not recreation for tourists or for retirees (the latter have the University Club, their shuffleboard courts, and city golf course), but for the "new" or "young people," from teen-age to the fifties. The issue re- volves around playgrounds and parks, access for boating and swimming purposes to Hiberna's lakes, and the tax-exempt status of some lands of the Hiberna golf course.

The discussion of the recreation question in Hiberna requires some description of the system of social stratification in the community. Although there is strong indication that the class structure is under- going fairly rapid change, the following is a very rough approximation to a characterization of the class system:

I. The "old guard" (long-time, wealthy, *rentier* residents, many no longer very active in money-making except for afternoon visiting in the branch offices of New York brokerage houses). The leader of the "bank group" in politics is, of course, a member of this class.

II. The substantial pensioner retirees.
III. Wholesale, retail, professional, and real estate entrepreneurs.
IV. "New" payroll elites.
V. White-collar salaried group.
VI. Craftsmen and service tradesmen.
VII. Negroes.

Although social stratification data were not a primary concern of ours, spontaneous comments of our respondents indicate that at upper and middle levels, at least, Hiberna is a very class-conscious community, and the perspectives of our respondents apparently help explain some of their responses as well as some of their policy orientations. The city attorney, for example, who seemed to identify strongly with the "old guard," referred quite unself-consciously to people in categories III and IV as "people who work for a living," although he did not seem to think of himself in that category.

The main reason for raising class structure in relation to recreation is that sociologists have properly stressed the key role of sociability interactions, including recreational ones, as indicators of social class membership. The "old guard" members apparently "recreate" at each others' homes and lake fronts; pensioners, at the University Club; categories III and part of IV belong to one or both of the two social clubs founded during the fifties: the dining and wining club, which has a swimming and tennis arrangement attached to it, and the local country club, which quite naturally emphasizes golf. The major potential clienteles for expanded public recreation facilities would be drawn from categories VII up through IV, with perhaps some III's.

The major points of division on recreation questions are fiscal in the sense of who pays versus who benefits, the "character of the town," and racial. On playgrounds and parks the fiscal issue is obvious, and opponents to expansion have sometimes used the threat of racial integration to thwart expansion in the program.

The question of access to the lakes is even more controversial, since it involves a major attempt to attenuate, if not destroy, by the "democratization of access," the class-symbolic character of the ownership of residential lakefront property. Public access to Hiberna's lakes is presently afforded by one small public beach and one public boat launching ramp with rather limited parking facilities. Once a boat owner has launched his boat, he is able, by means of interconnecting canals, to pass from one lake to another. The city maintains a lakes and canals police system to regulate registration, speed, safety, and muffler noise. Evidently, there are increasing demands from boat owners for more launching ramps, which are, of course, resisted by lake front owners in categories I and II.

Another problem of access to the lakes via ramps has been created by an illegal pre-emption of land by the very lake front property owners referred to above. Hiberna streets radiate out in spoke fashion from each lake, dead-ending right at the water line. The city had not in the past taken the pains to maintain these dead-ends which actually remain unopened and uncleared in a physical sense, although there is no question that they were platted as streets and dedicated to and accepted by the city years ago. Adjacent property owners, acting as "squatters," a term which, no doubt, would be repugnant to the "old guard" elite, claim that the city's right to the street ends lapsed over the years and that the street ends belong to them because of the city's failure to develop and maintain these ends. The younger element, which wants more boat launching ramps, points to these dead-ends and demands that the city "reclaim" these streets from the "squattings" of adjacent owners. Councilman Westerly, a lake front resident himself, although admitting the incipient explosiveness of the access question, delivered himself of the dubious opinion that the "squatters" may have acquired title to the city's unimproved streets by virtue of the city's neglect to open and improve them in a physical sense. No legal opinion appears that would support his view.

The golf club question involved some paternalism by the land company, which owns the land on which the last six holes of the city's golf club are located. The city owns the land occupied by the first three holes and the club house, which consists mainly of locker facilities. Access to the course is semi-public, through the payment of a greens fee. Hiberna golfers who do not belong to the local country club typically play the city golf club's nine holes. The land company heiress had threatened, if the city assessor proceeded against her grove property, to withdraw the land company's six holes and develop the land as an expensive residential subdivision. This threat, however, has apparently subsided, as the present mayor has so far apparently reached an accord with the land company heiress in getting the latter to accept a higher assessment.

In addition to the foregoing issues there are others of less importance, such as (1) regime; (2) race; (3) retirees; and (4) annexation and intergovernmental relations.

Form of government, i.e., strong mayor-council versus council-manager, has been an issue since the present hybrid charter went into effect in 1950. At the time of its drafting, the managerial forces apparently lacked either an understanding of the institutional forms of managerial government or the strength to put across a pure managerial charter. In consequence, several mayors during the ten year period of hybrid government have used their charter powers and their mayoral prestige to the hilt. The high rate of managerial turnover, as will be explained below, has also, in itself, made managerial government an issue, and during the early months of his administration Mayor Marvin Thomas, then in his strong mayor phase, recurred regularly in his newspaper column to the openness of the question regarding the choice of regime.

By all local testimony, Mayor Thomas stopped acting like a strong mayor after about a year, a development which may have resulted from the election of Admiral March to the city council. The Admiral was an authentic battle hero who received the highest award for fleet leadership under fire, and much more rare, he was a military man who read books on government with some understanding. Upon his retirement he decided to become an active citizen of Hiberna. He threw himself into Chamber of Commerce work and was soon elected to the city council in 1958. He was articulate, forceful, and succinct. When he spoke, the council and all of Hiberna listened respectfully. More than anything else, it was his leadership *de facto* of the council which cut Mayor Thomas down to just another council member. In addition, the Admiral got the council early in 1960 committed to the support of a charter amendment to eliminate the separately elected mayor and to replace him with an annually elected council president. Although most observers earlier in the year expected the electorate to ratify this proposal, fate intervened. The Admiral was stricken with a fatal disease, resigned from the council in September 1960, and died at just about the time of the December election. The amendment was defeated, as the rest of the council really did not care about this change as he had.

Mayor Morgan indicated upon his election that he would act like a strong mayor and keep office hours every day in the city hall, seeing and hearing out all citizens who might want to come to him. This lasted a matter of two or three weeks, and then the mayor lost interest. A busy lawyer involved in a good many local financial transactions, he found it far more convenient to refer the citizens to the city manager. Certainly the city council appears to have accepted council-manager government even if it has not accepted all the details of the doctrine. Despite a decrying of the report and recommendations made by a national firm of management consultants in 1957, the council and manager have moved steadily, if slowly, to implement many of the report's recommendations.

Race is not a strong issue in Hiberna politics. Two Southerners in official positions, Councilman Walters and Manager Grace (self-styled "Cracker boy"), both expressed more fear of integration attempts than did the non-Southern officials. Several respondents expressed the belief that a "better type of Negro" lives in Hiberna than in many other Florida cities. By this they did not seem to mean a higher proportion of senile Uncle Toms, but rather a class of home-owning Negroes, who, by virtue of prolonged association in domestic service with higher types of white persons had learned to behave. The stereotype here is of the highly educated Hibernan, whether retired or working, always setting a good example.

Walters is the only politician believed to pay much attention to the Negro vote which he says now numbers no more than 237, the last registration figure. Grace thought Walters had all the Negro vote; Thomas thought he had only the large Negro Masonic lodge, by virtue of Walters' Masonic fraternalism. Walters confessed to thinking of some new "gimmick" at each election time to keep the loyalty of those interested in him. The last time he ran, the "gimmick" he used to get the Negro vote was to send Western Union wires to all the Negro voters on election day appealing to them that he really needed them more than ever before. He had also hired all the taxicabs in town for that afternoon and ran a regular cab service to the polls from the Negro neighborhood.

Oddly enough, Walter thinks that race and religious hatred have greatly increased since World War II, and he believes this applies to "new people" in Hiberna. He attributes these emotions to Yankees as much as to Southerners. Walters has expressed dissatisfaction with the poor state of streets in Negro neighborhoods. This is apparently one of his manipulative proposals, which he publicly justifies in the name of economy of maintenance. A brief drive through the main Negro neighborhood suggests that Hiberna Negroes, although a light-year away from luxury, live in distinctly better neighborhoods than, say, most of the North or Central Florida Negroes.

The University Club has over the years shown quite a strong paternalistic interest in Negro improvement in Hiberna. One of its projects involved playground equipment. Another consisted of helping to get a Negro nursing home started. These activities would fit in well with the *noblesse oblige* attitude of the "old guard."

Grace and Thomas both referred to a public beach "incident" involving two teen-age Negro boys, not believed to be "agitator-inspired." The chief of police, albeit in the tradition of a front-line general, dispersed the boys in a persuasive, "noncoercive," nonbellicose manner, and received an anti-segregationist tongue-lashing from a white woman resident who had observed the incident.

Grace, the city manager, said the council's position on any attempted integration in city facilities would be a peaceful, law-and-order one which it would implement by closing down the affected facilities. Former Mayor Thomas said Walters was the most segregationist member of the council, characterizing him as a separate-but-equal man with equal emphasis on the "equal" and the "separate." Thomas, Grace, and Walters all thought that if Negroes attempted public school integration in Hiberna, they would receive substantial white support. Walters thought the support would come only from the retirees' group (obviously, in his thinking, from people whose children were long past school age), from University Club members who, as he put it, "did not understand the subtleties of the Southern situation." Thomas and Grace thought substantial support would be forthcoming not only from the retirees, but that many of the "new people" would accept and actively support school integation. Former Mayor Thomas said Admiral March might have publicly supported integration attempts on the ground that "what's good enough for the U.S. Navy is good enough for Hiberna."

Retirees constitute a problem as they do in so many retirement towns by reason of occupying their time scolding the city manager and members of the council on minor matters. Trees are one example. "Woodman, spare that tree," is truly the cry of the oldsters of Hiberna when the city makes any effort to remove trees for such purposes as street widening or sewer construction. The tree removal problem had become so sensitive in Hiberna that the city manager called a horti-culturist from the University of Florida to designate trees fit for re-moval and to write some articles for the local paper on the stigmata of the dying tree. This somewhat lessened the brouhaha over tree re-moval. But minor procedures that go off smoothly in towns with a younger population cause considerable uproar in Hiberna. For ex-ample, in order to facilitate trash removal the city manager issued an administrative regulation that the trash collectors would not remove branches of trees and shrubs that had not been cut into a certain maximum length. This led to dozens of irate calls from oldsters who quite naturally objected to the work of cutting up such branches.

Annexation has been no particular issue in Hiberna. A merger of the city with either the larger core city bordering it on one side or with a smaller suburban town bordering it on another is simply not in the cards. The annexation of a relatively large number of small fringe areas during the last ten years has, likewise, not been controversial, since fringe inhabitants wanted city service, which Hiberna does not provide to exurban customers, and the city fathers wanted expansion in the real estate tax base.

What has been a modest problem and what may, in the judgment of some respondents, become a larger one is the general question of inter-governmental relations with the core city, the bordering suburban town, and the surrounding county. A local college faculty member reported in 1958 that "planning in Hiberna continues to be carried forward as if the city were an island. . ." According to the manager, the present administration has established diplomatic relations with the State Road Department, the Board of County Commissioners, and the nearby suburban town, but these relations are apparently still in the talking, rather than in the performance, stage.

Councilman Walters spontaneously raised the question of intergovernmental relations during an interview with him. One of his pet proposals is a garbage-trash incinerator plant, to be privately financed (he had a Florida entrepreneur of some parts lined up, he thought). To meet the consultants' objections to the incinerators, Walters proposed to locate it so that he can sell its services to the central core city for part of that city's collections and to the suburban town in addition to Hiberna.

Managers of Hiberna and their Tenure in

(Full mayoral terms at

Mayors and Dates	Managers with Dates				
	Webb 1949– 2/3/50	Macy 2/3/50– 7/27/50	Ladd 7/27/50– 4/2/51	Stacy 4/2/51– 7/3/51	Pace 7/3/51– 2/16/53
Barnes 1/1/49–4/3/50	×	×			
Hector[1] 4/3/50–5/4/50		×			
Corey 5/4/50–1/2/51		×	×		
Hanley 1/2/51–1/8/52			×	×	×
Manley 1/8/52–10/6/52					×
Sinclair[1] 10/7/52–12/3/52					×
Roberts 12/3/52–1/2/55					×
Roberts 1/2/55–1/7/58					
Thomas 1/7/58–1/7/61					
Morgan 1/7/61–					

[1] Mayor pro tem

V

Since Hiberna adopted manager government in 1949, it has had eight full (i.e., not acting) managers, plus two short-term acting managers, and nine mayors, including two mayors pro tem. The chart below shows these two groups of officials in a time relationship to each other.

The mayors epitomize in certain instances the transfer of control from one clique to another. We begin the council-manager period in 1949 with Mayor Barnes, an "old guardsman" possessed of extensive land holdings and affiliated with a major public utility corporation in which he owned stock and which served the city. He was elected in 1948 under the previous mayor-council charter but carried over to the beginning of the manager period, resigning early in this period because of ill health. A temporary successor was replaced by Mayor Corey,

Relation to Mayors and Mayoral Tenure

three years shown in brackets)

Managers with Dates

Ladd 2/16/53– 1/4/54	Potter 1/4/54– 2/14/57	Parks 2/27/57– 4/8/57	Weeks 4/8/57– 2/18/59	Adm. March 2/18/59– 5/4/59	Grace 5/4/59–
✕	✕				
		$✕^2$	✕		
			✕	$✕^2$	✕
					✕

[2] Acting manager

elected only until the next general election could be held. Mayor Hanley was chosen at the 1950 general election to serve out the remainder of the Barnes term. With this sequence one full mayoral term is rounded out for three years. An "old guardsman" succeeded to the mayor's office in the December, 1951, election when Manley was chosen, but this faction lost its grip on city hall when Manley resigned at the end of ten months. A mayor pro tem served for two months until the December 1952 election could determine the succession.

The election of James Roberts in December 1952 marked a real change of the clique in control of Hiberna, for Roberts is a member of the "bank group." Roberts served the longest of any recent mayor, a total of five years. Always a strong-minded and strong-willed man, he rode herd on managers and councilmen alike, bulled through his policies, and chose at least one manager entirely on his own without reference to the rest of the council. Plenty of animosity developed against him especially during the full three year term to which he was elected in 1954. It was apparently a surprise only to him and to his "bank group" confreres that he lost the mayoral primary and did not even get into the run-off in November 1957.

In 1957 once again a change in clique control took place beginning with the mayor's election. Mayor Marvin Thomas belonged to neither antagonistic faction in Hiberna politics. Rather, he seemed to be interested in trying to cut loose from the commitments and orientations of both groups without indicating on his own part any new lines of positive policy development. The strong leader during the Thomas period was Admiral March, who had broken with the "bank group" that had originally backed him.

The "bank group" returned to power in December, 1960, when Lester Morgan defeated Marvin Thomas and pulled two councilmen, Westerly and Billow, into his orbit. The new councilman elected to fill out Admiral March's unexpired term was neither "old guard" nor "bank group" but came out of Junior Chamber of Commerce activities and appeared to be groping for a policy orientation of his own. Once the controversial cooperative apartment house rezoning case was out of the way, Mayor Morgan seemed to lose most of his interest in providing policy leadership. Perhaps with this and the way opening up for conversion of the land company's grove land into a "luxury" subdivision area, the "bank group" may have accomplished virtually all that remained on its agenda from the days of the Roberts administration, and it may possibly have nothing else to offer in the way of positive policy for some time. A number of attractive new investment opportunities will have been opened up by these moves alone.

Turning from mayors and their clique affiliations to the city managers of Hiberna since council-manager government was adopted, the chart on manager-mayor terms shows the short average tenure for managers in this community and the close correlation between the beginning of a new clique and the firing of a manager. There have been eight managers plus two short-term acting managers in an eleven year period. The average tenure for Hiberna managers in this eleven year period is 16.2 months. But a detailed examination of the reasons for termination of the various managers shows that six were dismissed and only one prior to the present manager, who is still very much in the saddle, left voluntarily. One of the other six, it is true, resigned, but the resignation was effected quickly to avoid a dismissal the manager knew was planned. Only three managers — Pace, who started as an acting manager, Potter, and Weeks — had served one year or more prior to the service of the present manager. Ladd's two periods of service were divided by military duty. At least three of these managers, probably more, were local residents at the time of their appointment.

Manager terminations in Hiberna have resulted from two different sets of factors: (1) changes in clique control, and (2) personal rivalries between managers and strong mayors who wanted to act like mayors under the mayor-council plan. For example, under the first rubric of changes in clique as a cause of manager dismissal, Roberts symbolized the assumption of control by the "bank group" in late 1952, and he quickly effected Pace's dismissal early in 1953. Once again under Mayor Thomas, who was not a member of the "bank group," the council gradually repudiated "bank group" domination and sufficient opposition was generated to dismiss Weeks who had been put in by Roberts during the period of "bank group" dominance. The leading figure in the dismissal decision and the hiring of the present manager was Admiral March. Once again in 1961 the "bank group" called the turn on manager tenure, but this time it was the reverse of a firing. Despite the fact that the present manager, Grace, was put in by a council not controlled by the "bank group," the latter clique decided, according to some prominent members of the faction, that frequent manager change had created a bad "image" of Hiberna among such solid business firms as they wish to attract to Hiberna. Therefore, it is reported that the "word has been passed" that Grace is to be retained and the council must get along with him at all costs.

Under the second rubric of mayor-manager rivalries, those in city government at the beginning of the decade of the fifties report that Webb and Macy were both fired summarily by Mayor Barnes because the mayor "couldn't get along with them." Stacy, who was brought in from outside and was Hiberna's first professional manager, was fired quickly by a strong mayor who resented his independence of views. It is impossible to attribute Stacy's dismissal entirely to friction with a strong mayor as Stacy did things as a professional manager that were intolerable to the "old guard," and one could probably pinpoint his dismissal to policy differences as much as to friction with the mayor. Pace, a local man employed in a minor capacity at city hall, was first made acting manager and then under the next mayor, of the same faction, promoted to manager. The two were very close, lunching and golfing together frequently. But when the patron mayor, Manley, resigned and was followed by a change in clique control, Pace was out on the basis of a power exchange and not for personal reasons. It was clear to us that Potter had serious friction with Mayor Roberts and was forced to resign.

Of course, there is another factor to be considered in connection with manager tenure in Hiberna. The city showed no disposition until the employment of the present manager to pay for minimal competence in managers. Those who were employed could not be said to have represented the top talent available for a city the size of Hiberna. The present manager receives a salary of $10,200. How much this indisposition to pay anything approaching the "going" rate for managers stemmed from lack of understanding of modern management or how much from a covert, deliberate desire to sabotage the manager system, we did not determine.

It is impossible to discuss city managers of Hiberna or the change in the climate of councilmanic opinion with respect to the manager without taking note of the crucial role played by Admiral March. Most respondents readily attributed a change in councilmanic behavior to the election of the Admiral in late 1958. A vastly admired public figure as an authentic battle hero, he was also a modern civic hero who persisted in serving his community even as he was dying of lung cancer. He sought to apply the textbook principles of council-manager government to Hiberna. During his three months' service as interim manager between Weeks and Grace, he really shook up City Hall. Opinions differ as to the Admiral's capacity as a manager, and his qualities as a policy leader, but not as to his widespread public popularity. It is clear, however, from the mere matter of the record on actual reorganization of functions during his short tenure, that the Admiral got things shipshape. He reorganized and consolidated the number of departments and reduced the span of control, so that Grace could take over with a minimum of difficulty. Reorganization, which is often a "sticky business" at best for a manager to effect, was obviated for Grace by Admiral March's decisions.

With the Admiral's election to the council, the manager system picked up perhaps its strongest supporter, and the community and the council moved for a time toward down-grading the position of mayor and strengthening that of manager. The mayor was deprived of his office in city hall; the manager's power to appoint department heads was, on paper at least, made unqualified; and his powers to spend without specific council authorization were enlarged. March even got the mayor, along with his fellow councilmen, to agree to a charter proposal to do away with the separately elected mayor.

Experience with "true" manager government thus dates only from Grace's appointment, for Grace is a young professional recruited under Admiral March's prodding from another Florida city. We had the impression that Grace is operating approximately by the book, but that he is far from aggressive and probably feels, in fact, fairly insecure with both the mayor and the council. He regularly initiates policy proposals, as the council expects him to do, but he stays away from recommendations on touchy matters. He is keenly aware of the police chief. Although the manager gave us the impression that he himself had a strong recreation program, Mayor Thomas describes Grace's main interest as sanitary sewers and implied that Grace dragged his feet on vigorous recreation expansion. The latter issue is, of course, far more touchy in Hiberna than the former issue. However, most council members apparently do not mind Grace's going slowly on controversial recommendation. Some councilmen believe that he is not aggressive enough on relatively settled matters, that he still runs to them on too many little things, and that when he confers with them, he talks too long, making his points more repetitively than is necessary. But on Grace's side it should be mentioned that he lost his strongest supporter when Admiral March died, that Mayor Morgan was openly hostile to him and made him a campaign issue, and that he has had an attrition among councilmen by virtue of age, death, and political ambition that has left him with only Westerly of the group in office in 1960. Even his critics believe that Grace is, on the whole, doing a very good job.

Grace circulates the council agenda at least two days before an executive session. He usually makes detailed recommendations on each item. Since most councilmen do their homework on the agenda, the executive sessions do not last long. These sessions incidentally have, as remarked above, been opened to press and public recently and are called "work sessions." Such sessions lead to: (1) compromise at the session; (2) postponement (not definite) of hard questions; and (3) occasional disagreements at the public meetings.

Grace's budget practice is pretty standard. He draws up the budget and gives it to the council before the press gets it. In 1960 he used a double budget. Grace told us he gets no cues from the council on what to put in or leave out, although a council member averred that councilmen do give him cues. Cuts and increases are negotiated among councilmen, manager, and department heads, according to another councilman. Indeed, the powerful police chief, who resented the elimination of his car allowance when he obtained a large salary increase in 1960, recovered his car allowance retroactively with the help of one of his close friends on the council.

On hiring and firing, councilmen in the past have interfered without compunction. The council still appoints the police and fire chiefs although, says Grace, this will probably change when the present chiefs retire. There is some contradiction about Grace's manner of appointing department heads. Grace declared that, when he first came, he "shook up" the departments and got new heads. Others reported that the council had shown considerable dissatisfaction with the previous manager Weeks because he was too "weak-kneed" in dealing with poor department heads and that the council wanted action from Grace. When a new man is hired, the procedure followed thus far with Grace is that the council gives the nod to the man they want after Grace has worked up the dossiers and he and the council together have reduced the prospects to the "top three." Grace then appoints. Maybe the reconciliation of the contradiction between his declaration that he had an unfettered appointment power and councilmen's description of appointments comes to this: the way described by councilmen is the way utilized before the charter amendment of 1959 and the way described by Grace is the way set forth in the new amendment, but there have not been department head appointments since the new amendment was adopted.

The picture of Grace that emerges is that he is playing slowly and carefully and trying to avoid controversial questions. He is frank in stating that his personal career can be boosted by getting a reputation as the man who licked the turnover tendencies in Hiberna by staying at least four years (he has now served three years). Then he expects, as a careerist, to move on to a larger city that will offer a higher salary. Some of our informants were quite candid in saying that they thought Grace would eventually leave because of salary. While he stays, and if he stays, he can still be an effective manager simply by being allowed to remain as manager and to pick up much if not all the "slack" in the sense of catching up on the backlog of municipal services characteristic of Hiberna. If all Grace does is to install sanitary sewers to replace septic tanks, he will have an achievement of quite controversial dimensions that can well contribute to the advancement of his managerial career. Sanitary sewers are basic to urban living, although highly controversial in Suburbia. If Grace can develop a major sewer program, he will have demonstrated marked leadership qualities.

VI

Has Hiberna come any nearer to the settlement of the basic question that has racked the town — what kind of town shall it be? Possibly it has, in the sense that the 1960 election, with the return to power of the "bank group," meant the elimination from further consideration of the alternative of an estate town. It would seem that the 1957 election eliminated the alternative of flamboyant tourism. It is still possible that it can be a retirement town, but in the future it can be a retirement town only on the terms laid down by either the "bank group" or the dormitory suburbanites if the latter are ever rallied to play a part in the government of the city. In other words, it will be a retirement town with some large cooperative apartment houses studded here and there along its lake shores in the midst of some additional middle class type subdivisions where an estate of groves and screaming peacocks now holds the public at bay.

An addition has been built to the newest of Hiberna's hotels, and the "tone" is that of a motel, a fact which seems to augur the "bank group's" emphasis on quiet tourism and state conventions of modest size. The brash tourism of Mayor Roberts may be discarded — although that is not yet absolutely clear — but low-voltage tourism may even be expanded. As to the expansion of recreational facilities, the dormitory suburbanites are going to have to fight for them as that dimension of Hiberna's future has certainly not been disclosed. After all, the dormitory suburbanites are not organized as a clique and were not even registered to vote in city elections until 1960. Until there is an ultimate resolution of the question of the kind of town Hiberna shall be, there will be only lulls in the rapid turnover of managers. Although the "bank group" is committed to keeping and getting along with the present manager, the history of manager tenure would dictate that if ever the dormitory suburbanites should force a resolution of city services that they desire upon the city and take over city hall, the "bank group's" manager will go. But for the immediate future the "bank group" rules, and the "old guard" is less strong each day as the changes produced by the "bank group" have a "feedback" effect.

The latter point of "feedback" may be illustrated by zoning. Once the first "breakthrough" is made in a strict zoning system, other variances are always much easier to achieve as the attack against variances has been sapped by the first victory and a cumulative effect of defeat builds up. So it is with zoning in Hiberna as a result of the old hotel-cooperative apartment house fight and the opening up of middle-class subdivisions by developers tied to the bankers in search of capital investment.

So the town changes. Maybe it is stabilizing. New money, new faces, new methods of politics have their effects. The question is are those effects deep or superficial?

9

Estiva

The present community of Estiva began in the mid-1880's as a speculative project in real estate and tourism. It is one of three adjoining coastal towns that are both recreational and residential areas for Monroe, a nearby major city. Estiva is separated from the mainland by a wide bay used for deep sea shipping and is actually located on a spit of sandy beach. At the time of its founding the coastal towns in that part of the peninsula still attracted a substantial winter tourist trade. A syndicate of Monroe businessmen apparently decided to begin a beach development, designed to accommodate summer as well as winter visitors.

The development syndicate secured a charter in 1883 to construct and operate a narrow-gauge railway, the Sea Line, from East Monroe to Monroe Beach, as the projected resort was then named. The plat having been filed, and the completion of the railway only a month away, the syndicate in November of 1884 began the sale of lots. Business was brisk, and by 1886 the sydicate had constructed the Ocean Queen Hotel, a large, year-round (centrally heated), electrically lighted, and, unfortunately, inflammable structure.

For four years, the Ocean Queen served as the summer center for the social elite of Monroe. How well it did as a winter tourist hotel is not known. In the summer of 1890, however, the hotel burned completely, as did the terminal of the railway, located on the hotel grounds.

This disaster seems to have destroyed the syndicate's efficacy. The railway stayed in financial difficulties until 1899, when the Coast Line Railway purchased the narrow-gauge line. Within six months, the merged railway system had converted to standard gauge, sent in its first train to Monroe Beach, and an extension of the railroad northward from Monroe Beach was started.

Although the coming of the coastal railway seems to have revitalized the beach area, Monroe Beach did not acquire another "elite" hotel to replace the Ocean Queen. The Coast Line Railway erected *its* exclusive hotel at what was later called White Sands Beach, some miles to the north of Monroe Beach, and Monroe Beach's later development came as a popular summer resort.

In 1907 the community acquired its first municipal charter, and in 1910 the county began laying a road from Monroe to Monroe Beach. The 1920's saw completion of a bridge across the bay that separated the mainland from the coastal spit on which Monroe Beach was located, and of a broad paved highway to the beach area. The consequent increase in the flow of summer resort visitors stamped Monroe Beach with its character as a summer resort for the masses.

The town's name was changed to Estiva in 1935. Two years later Estiva failed in an attempt to consolidate with White Sands Beach, a newly incorporated municipality then adjoining Estiva on the north. In 1931, Estiva itself had undergone division, when the legislature granted a charter to a new municipality, Azalea Beach, formed from the northern portion of Estiva.

This fission and failure at consolidation were not due simply to an excess of particularism. Persons long resident in the area have been familiar with the distinctive civic character displayed by each of the three beach municipalities. These characters have been closely correlated with the differing resort clienteles of the three communities. In oversimplified terms, White Sands Beach has been a socially selective or "elite" resort; Azalea Beach, a relatively decorous, "family-centered" resort; and Estiva a carnival, honky-tonk, "popular" resort. Both at White Sands Beach and at Azalea Beach, therefore, there has been a long-standing community interest at variance with the putative carnival interest in Estiva, and the separation has undoubtedly reflected an unwillingness of the two separatist municipalities to come within the loose zoning and land-use controls of Estiva.

II

Until some time during the 1930's, Estiva's resident population for census purposes, as Table 3 shows, never exceeded five hundred.

Although we do not have detailed data on the 1920's, it seems reasonably clear that during that period a number of concessionaires began to operate eating stands, penny arcades, bathhouses, amusement parks, and other carnival types of business along a beach-front boardwalk. It was during the same period, we speculate, that the owners of boardwalk real estate, of summer cottages and apartments, and of some of the concessions emerged as the leadership clique to which we

Table 3

Estiva Population, 1910–1960

Year	Population	Percentage Increase	Year	Population	Population Increase
1910	249	—	1940	3566[b]	—
1920	357	43.4	1950	6430	80.3
1930	409	14.6	1960	12049	87.4
1940	4929[a]	1105.1			

Source: U. S. Bureau of the Census
[a] Includes 1940 poplation of Estiva and Azalea Beach
[b] Includes only 1940 poplation of Estiva

later refer as the "boardwalk crowd." Further, it appears that it was during this period that the clique assumed its role as the ruling group in Estiva's politics. We also judge that the role of the small resident population in community decision-making was not exclusive, since the city charter allowed nonresidents who owned real property in Estiva to vote in municipal elections and to hold municipal office.

In the decades before the depression, the rate of increase in Estiva's resident population was considerable, although the absolute numbers were rather small. Since 1930, however, both the rates of increase and the absolute numbers have been larger. The 1940 Estiva-Azalea Beach population was twelve times that of 1930, and during each decade since 1940, the population of Estiva has approximately doubled.

These increases in population do not mean that Estiva has simply become a bigger, brassier, more popular honky-tonk and summer resort. Instead, what they represent in large part is a long-term, continuing invasion of the old carnival town by dormitory suburbanites, who reside in Estiva and commute to work in Monroe.

During the early part of the depression, it appears, some owners of beach apartments and cottages found it desirable to try to rent their seasonal properties on a year-round basis, and a number of Monroe families found it economical to "move to the beach" and commute. What may have begun as a temporary expedient changed, during the last half of the decade, into a building boom.

As Table 4 shows, one-third of the dwelling units enumerated in the 1940 housing census of Estiva were constructed after 1934.

Although the construction of seasonal housing may have continued during the 1930's, that sort of construction can hardly have accounted for the bulk of new housing units, since the enumeration of 1940, completed before the beginning of the impending summer season, reported only 13.4 per cent of all dwelling units in Estiva as being then seasonally vacant and for rent.

If this argument insufficiently establishes the occurrence of the suburbanites' migration to the beaches, two additional pieces of evidence may do so. During the last half of the 1930's, the bus company operating in Monroe inaugurated regular and frequent service between that city and the beaches. By the time the decade closed, the county school board had erected a high school in the beach area.

As Table 4 indicates, residential construction and, presumably, population growth, slackened at Estiva during the war, only to resume vigorously during the last half of the 1940's, even though not all the data appropriate to illustrate it are yet available from the 1960 census.

Among the available data, the most relevant, perhaps, are of two kinds: those that illustrate the socio-economic character of the population of Estiva, and those that deal with the vital processes. Table 5 contrasts selected socio-economic characteristics of the populations of Estiva and Monroe. In general, both in 1940 and 1950, people in the beach community were somewhat more "white-collar," more "middle-classish," "better off" than those in the central city, and the intercity differences in social class presented in the table appear to be widening with the passage of time, although those in economic status, at least as to median income, seem to have disappeared.

The two vital processes considered are birth and death, and the statistic used here to symbolize them is the fertility ratio. The numerator of this ratio, as usually defined, is the number of children under five years of age at a particular time in a particular community. The denominator is supposed to be the number of females of child-bearing age, variously considered as beginning at age 15 or 20 and ending at age 44 or 49. The denominator here used runs from age 15 to 44,

Table 4

Distribution by Year of Construction of Estiva Dwelling Units 1940 and 1950

1940		1950	
Year Built	Percentage of Dwelling Units	Year Built	Percentage of Dwelling Units
1919 or earlier	15.0	1919 or earlier	4.1
1920–24	17.0	1920–29	17.0
1925–29	17.4	1930–39	33.9
1930–34	17.1	1940–44	9.3
1935–40	33.4	1945–50	35.6

Table 5

Selected Socio-economic Characteristics of Estiva and Monroe
1940, 1950, and 1960

Socio-economic characteristics	1940 Estiva	1940 Monroe	1950 Estiva	1950 Monroe	1960 Estiva	1960 Monroe
Percentage of males in white-collar occupations	43.2	39.4	50.7	37.8	48.8	31.6
Median family income year	–	–	$2,466	$2,164	$3,043	$3,048
Median contract (1940) or gross (1950) rent month	$25.05	$18.79	$52.70	$38.69	a	a
Median home value	$2,900	$3,610	$8,729	$6,943	a	a

ª Not available

and the ratio is computed only between white children and white females.

Table 6 displays the long-term decennial fluctuation in white fertility for Estiva, Monroe, and the urban population of Florida.

The fluctuations in the urban fertility ratio simply confirm what is already known about fluctuations in the birth rate during the past thirty years; they probably reflect, as well, some decline in infant mortality. Insofar as the Estiva data for 1930 are firm data, the long-

Table 6

Fertility Ratios, White Population of Estiva and Monroe, and White Urban Population of Florida, 1930–1960

Year	Estiva	Monroe	Florida Urban
1930	277.3ª	314.3	325.5ᵇ
1940	275.1	246.7	239.6ᵇ
1950	437.7	382.4	365.4ᵇ
1950	–	–	389.6ᶜ
1960	544.8	423.9	478.1ᶜ

ª An estimate based on data from a precinct containing Monroe Beach and some unincorporated area. The available data did not separate the age-sex distributions for whites and nonwhites, nor for incorporated and unincorporated parts of the precinct.

ᵇ Old definition of "urban."   ᶜ New definition of "urban."

term Estiva fluctuations parallel the Florida urban and the Monroe fluctuations.

More to the point of the present study, however, are the inter-community comparisons at the time of the same census. From 1940 onward, the white fertility ratio in Estiva consistently and increasingly exceeds the fertility ratio in Monroe and in the entire urban population of Florida.

Given these data as well as the interview materials, one can denominate two of the three major resources in the economy of Estiva. The first is about five miles of ocean beach, wide and, at low tide, hard enough for cars to drive on. The real estate, lodging, and commercial interests concerned with the beach need no detailed description. The second economic resource is the dormitory suburbanites themselves, leading a familistic style of life, whose economic role as consumers of housing, retail commodities, and personal services should be obvious.

The third major economic resource, whose existence our interviews alone determined, is the W. W. Brow and Sons Construction Company. The Brows are an "old family" in the Monroe Beach-Estiva area, and the company has been in existence for some sixty years. Although it has participated in local contracts, the bulk of its work during the last twenty years has been done on military and nonmilitary contracts at some distance from Estiva. The firm is the largest single employer of labor in Estiva; indeed, it is the only firm of any size in the town.

III

At the time of our study, Estiva was operating under a council-manager charter granted in 1937 by special act of the Legislature. Although the grant of the charter antedates the period covered by the study, we speculate that the charter of 1937 which supplanted a mayor-council arrangement and abolished both absentee suffrage and office-holding, represented a concession by the then dominant boardwalk interests to the incoming dormitory suburbanites.

As adopted, the charter provided for the biennial election of a designated mayor and six councilmen at large. All elections were by plurality, and the highest six candidates for the council were the winners, with no designation of seats or positions for which particular candidates ran. In 1953 and 1959 the voters rejected charter amendments that would have lengthened the mayor's term to four years and required council candidates to file for designated seats. In rejecting the 1959 proposed amendments, the voters also rejected proposals to increase council terms to four years, to stagger council elections so that half the seats would be filled every two years, and to require primary nominations in elections involving more than two candidates, with the two highest primary candidates pitted against each other in a run-off election.

A further attempt to introduce stability and continuity into the governmental structure finally succeeded. In 1961, the legislature amended the charter to effect the following changes: (1) lengthen terms of all elective offices to four years; (2) require council candidates to run for a designated seat; (3) require run-off elections where necessary to insure majority nomination and election; and (4) stagger council elections so that half the seats would be filled every two years.

Under the manager charter of Estiva, the separately elected mayor is nominally a council president and ceremonial head of the city, and the role of policy initiation is the manager's. In point of fact, a variety of relationships has existed between various mayors and managers during the period covered by the study. Amos Jameson, mayor in the periods 1947–49, 1951–53, 1955–57, and 1959–61, took very seriously his real or assumed executive and directive powers as mayor, and increasingly, during the research period, Jameson acquired the reputation of being the "hatchet man" to bring down strong managers. R. O. Brow, mayor from 1953–55, worked harmoniously with one of his former and later employees, Ben Crow, as manager. Brow has also continued on some occasions when he was not mayor, to work well with, and perhaps to manipulate, managers in whose selection he had no discernible voice. Other mayors, notably Mason Bell (1957–59) were willing to leave to the manager not only a policy-initiating role, but also the responsibility for publicly advocating and defending policies adopted by the mayor and the council.

On paper the manager occupies a strong position *vis-à-vis* department heads. Only the city clerk is an elected department head independent of the manager. All other heads are appointed and removable by the manager, with the approval of the council.

As matters have worked out, however, manager-department head relationships are by no means consistently hierarchical. The present city clerk, a Brow man, gets along with those managers whom Brow endorses, and he does not see eye to eye with those whom Brow scorns. When in 1950 a manager would not fire a police chief whom a council majority wished dismissed, the council failed to acknowledge the manager's charter-granted right to propose a firing. Instead, the manager's refusal to fire led to his own forced resignation. Department heads have, on occasion, been caught up in conflict over personnel policy between the manager and city employees. Moreover, managers have not always been able to prevent department heads from influencing the votes of their employees in councilmanic elections.

IV

There are rather few registered Republicans in the county election precinct that Estiva entirely comprises. Nevertheless, as Table 7 shows, the beach community exhibited marked tendencies toward presidential Republicanism during the twelve years ending in 1960. These tendencies, pronounced in each postwar comparison between the presidential vote in Estiva and in Monroe, are tendencies shared by many Southern, white, middle-class areas. They are also, of course, further evidence of the middle-class, suburban character of the population of Estiva.

If these data suggest an emergent postwar consensus in Estiva that endorsed either the presidential Republican Party or the public image of Dwight D. Eisenhower or that deprecated the "welfare state," this consensus by no means extended to matters of local political concern. The earliest evidence of more or less organized local political competition during the research period does not appear until 1949. Since that time, Estiva has acquired in the state a modest notoriety as a city of extreme political instability. Between 1949 and 1961, the city underwent seven power exchanges; that is to say, there were seven occasions on which control of the city government and its policy-making authority passed from one leadership clique or faction to another.

Table 7

Percentage Distribution of the Major Party Vote for President, Monroe and Estiva, 1932–1960

| | *Estiva* | | *Monroe* | |
Year	*Democratic*	*Republican*	*Democratic*	*Republican*
1932	81.3%	18.7%	72.2%	24.8%
1936	86.8	13.2	83.5	16.5
1940	83.6	16.4	81.8	18.2
1944	76.2	23.8	74.6	25.4
1948	66.1[a]	33.8	75.1[b]	24.9
1952	38.2	61.8	56.4	43.6
1956	41.3	58.7	52.1	47.9
1960	52.4	47.6	59.6	40.4

[a] Includes 1.4 per cent for Wallace, 39.3 per cent for Truman, and 25.4 per cent for Thurmond.

[b] Includes 2.3 per cent for Wallace, 48.9 per cent for Truman, and 23.9 per cent for Thurmond.

To understand the political development of Estiva it is necessary to outline its political structure as it existed at the time of our study and as it had developed up to that time. Respondents in our interviews identified three major foci of power and influence in the town. These foci correspond to the three major economic resources of Estiva that we have already enumerated.

In terms of the history of Estiva, the oldest of these congeries of interest and influence is the leadership clique consistently referred to as the "boardwalk crowd." Although estimates differed as to the precise number of leaders in the boardwalk inner circle (the range of estimates was from six to fifteen), respondents were fairly well agreed on three features of the boardwalk crowd: (1) it had been a power in Estiva for a long time (presumably since the 1920's) and had largely run the town until after World War II; (2) the major economic interests of the clique were beach-front and other valuable real estate, boardwalk concessions, an amusement park, and, correlatively, large numbers of summer resort visitors; and (3) the Estiva Chamber of Commerce is and has long been simply a mouthpiece for the boardwalk crowd. Clustered around the boardwalk leaders were, and are, various owners of seasonal rental housing west of the beach front, a varying number of motel owners, and a varying number of small retailers along Main Street (one block west of the beach front) and along the several streets running west from the beach. Some Estivans, particularly R. O. Brow, a former mayor who has operated politically both in cooperation with and in opposition to the boardwalk crowd, showed a nostalgic tendency to romanticize the prewar boardwalkers as being somewhat more "responsible" and less "carny" in orientation than the postwar boardwalkers. This may be true as to responsibility, but both interviewers, who grew up in the area and who visited Estiva many times during the 1920's and the 1930's, agree that the resort operation in the town has had a "carny" atmosphere for at least thirty years.

The next earliest leadership clique or faction in Estiva is one that presently centers around R. O. Brow, president of the W. W. Brow and Sons Construction Company. During World War II, R. O. Brow succeeded to the presidency of the firm.

The political power of the Brows in Estiva seems to have stemmed largely from the firm's local reputation and, probably, from the votes of its employees, many of them Negroes. Our impression of the internal personnel policies of the firm is that they are paternalistic and charismatic, with the expected focus on the person of the president. For example, during our interview with R. O. Brow on a Saturday in his office, when the firm nominally was closed, he managed to see several of his employees (all happened to be Negroes) to whom he dispensed a sort of benevolently baronial justice.

Although the firm had no particular resort interest, the Brows apparently for a long time were of the boardwalk crowd, if not in it. As late as 1950, R. O. Brow successfully managed a bitter recall election on behalf of the boardwalkers. By election time in 1953, however, he had broken with the "carny" operators, as he contemptuously referred to his former political associates, and had successfully put in office an administration based on the votes of the dormitory suburbanites and headed by himself as mayor.

Although narrowly defeated for re-election as mayor in 1955, Brow remained a power. During the caretaker or stalemate government of 1959–1961, he had great influence over the city manager, Robert Poore, who died midway during the caretaker period. A Brow man, moreover, was elected mayor in 1961.

The most recent faction in the political history of Estiva is that comprised, in the mass, of the dormitory suburbanites. The leadership of this faction is not particularly cohesive. In the early 1950's local Protestant ministers and laymen agitated the suburbanites over "sin" issues. Brow's two campaigns for mayor, as well as that of Mason Bell in 1957, were heavily oriented toward voters in this aggregate. Despite this fact, not all suburbanite leaders (or councilmen) are necessarily Brow men. For this reason, the suburbanite faction is treated as a separate clique, even though Brow and the non-Brow suburbanite leaders have been, in effect, in coalition since 1953. The strength of this clique (or cliques) lies in the number of suburbanites in the community; its weakness, according to some informants, lies in the relative political apathy of the suburbanites as voters, and in their ambivalent tendencies to want improvements in services and low taxes. If there is a formal association in Estiva that fronts for the suburbanites, it is probably the Board of Realtors, most of whose members are interested in residential development, in a regular volume of residential real estate transactions, and in "morally wholesome," non-honky-tonk tourism. (The new Brow mayor is a realtor.)

One major political leader in Estiva, former mayor Mason Bell, refused to see the suburbanites as a separate faction. Bell, an intellectual lawyer and the scion of an old boardwalk family, argued that he could see little difference between the policy orientations of persons alleged to be suburbanite leaders and those of boardwalk leaders, and he strongly intimated that the division was a factitious one devised by R. O. Brow, in 1953, when he broke with the boardwalk crowd and first ran for mayor. The interviewers questioned Bell closely on this point. They suggested that, in fact, his role as mayor as well as his own personal style might have led him to bridge the division between boardwalkers and suburbanites. They recalled to his attention his freely acknowledged sociability with leaders of both groups. They suggested that, for these reasons, he might have been far less sensitive to the distinctions between the two cliques than a more zealous factionary would have been. Bell acknowledged the intellectual possibility of this conclusion but remained of his original conviction.

Bell was our only respondent who denied the existence of both boardwalk crowd and a suburbanite faction. Despite our great admiration for his intellectual incisiveness, we reject his analysis in this instance in favor of the almost unanimous testimony of our other respondents.

The emergence of competitive politics in Estiva was a consequence of widening division in the community. At a relatively pedestrian level of observation, the division was reflected in obvious conflict over the "moral wholesomeness" of the community. This was conflict over alleged governmental tolerance of drinking and dangerous driving on the beach, violations of closing hours for bars, and gambling and prostitution. There was also an equally obvious conflict over accumulating deficits in the provision of traditional municipal services such as paving, utilities, and sewerage.

From a more stratospheric vantage point, the grand issue in the politics of Estiva for at least twelve years has been the kind of town it shall be. Shall it be a suburb or a resort? How can the suburban interest and the resort interest be blended? Although this basic issue is by no means clearly articulated in every election campaign — because Estiva politicians, like others, are not always fond of drawing sharp lines — it is an issue clearly present in the minds of most clique leaders. Moreover, the issue tends to ramify and find specific expression in many of the projected programs and budget items that have become politically controversial.

On the grand issue, the two most relevant factors are the steady increase in the number of suburbanite residents and the steady decline in the economic health of the resort industry. Although there may be suburbanites who would like to see the community go out of the resort business and the beach become the more or less exclusive purlieu of the permanent residents, we found no leader in any clique who was seriously willing to advocate such an extreme "solution" of the resort question.

Clique conflict over resort policy has tended to revolve, instead, around the question: What kind of resort? "Mass" (inexpensive) or "select" (expensive)? "Carny" or decorous? "Wide-open" or "regulated"? Boardwalk factionaries were by no means unanimous on this question; suburbanite leaders tended to prefer the second alternative of each pair presented.

Because the "carny" segment of the resort interest regarded its members as having, by ancient prescription, a vested right to operate a mass resort, these members were afraid of changes in land-use policies — as, for example, under an urban renewal program — that would alter the character of the resort. The "carny" segment, moreover has tended to explain the sickness of the resort industry in terms of the intermittent hostility of suburbanite administrations to mass tourism.

Anti-"carny" leaders have argued that the "carny" aspects of the resort industry (1) make the beach undesirable and unsafe for use by suburbanites and their children; (2) corrupt the police force and create disrespect for law; and (3) deserve little support from the city government, since "carnivalism" is dying a natural death which should, if anything, be hastened, not postponed.

The other main problem or grand issue in Estiva politics amounts, so to speak, to a continuing "crisis of regime." The approximate equivalence in the power of the resort interest and the suburban interest and the plurality election of councilmen have apparently led to "chancy" election results. Because the prospects of success at the next election have been unsure and the stakes of municipal politics so high, an incumbent government has usually tried to "go for broke," or to embark on irreversible "crash" programs, or to nail down in irrevocable terms, if possible, a policy all too nakedly based upon the interest of the clique in control of the government. The naked extremeness in many programs has apparently alienated enough "swing" voters to produce a regular, biennial overthrow of the "ins." And, in viciously circular fashion, the prospects of alternation have tended to increase the extremeness of programs.

As a result, Estiva acquired during the 1950's a reputation for political instability. This reputation was forcefully brought home in 1960 to most clique leaders. A national chain of "luxury" (i.e., expensive) motels had decided to locate one of its units on the beach in Estiva. Many leaders in both the suburban interest and the resort interest favored the coming of a "quality" (i.e., expensive) motel to the community. Negotiations for mortgage money collapsed, however, when the mortgage brokerage firm involved told the prospective borrowers that Estiva was too unstable and unreliable politically for a luxury motel there to be a good risk.

Against the frame of reference described above, the examination of specific conflicts in the electoral, managerial, and regime politics of Estiva takes on additional meaning.

VI

"Moral wholesomeness." Competitive politics came to Estiva in the municipal elections of 1949. At that time, a new leadership clique, composed largely of ministers in several Protestant churches serving the beach area and claiming to speak for the "decent" dormitory residents, won three of the six seats on the council. Although the postwar increase in Estiva's population had produced large deficits in the quality and extent of the usual municipal services — streets, sewerage, and utilities — the new council faction seemed less interested in these things than it was in "sin" and morality questions.

Launching a strong attack on the alleged existence of police graft, prostitution, gambling, and illegal liquor sales, the new council faction, by vigorous public moralizing, swung a wavering boardwalk councilman to their side, and demanded that City Manager Ben Crow discharge the police chief. When Crow refused, the council forced his resignation and in March, 1950, selected a new manager, Richard Moore, who discharged the police chief and replaced him with the man who is still serving as chief.

The boardwalk crowd then began circulating recall petitions against two of the minister clique's councilmen, with the latter clique retaliating by starting recall petitions against Mayor Ames and the two "loyal" boardwalk councilmen. At this stage, R. O. Brow, with the backing of the boardwalk crowd, called for a "complete" recall election.

Under the charter's recall provisions, the name of each official whose recall was sought went on the ballot; the voter was given the choice of favoring or opposing the recall. Recall proponents could also file candidates to oppose each official whose recall was sought, and voters who favored recall of an incumbent could also vote for his opponent.

By the time of the election, in the summer of 1950, each side had a full slate of candidates for the mayoralty and six council seats. Brow, who managed the campaign for the boardwalkers, brought off the difficult feat of educating the voters in the intricacies of choice presented them by the ballot.

In the event, the incumbent mayor and two councilmen, all "loyal" boardwalkers, were retained in office by rather wide margins. The three minister clique councilmen and the "wavering" member were recalled by fairly close margins and replaced by reliable boardwalkers.

Manager Moore took the hint and formally resigned. His successor, Charles Snow, held office for ten months, when he was replaced, upon resignation, by Ben Crow, whose refusal to fire the police chief had been an early event in the developing recall crisis.

Although the boardwalkers had defended the integrity of the dismissed police chief and had decreed the "injustice" of his loss of pension rights upon his discharge, they did not move to replace the new chief and restore the old one.

Estivans disagree concerning the present prevalence of "sin" in the town. Former City Manager Earl Mays (1957–59) hired a special investigator to check into suspected police graft, but the only result of this investigation was an intense dislike of Mays by the patrolmen. The late city manager, Robert Poore, (1959–60) and incumbent councilman, Blaine Frank, both agreed that the present police chief, though a "nice guy," does not really run his department; the patrolmen, they say, "run him." Frank then went on to say, "We don't pay our policemen a living wage, so they've got to steal." Poore said that there were few prostitutes or illegal liquor operators in town.

Of the two statements, Frank's seems the less likely to be distorted by self-interest and the more likely to lack a detailed factual base. Although Poore presumably had more detailed knowledge than Frank, his agreement that the cops "run" the chief seems difficult to reconcile both with his statement about the relative lack of "commercial sin" in Estiva and with another statement in which Poore referred to the chief as a "professional" chief and to the present police department as "nonpolitical."

If the importance of the traditional commercial vices has declined in Estiva since 1945 — and it seems quite possible that this is so — we think that the decline is attributable more to the long-term illness and decline of the resort industry than to the replacement of one police chief by another in 1950.

When R. O. Brow ran for mayor in 1953, he raised the "sin" question, particularly in regard to the sale of liquor at illegal times. The question of public drinking and drunkenness on the beach itself came to a head during the Bell administration (1957–59), and the city has since consistently enforced an ordinance forbidding drinking on the beach. Our tentative judgment would be that "sin" has become a dead issue; middle-class suburbanite morality in respect of the commercial vices has probably come close to prevailing; and commercial "sin" has probably become almost nonexistent.

Traditional services and public works. One choice that would have confronted any anti-boardwalk ticket in 1949 was whether to go after "sin" or to liquidate some of the deficits in paving, sewerage, and utility services that the suburban boom had produced. The ministers' clique made its choice with results already described, and control of the city reverted to the boardwalkers. The reversion slowed down but did not prevent liquidation of these deficits.

In 1949, during the last Ames administration, postwar expansion of the city's electric distribution system began. Further expansions took place during the Brow (1953–55) and Bell (1957–59) administrations. Although these expansions were not highly controversial, there was boardwalk opposition to each of them. The rationale of the opposition is not hard to understand. Each expansion was financed by revenue certificates, to whose retirement future utility "profits" were pledged. Since most of the expansion went into new residential areas, and since the charges against future utility "profits" represented a reduction in the future "contributions" of the utility to the general revenue fund, the expansion program to that extent made it difficult to keep real estate taxes from increasing. Some boardwalkers still grumble, too, that the electric utility's rate structure discriminates against commercial or boardwalk users, in favor of residential consumers, although the seasonal character of much boardwalk business makes such a charge difficult to substantiate.

The major postwar "crash" programs in other public work areas — water treatment (removal of sulphur), paving, extension of sewerage, and construction of a sewage disposal plant — occurred during the Brow and Bell administrations. These programs were differentially controversial, but each involved some boardwalk opposition. Although the sewerage and paving projects were financed in the main by special assessments, each had a general revenue fund appropriation behind it as well. Since much of the expansion took place in residential areas or for the benefit, in numerical terms, of suburbanite users, boardwalk opposition is not hard to understand.

Public finance. A public budget's allocations of burdens and benefits are always political even when they are only potentially controversial. Since 1953, the allocations have been actually controversial in Estiva.

The main sources of municipal revenues are the general property tax, utility profits, an excise on utility bills, and rebates from a state excise on cigarettes. The first two are within the power of the city to manipulate. Maximum yields from the last two are set by state law.

Controversy in the public finance area thus revolves around the relative proportions of public revenues that should come from the property tax and from utility profits. It seems likely that much of this controversy is "unreal" in the sense that the relative incidence and regressiveness of these two taxes have not been conclusively demonstrated. Despite this "unreality," clique leaders tend to have definite preferences for these two taxes. In general, boardwalk people favor manipulating the rate structure of the electric utility so as to increase utility profits, and they oppose any increased reliance on the property tax. Suburbanite leaders tend to take opposite positions.

The main reason that suburbanite leaders prefer to rely on the property tax is that, under the Florida Constitution, five thousand dollars of the assessed valuation of each homestead (owner-occupied residence) is exempt from the general property tax. The exemption does not apply to tenant-occupied residential property or to commercially used real estate. It is thus possible for the boardwalk interest's leaders to argue that the general property tax discriminates against them and in favor of home-owning suburbanites.

Any substantial reliance on the property tax raises political questions about assessment procedures. The incoming Brow administration in 1953 found real estate assessments at the level of about 50 per cent of estimated "fair market value." The legal standard to which assessments are supposed to conform is 100 per cent of fair market value. Supported by most of the council, the Brow group raised the level of assessment to over 90 per cent.

Our informants disagreed about the role of the reassessment per se in contributing to Brow's defeat in 1955. The Brow administration, after the assessment was completed, raised the rate of taxation from five to seven mills. (This would amount to increasing the annual property tax on a $15,000 owner-occupied residence from about $12 to about $60. Comparable figures on a $20,000 home would be from $25 to $91.) Some informants argue that it was the raise in millage, others the raise in assessment level, that produced anti-Brow votes among suburbanite residents.

Annexation. As earlier indicated, there was an unsuccessful attempt to consolidate the beach communities in the 1920's and a fission of Estiva in 1931. Consolidation was tried aagin during the Ames administration in 1949. On the referendum then held, the voters in Estiva endorsed consolidation, while those in Azalea Beach and White Sands Beach rejected it.

Most segments of the community in Estiva support consolidation for the same reason that sophisticated central city dwellers would like to absorb adjacent suburbs: the "outlanders" use expensive city services without adequate sharing of costs. Public officials in Estiva complained to us that permanent and transient residents from both Azalea Beach and White Sands Beach used Estiva parks and other public recreation facilities (both resident- and resort-oriented) without payment for the construction or upkeep.

"Honky-tonk carnivalism" in Estiva has already been suggested as a factor that keeps the beaches' municipal separatism alive. We would judge, however, that even if the "carnies" in Estiva some day close their remaining stalls and tents and silently steal away, the separatism might persist. What motive other than the desire to assume a share in costs could impel Azalea Beach and White Sands Beach voters to favor consolidation, when public authorities in Estiva can devise no feasible way to bar Azalea Beach and White Sands Beach residents from public recreation facilities intended for resi-

dents of Estiva, or to bar resort visitors to Azalea Beach or White
Sands Beach from public resort facilities designed for Estiva visitors?
  Land use and community development. Several policy questions
may be subsumed under this catch phrase, and about them rage what
are probably the bitterest conflicts in Estiva politics. Since public
recreation is an important factor in the community development of
middle-class suburbs, and obviously of resorts, recreation policy is
intimately embedded in this policy area. The policy question here is
the optimum allocation of public recreation facilities and expenditures
between suburbanite residents and their children, on the one hand,
and resort visitors on the other. The question is complicated by controversy over the kind of resort clientele Estiva should try to attract.
This controversy merges imperceptibly into the grand issue of Estiva
politics: what kind of town shall this town be?
  Estiva was originally platted with a gridiron of narrow streets running parallel and perpendicular to the beach. At low tide, the beach
itself has been used as a street and as a parking lot. The land-use
history of the community has been rather chaotic, as there was no
zoning ordinance until 1949. Beach-front real estate has usually
been used as the site of motels, lodging houses, restaurants, and a
boardwalk with "carny" stalls and concessions. Some of our informants told us of the decline during the 1950's of both carnivalism and
the motel business, and their interviews were full of the details of
plans to "clean up the boardwalk," to "redevelop the downtown area,"
to attract one big beach-front business of genuine elegance and of a
manifestly wholesome moral tone, whose coming would set off a
genuine redevelopment of the resort.
  During the 1950's, the Brow (1953–55), Jameson (1955–57), and
Bell (1957–59) administrations took various steps designed to promote community redevelopment. In the election of 1955, in which
the Brow administration went down to defeat, Brow's two proposed
general obligation bond issues were also lost. Despite the bitter fac-
tionalism in the community, one $600,000 issue — which packaged
a fishing pier, a municipal golf course, playgrounds, and a municipal
swimming pool for Negroes — came close to winning. It lost by only
109 votes out of 1,313, presumably because it contained something
for everybody. The other issue, for a municipal auditorium intended
for convention business, was severely defeated, 751 to 552.
  A year later, the new Jameson administration broke up the package
into four revenue certificate issues, all of which lost by votes of about
1,000 to 600. Antiboardwalk leaders expressed skepticism to us concerning Jameson's "sincerity," since he refused a packaging presentation, but more detached observers suggested that many "outs" simply

refused to support policies proposed by the "ins" even where they agreed with the policies.

The Bell administration took a piecemeal approach to recreation and community development questions. It built a municipal golf course out of surpluses, and constructed a Negro swimming pool. The latter was designed not only to keep the relatively small number of Estiva Negro voters tied to the leadership of the suburbanite interest, but also, hopefully, to keep local Negroes off the beach and out of the ocean.

The Jameson "stalemate" administration of 1959–61 sold the golf course to private interests because it did not want to run the risk of having the course racially integrated. That administration also saw the beginning of serious enforcement of an ordinance banning drinking on the beach, and of an unsuccessful movement in 1960 to ban the driving and parking of automobiles on the beach; it also brought about the hiring of a city planning consultant to work with the State Development Commission in devising a program for downtown redevelopment.

In short, the twelve-year agitation over community development since 1949 has produced three concrete results: a zoning ordinance, a swimming pool for Negroes, and prohibition of drinking on the beach. It seems quite clear, however, that the leadership in the suburbanite interest has major objectives that run sharply counter to the interest of many boardwalkers.

A new Brow-suburbanite administration came to power in the municipal elections of 1961. Headed by Mayor James Marshall, realtor and former Brow councilman, the new administration immediately announced a redevelopment plan designed, as a news story put it, "to upgrade the heart of the city in both appearance and moral climate," and to accord with what was said to be a "national trend to large motel developments and family-type amusement zones. . . ."

Within five weeks, the Marshall administration took its plan to the freeholders in a referendum on a substantial ($1,200,000) general obligation bond issue designed to help finance the redevelopment plan. The state law stipulates that approval of a bond issue requires a favorable vote by a majority of all freeholders registered to vote. Although the vote cast for this bond issue was heavily in favor of the issue, it was barely over the required majority of registered freeholders. When Mayor Marshall tried to market the bonds authorized at this referendum, the bond houses with whom he dealt refused to buy the bonds. The bond houses had no faith in Estiva bonds authorized by such a bare majority.

Disappointed, but not daunted, the Marshall administration called another general obligation bond election on the same issue in the early spring of 1962. Both the turn-out and the support for the new issue were regarded as sufficient to overcome, with the money lenders, Estiva's long-standing reputation for political instability.

Regime and form of government. As noted earlier, Estiva operated during the entire research period under a system of plurality elections for mayor and councilmen. In consequence, the municipality was easily subject to, and in fact underwent, an alternation in control of the government every two years. Moreover, the two principal leadership cliques, even when they put a full ticket in the field, frequently had to "put up with" minority councilmen who had campaigned as independents. Some of the later were described by informants as "real lulus," and some suburbanite leaders bemoaned what they regarded as a long-term decline in the overall quality of council candidates.

Charter revision to provide for election to designated council seats for four-year, overlapping terms was sponsored by the boardwalk administration of Mayor Jameson in 1953 and by the suburbanite administration of Mayor Bell in 1959. The voters defeated both sets of proposed charter proposals in the referenda. Our informants explained both defeats in terms of bitter "outs," joined by "swing" voters, voting against the "ins." Following the defeat of the 1959 proposals, and the replacement later that year of Mayor Bell's government by a stalemate administration (a boardwalk mayor, one boardwalk councilman, three "in-betweeners," and two Brow-suburbanite councilmen), the question of charter revision again emerged.

Over the next year and a half, an advisory citizen's committee on charter revision met from time to time. Its deliberations were greatly facilitated when the "luxury" motel project earlier referred to collapsed, and the committee, by all accounts, included leaders from "all" existing major and minor cliques in the city. By the time the county legislative delegation left for the 1961 session of the state legislature, the "all-faction" citizens committee had agreed on revision in the election system and, more importantly, had agreed not to require a referendum for putting into effect the local bill embodying the charter revision. The delegation thereupon passed the bill under the legislative courtesy custom that prevails in Florida on local legislation.

In addition to the electoral system, the question of manager government itself has been a running, if subdued, issue for several years. The main opponent of manager government has been Amos Jameson, a boardwalker and four-time mayor (but never able, as his opponents point out, to secure two consecutive terms). Jameson envisions the mayoralty as the preserve of a strong leader, and he has a local reputation both for "meddling" in managerial matters and for serving as the "hatchet man" against managers inherited by some of his administrations from preceding ones.

When interviewed, Jameson alternated between a preference for a strong mayor form and for a plural commission executive, with a separate council, as in Monroe. In any event, Jameson regards the manager as only a chief administrative officer, not as an initiator of policy proposals. Although Jameson and some other boardwalk leaders dislike manager government, they were our only informants who thought they had a chance of getting charter revisions to redefine the manager's role.

VII

During the entire period covered by our research Estiva operated under the council-manager form of government. Since January 1, 1945, the city has had twelve full (that is, not acting) managers. During the same period, including the election of 1961, the city government underwent seven power changes. Since these two factors are connected, some detail about each of them is necessary in order to illuminate the connection.

The first power exchange occurred in 1950, when the "wishy-washy" boardwalk councilman destroyed the boardwalk majority in the government by defecting to the church crowd, and giving it a council majority. This was followed by another power exchange the same year, when the recall election returned a solid boardwalk government to office.

Beginning with the election of 1953, there has been a power exchange at each biennial election: to suburbanites in 1953, to boardwalk to 1955, to suburbanites in 1957, to stalemate in 1959, and to suburbanites probably sometime before the 1961 election, when the suburbanites regained control of the government.

Many, though not all, manager terminations parallel these exchanges. Manager Harp, the first incumbent under the manager charter, voluntarily resigned in 1946 after eight and one half years' service. He died three weeks later. Manager Prow voluntarily resigned in early 1947, after having used his job to wait out a better job offer.

Manager Stow, appointed in 1947, during one boardwalk administration, was forced to resign in 1948, during the next, because of friction with the new mayor, Amos Jameson.

Manager Ben Crow, a boardwalk manager, was forced to resign

after the church group ordered him to discharge the police chief and he refused to do so. Manager Moore, the church group's manager who accomplished the discharge of the police chief, was forced to resign when the boardwalk clique regained control of the government in the recall election.

Manager Snow, the next incumbent, voluntarily resigned to make way for Crow's return. The latter spanned the Jameson administration (1951–53) and the Brow administration (1953–55). He was removed in 1956 after a Jameson boardwalk administration had again come to power in late 1955. Both Managers Glow and Plow, the two Jameson-administration appointees, voluntarily resigned their jobs for better ones elsewhere.

The Bell administration (1957–59) inherited an acting manager and appointed Manager Mays, who was removed after the stalemate Jameson administration came to power in 1959. The council then named as manager Robert Poore, who died in 1960. He was succeeded by Manager Ray, who has so far (July, 1962) survived the change from stalemate to Mayor Marshall's suburbanite government.

VIII

Although political speculation is hazardous, we feel impelled to speculate about the recent past and the future of Estiva. The collapse of the luxury motel mortgage negotiations seems to have shocked almost all leaders in Estiva. In financial terms (that is, in terms respectable and understandable to most of the leaders), the collapse vividly showed Estiva to its leaders as others saw it.

We judge that the Brow-suburbanite clique was able to use the motel fiasco to split the boardwalk crowd, to isolate the "carnies" in it, and to leave them with no one to dominate but themselves. In doing so, the Brow group seems to have been able to forge a successful coalition based on suburbanite and Brow Construction Company votes and on the blended interests of suburbanites and promoters of an upgraded resort.

Only the isolation of the "carnies" in near-impotence, it seems to us, can explain the near-unanimity of the citizens charter committee, the agreement of the legislative delegation not to require a referendum on the charter revisions, the clean sweep of mayor and council seats by the Brow-suburbanites in 1961, and the Marshall administration's success with its two redevelopment bond referenda.

We can, presumably, speak of the recent emergence of a new community consensus in Estiva, on what kind of town its citizens wish it to be. If this is so, the stabilization of the new consensus will mean that Estiva politics will have ceased to be what we call "competitive" and will become what we call "monopolistic." This does not mean that municipal elections will necessarily cease to be held, or that individual candidates will not try to "crash" the new ruling group via the electoral route, or that "personality" or "popularity" contests between opposing candidates will not take place.

What the new consensus does mean is that, in the absence of certain factors, there is not likely to be interest-based electoral politics in Estiva. Among the "certain factors" would be such things as: (1)

Managers of Estiva and their Tenure in

Mayors and Dates	Managers with Dates					
	Hays[1] 1/15/38– 5/1/46	Prow 7/1/46– 2/28/47	Stowe[2] 7/24/47– 6/22/48	Crow[2] 7/12/48– 2/5/50	Moore[2] 3/6/50– 8/30/50	Snow 8/31/50– 6/16/51
Ames 1945–1947	×	×	×			
Jameson 1947–1949			×	×		
Ames 1949–1951				×	×	×
Jameson 1951–1953						
Brow 1953–1955						
Jameson 1955–1957						
Bell 1957–1959						
Jameson 1959–1961						
Marshall 1961–						

[1] Retired   [2] Forced to resign

catastrophe (the drastic erosion and destruction of the beach, for example); (2) some long-term secular process (such as a change in the character of the suburbanite population) not now observable; or (3) the ineptitude of an incumbent administration in continuing to "do justice" to the amenities interests of the suburbanites and the promotional interests of the proponents of "quality tourism." Pending the injection of such factors into the situation, Estiva seems to have achieved a working consensus that will probably "de-politicize" its local politics.

Relation to Mayors and Mayoral Tenure

Managers with Dates

Crow[3] 6/15/51– 7/20/56	Glow 11/1/56– 8/15/57	Plow 8/15/57– 10/9/57	Mays[3] 11/25/57– 11/5/59	Poore[4] 11/15/59– 8/60	Ray 11/60–
X					
X					
X					
X	X	X			
			X		
			X	X	X
					X

[3] Removed   [4] Deceased in office

10

The Politics
of the Town

The reader of these profiles by this time will be ready to form some conclusions regarding manager tenure and community politics. We wish to summarize the findings of these eight case studies, based upon intensive field interviews, and of the materials from a questionnaire we sent to all Florida city managers.[1] The data upon which we base our conclusions, therefore, are more extensive than those available from a reading of the foregoing case studies alone.[2] However, we believe that by a careful reading of the cases the reader can come to substantially the same conclusions as we did.

Politics and Manager Tenure

1. *Manager tenure and turnover are positively related to power exchanges*

When clique control of a city council changes, either by means of the electoral process or through a realignment of forces on the city council, the city manager associated with the old alignment is normally replaced by a manager named by the new leadership faction. The factors underlying the firing of the old manager and the hiring of a new manager are fairly clear. Managers tend to play major policy roles in the community's decision-making process, and in this par-

---

[1] A copy of both the questionnaire and our interview schedule may be found in the Appendix.

[2] See the *City Managers in Politics*, published by the University of Florida Press, 1962, for a detailed delineation and analysis of these extensive data.

ticipation they tend to incur political hazards. We found that all managers in our case-study cities were involved to a greater or lesser degree in the shaping or vetoing of public policy. When a manager participates in the policy process, we found that he tends to be identified, whether justly or not, with the majority clique that hired him, and he is regarded as expendable upon that clique's defeat or threat of defeat.

An additional factor must be considered in connection with politics and manager tenure. That factor is the differentiation of reasons we found to exist for terminations according to the political style of the community. Of all manager dismissals in our profile cities, the overwhelming majority in cities with a monopolistic style of politics could be traced to what we call "palace" considerations, i.e., trouble with the mayor or boss. On the contrary, in cities with a competitive style of politics all but one dismissal could be attributed to electoral reasons, i.e., a power exchange in clique control or a power play to try to forestall a power exchange.[3]

Our explanation, of course, implies that managers, whether consciously or not, come to be identified with the aspirations of particular interests in a community, and when new interests replace old interests in control of a city council, a new manager will replace the old one. Although, after reading the case studies presented here, this explanation might seem simplistic, we think it far less trivial than explanations of manager tenure and turnover offered by managers themselves or some proponents of the plan. These latter explanations are that managers lose their jobs because they lack sufficient training in public administration; because of the rise of "unfortunate" personality conflicts between the manager and one or more councilmen; because a manager urges on the council the "right way" to pick up trash rather than allowing them to "dictate" the "political way"; or because "people don't understand the way that the plan is supposed to work." Any or all of these latter types of explanations we found to be superficial rationalizations of the intrinsic political struggles of the community.

We suggest, as supportive of our finding, the dismissals of managers in Center City, Estiva, Hiberna, Dorado, and Eastbourne and the correlation between discussion of manager dismissal in Floriana and the

---

[3] A power play, as we define it, is a manager dismissal by an incumbent clique under fire for the express purpose of drawing that fire away from the clique councilmen in the next election. A power exchange is the supplanting of the majority clique by a rival clique, usually through an election. Sometimes a power exchange may occur through the process of co-optation of one or more councilmen by a particular clique.

expanding strength of the new rival clique. As a matter of fact, of twenty-two power exchanges that took place in our case-study cities during the fifteen-year period studied, twelve directly resulted in manager dismissals. Three other dismissals were effected in power plays anticipatory of power exchanges. In one exchange the incoming clique had already placed its man in the managership. These figures show the relatively strong relationship between a change of clique control and a manager dismissal. The table shown here is explanatory of the conclusions we have drawn.

Table 8

Power Exchanges and Manager Terminations

Item	*No.*
Power exchanges during the research period	22
Power exchanges followed by an involuntary termination	12
Power exchanges not followed by an involuntary termination	10
Reason for non-occurrence of a termination following a power exchange:	
The incoming clique was satisfied with the incumbent manager because —	4
In a power play it had already installed its man before the power exchange occurred	(3)[a]
He was allied with the leader of the successful clique	(1)
The incoming clique inherited an acting manager	1
The incumbent manager, because of his political leadership and sponsorship of city employees, operated from a power base independent of either competing leadership clique	2
No explanation could be ascertained	1
The incoming clique, avowedly in one case and apparently in the other, was sufficiently committed to the "city manager idea" not to fire the manager whom it found in office	2

[a] Numbers in parentheses included in totals for class of phenomena.

2. *Manager tenure tends to be longer in communities that have a monopolistic style of politics than in communities that have a competitive style of politics*

Our definition of a monopolistic style of politics requires that over any given period of time there be only one leadership clique represented in the formal decision-making institutions of the community and that during this same time period there be no other leadership clique in effective competition in the community. This definitional requirement, however, does not preclude the replacement of one monopolistic regime by another. In other words, a power exchange can occur with the replacement of one monopolistic clique by another monopolistic clique as well as by the displacement of monopolistic politics by competitive politics. The point is that power exchanges, by the very nature of the level of interest conflict, occur less frequently in monopolistic communities than in competitive communities. Accordingly, manager tenure tends to be longer in monopolistic communities than in competitive communities.

In the monopoly community the leadership clique normally represents the dominant interest or set of interests in the community. Interest conflict does exist within a monopoly community. However, the level of interest conflict is low enough so that differences can be accommodated within the single leadership clique. In the competitive community, on the other hand, the level of interest conflict is high enough and the interests perhaps are divisive enough so that accommodation cannot occur within a single leadership clique. Consequently a polarization of interests occurs, making possible the rise of a competing faction or factions on a permanent basis.

The existence of conflict over the question of "what kind of town shall ours be" — a type of conflict which we label *regime* conflict — is a conflict of interests of such scope and depth that it normally can not be contained within the confines of a single leadership clique. In most instances the case-study communities that had not settled this important question were competitive communities that were highly unstable in a political sense. Only one community which had not, at least for the moment, resolved this fundamental issue — Orange Point — was a monopoly community. However, it is essential to point out the "bossed" character of politics in this community. We would speculate, then, that either a high degree of competition or "bossdom" characterizes communities which have not solved the regime conflict. In either case, manager tenure appears to be shorter in this type of community than in either monopoly communities or competitive communities that do not face a resolution of regime conflict.

3. *Local-amateur city managers have a longer average tenure than outside professional managers*

The professional city manager (who is normally a nonlocal) is a careerist. His training and the achievement norms characteristic of those active in the professional organization essentially require that he be constantly moving "upward" — from smaller to larger city. The professional, by training and organizational orientation, is motivated to seek status and prestige and is restless to move on to a larger city with "more and bigger problems to solve." In such moves he finds his career satisfaction and to such moves manager dismissals, as a result of changes in factional control of the city hall, offer no impediment. The manager is a part of a rare profession in which firing is in many instances a badge of honor.

The outsider-professional's power base in the community is usually far less secure than that of his local-amateur counterpart. The local-amateur usually has acquired some factional or clique ties before he assumes office, and this membership normally gives the local-amateur a fairly secure political base from which to maneuver while in office. The weakness of the outsider-professional's power base in the community is demonstrated by the fact that the clique or faction that brought the professional to the community is itself insecure in its political grip and cannot be depended upon. If the "political going is rough," it is far easier for a clique to rid itself of an outsider-professional in an attempt to shift unpopularity away from the clique and to the manager than it would be to fire a local man who holds membership in the clique. The professional city manager then, has no stable power base from which to fight his enemies and, indeed, no political weapons except, perhaps, his public "image" as a professional.

Our questionnaire data show that three-fourths of all the professional managers had an average job tenure as managers of less than four years and one-fourth had an average job tenure in excess of four years. For amateur managers these proportions were exactly reversed, with three-fourths falling into the long tenure category. For outsiders the findings were almost identical to those for professionals: 71 per cent had less than four years average job tenure and 29 per cent over four years. "Locals" were even more preponderantly long tenure than amateurs: 88 per cent over four years average tenure and only 12 per cent under four years. The reader need merely recall the long tenure for local-amateurs in Floriana, Dorado, and West-bourne and the short tenure for outsider-professionals in Estiva, Hiberna, Eastbourne, and Orange Point.

Finally and perhaps most important, the local-amateur usually is found in communities which have a monopolistic style of politics, while the outsider-professional usually is found in communities that have a competitive style of politics. We believe that monopolistic communities find it easy to adopt and use the manager plan because this form of government usually cements the acceptance of a member of the ruling clique as the theoretical administrative head of the community. The relatively long intervals between power exchanges in monopoly communities, then, help explain the correspondingly long tenure of local-amateur managers.

4. *Although a high rate of population growth is related to a short-
ening of manager tenure, population growth is not a sufficient
explanation of manager tenure*

Factors other than gross population increase must be taken into
account. Are the same types of people moving into the community
as have lived there before, or are the newcomers different from the
older inhabitants? An influx of people with differences in income,
class, or expectations from the pre-existing majority is crucial. New
economic groups, different social classes, and age realignments are
likely to represent new interests in the community and, insofar as
they do, they alter the old interest structure of the community. For
example, the movement of a large number of white-collar workers
into a tourist-oriented community may cause serious interest conflict.
It is interest conflict which in-migration produces and not growth per
se, which helps explain variations in manager tenure. A community
may treble in size without affecting manager tenure if the growth
merely represents an increase in the same kinds of people who were
predominant in the community. On the other hand, a much smaller
rate of growth may have drastic effects on the politics of the community if the new people bring with them new expectations and interests or style of life which they attempt to express politically.

For instance, the town of Westbourne maintained a substantial rate
of population growth during the case-study period. But those who
moved to Westbourne appeared to share the same interests and expectations as those who had preceded them to the community. The
substantial addition of new people to the community did not endanger
the community style of politics nor did it affect the tenure of the city
manager. On the other hand, in Hiberna, a politically unstable city,
the "estate" owners and retirees, long the dominant political group,
were challenged by the influx of younger suburbanites. In Dorado a
different income level represented among more recent retirees caused
a political "revolution."

Left unanswered in our analysis is the question of timing. For
instance, are there discernible patterns in the length of time it takes
for new interests to receive political articulation in a community? Are
the time periods different under different styles of politics?

5. *Separately elected mayors are a political hazard to managers*

The towns of Estiva and Hiberna provide ample documentation for
the conclusion that the separately elected mayor can and frequently
does shorten the manager's tenure. Such tenure threats from the
mayor are, of course, in addition to dismissals based solely upon

changes in clique control. The third case-study city with a separately elected mayor, Dorado, cannot be classified as supportive of our conclusion because the change in mayor and manager coincided with a change in clique control and the old manager had been a campaign issue. Eastbourne has too recently adopted separate popular election of the mayor to provide evidence in either direction. Our questionnaire data support the Estiva and Hiberna findings. Table 9 explains the relationship discussed.

Table 9

Community Tenure of Managers by Manner of Selecting Mayor*

Community Tenure	Method of Selection	
	Percentage by Council	Percentage by Voters
2.0 years or less	26%	40%
2.1–3.9 years	23	38
4.0 years plus	51	22
(N)	(43)	(32)

* Community tenure means the average number of years for all managers in a particular city since 1945 or the inception of council-manager government. Acting managers were not counted.

6. *Developmental sequence*

Finally, the set of concepts used and case-study materials suggest a rather developmental sequence. We conceive of the typical monopolistic community as being transformed into the typical competitive community. The monopolistic community is relatively small in population with a single leadership clique, of which the city manager, a local-amateur, is a member. The competitive community is larger in population, with two or more leadership cliques and employs an outsider-professional as a city manager, who may or may not become a member of the leadership clique. The change from monopoly to competition appears to be associated with an influx of population which brings with it a new set of interests, but change can also be associated with an influx of outside money or with the emergence of a new and competing clique made up of a different generation.

Tendencies in Community Politics

Transferring our attention now to a broader context, we must ask what our case studies may suggest by way of possible tendencies or sequences in community politics. The professional manager, as a political leader, must operate in a variety of political settings. What are some of the characteristics of these settings? A few generalizations would appear to us to be valid at this point, particularly in relation to the idea we have posed of differing economic and social orientations providing an explanation for conflict as towns grow.

As we indicated above, conflict over destiny of a city — what we have called regime conflict — is basic to all other serious divisions in a community. It reveals the principal group alignments because these groups develop around the various alternatives open to the community as paths of future growth. The groups that occur to the reader are retirees, banks, developers, and touristic interests — with occasionally industry groups. Let us recapitulate from the case studies the active role each appears to play in local politics.

1. *Retirees*

Westbourne and Eastbourne contain a fairly large proportion of retirees who do not articulate a distinct policy view of the community. On the other hand, Dorado does show a polarization around retirees. Hiberna's retirees are political activists but aligned with the more influential and more dominant "estate" group and not major contenders themselves for control of community destiny. Why these differences?

Once again, we recur to the theme of socio-economic differences between groups as the major factor providing a different *Weltanschaung* and, therefore, a different policy choice. Dorado's retirees represent, for the most part, upper middle-class to middle-class pensioners who like the town as it is and are openly averse to much growth. The millionaires were in Dorado in force well before the upper middle-class retirees and are really responsible for the latter group being in the town. The unanticipated consequence of construction of the first cooperative apartment house by a millionaire developer was to introduce the first tax-conscious pensioners to the city. As pensioners, the retirees are acutely aware of the inflationary trends of the times and fear tax outlays for growth programs. They want their present investment in a Dorado home or apartment fully protected by means of a strict zoning. They resent subsidization of growth programs that benefit others. Pitted against them are the millionaire developers and small businessmen, both of whom require population growth either to turn large capital investments to a profit or merely to survive in ordinary Main Street business competition. Each of these groups defends the use of governmental favors to the developers as a way of promoting the kind of enterprise that will attract in-migrants and tourists to the town. Ironically, the more successful the developers are in selling homes or apartments to retirees, the more strident becomes the conflict between themselves and the retirees over town policy.

Westbourne began as an upper middle-class community and through strict zoning has continued to attract that class alone. It not only lacks a millionaire contingent with exploitative goals, but by means of zoning its small business community has been kept too small to muster any force for policy-making. Westbourne's retirees, therefore, simply brought "more of the same" to a community already deeply dedicated to a simple and clear set of goals.

Eastbourne represents the other side of the coin on zoning — no plan, no pattern — but a similar class unanimity that keeps retirees as one with original residents. Eastbourne's original population of poor to modest rustics had a low level of expectation as to community services. They could easily absorb the influx of working-class retirees, subsisting on Social Security pensions or little more, who live in trailer parks or in old and inexpensive housing. Such retirees want no services except a few inexpensive shuffleboard courts as they hope for minimal taxes.

Hiberna's retirees, although essentially in a different income group from that of the "estate" owners and *rentier* group, share the desire of both of these to maintain the status quo and to repudiate growth programs. They like Hiberna as it has been, with minimal governmental services and low costs. The retirees have their clubs and crafts activities and want no expansion of recreation opportunities for younger residents. Hence, the pensioners form an integral part of the political "old guard" of Hiberna. All of this underscores the point that retirees do not become a separate political group or even become politically active with others unless they have a set of socio-economic goals divergent from those of other major groups in the community. So long as their socio-economic goals are identical or harmonious with those of the other groups, conflict remains at a low level and they remain politically quiescent.[4]

2. Banks

Banks in a number of our profile cities provided the leadership or

---

[4] Cf. Frank A. Pinner, Paul Jacobs, and Phillip Selznick, *Old Age and Political Behavior* (Berkeley: University of California Press, 1959). This is a study of the political activism of the California oldster group subsisting on public assistance. In contrast, the Florida retirees living on either OASI or private pensions, or both, have remained politically inactive at the state level as they share the orientations of the "Cracker" majority in the legislature to keep state government expenditures low and could not, in any event, improve their pensions through state activity.

foci for coherent political cliques. The exceptions are Dorado, East-bourne, and Estiva where banks played no discernible role in city politics. That a bank should play a central role in organization of a political clique in a small or medium-sized city is comprehensible and to be expected in the light of any bank's canalizing role in determining kinds and rates of investment, and hence of economic activity, in the city. In a larger city with major industrial corporations, such business corporations may possess financial ties outside the city that may be woven into the fiscal development of the city or, on the other hand, major banks may be so numerous and competitive that it is impossible for competitive politics to be focused around any one or two banks. But the smaller city, except in the case of Center City, seldom has financial alternatives. There, through a "deal" for financing a large public works program, the very threat of an outside bank entering Center City had the political consequence of mobilizing the "old guard" investors in local banks in the council election. A power exchange resulted from such "old guard' mobilization. Little or no evidence could be adduced, however, to indicate any sustained political effort by Center City banks once they had successfully fought off outside competition. Perhaps the fact that the character of Center City has long been settled is related to the normal quiescence of local banks in Center City politics.

But Hiberna, Westbourne, Floriana, and Orange Point all demon-strate in their politics the central role banks may play, especially on the question of town destiny. The challenge to the monopolistic clique ruling the town as well as to the goals of the town came in each of these communities from another clique organized around a bank. The fact that in Westbourne and Orange Point the bank group was not in the long run successful in its objectives either of ruling or changing the city's character still does not alter the significance of the fact that a bank in each case was the focal point around which a "revolution" in regime was attempted.

But, one might well ask, why was this not the case in Dorado, East-bourne, and Estiva? Each offers a sound reason for deviation from the point made about the others. In the case of Dorado, although the organizer of the town's first bank was the long-time mayor and surro-gate for the millionaires who provided the capital for his bank, the millionaire developers launched projects of such magnitude and them-selves had access to sufficient outside sources of capital, that the local bank was "peanuts" to them and incapable of handling their needs. Because the local bank was far more dependent on them than they on the bank, the millionaire developers provided the status and leadership requisite to cement together a political clique in which they were superordinate to the bank. Eastbourne offers the reverse situation —

a very poor town, with the only bank financed by a non-city group. There are no real potentialities for investment opportunity within the city, and the bank, therefore, is not too closely tied to local politics except to keep the channels open through Bray attorneys to the ruling Bray clan. Estiva has always depended for its financial institutions upon branches of Monroe banks, which are oriented to the politics of the central core city and not to a "carny" atmosphere suburb.

3. Developers

Although developers and allied realtors seem especially ubiquitous in community politics in Florida, certainly the large scale developer of suburban real-estate — both residential and shopping center type — has become a national phenomenon. The stakes are so high in the way of benefits local government bodies can confer that it is not surprising to find developers organizing coherent political cliques. Such cliques are always oriented around "growth" as a positive good for the city. They may be instrumental in forging political alliances with small businessmen in the local chamber of commerce, as in Dorado and Hiberna. Where developers are centered in another city and have moved on in their operations, as in Westbourne, they may leave no imprint on the city's politics. But where they are not only resident but still operative within the city, they soon by their very operations produce countervailing pressures. In Dorado such countervailing pressures have come from the pensioner retirees; in Hiberna the dormitory suburbanites as well as the "old guard" have furnished opposition to the "bank group," which is essentially a real estate-developer group. The interesting thing in both Hiberna and Dorado is that the "old guard" has itself been aligned with the original land developers and, indeed, was brought in by the land company. The Dorado developers today are in conflict over the class of buyer to which to appeal and hence in conflict over the "rate of growth" and direction of change in the town.

4. Touristic Interests

Usually small businessmen in Florida hard pressed in retail competition utilize the local chamber of commerce to push hard for tourism. Such drives may gain support, both financial and moral, from bankers and developers interested in investment. Often a drive for tourism will stimulate opposition to the rising government expenditures sought by tourist-minded interests for recreational, highway, and other projects not geared to the needs of local residents. The other reason for opposition is that encouragement of tourism usually leads to rezoning requests, an issue calculated to stir local residents near affected areas to a frenzy of reaction because it touches upon both esthetic and economic values dear to them.

A city that has an industrial orientation seldom manifests much serious interest in tourism, as witness Floriana and Center City. But cities that are residential centers and possess environmental advantages are often caught in the struggle over whether or not to promote tourism. As a matter of fact, emphasis on tourism alone is not necessarily productive of community battles, as is attested by the acceptability to the entire town of Dorado's plush beach-front hotel and Hiberna's sedate old lake-front hotel populated by a superannuated clientele. These two cities were precipitated into battles over facilities of a more popular variety that would attract budget-minded tourists. In the case of Hiberna such facilities were an outdoor theater, civic center, and swimming pool, and in the case of Dorado the battle was joined over improvement of a beach-front park near private homes and expensive cooperative apartments. In Estiva the recent history of the town's conflicts has centered around the efforts to change the orientation of touristic interests from "carny" to respectable middle-class. Doradans exhibited little concern over a convention-type hotel to bring in year-round tourists or a yachtel, but they do not wish to encourage the masses to get on the beach. To a city like Orange Point at the bottom of the social and economic scales the battles in Dorado and Hiberna would be meaningless, but once again the reader must remember that tourism, like the general issue of "growth," is controversial when it means bringing into the community people of a different social and economic class from that of the major political clique.

Suppose we conceptualize the politics of our communities in another way than through group orientations. Issue itself might provide a common thread of analysis, but issue would lead us back to groups and their attitudes on issues. What are the divisive issues that create conflict in local government? When do these issues emerge? At the risk of appearing simplistic, we can remind readers of the rather general division in all our cities except Westbourne over the tax rate because this issue had back of it in all instances the demands for services by some groups in the city that ran into collision with other groups of persons uninterested in amenities of urban life or "social welfare" concepts, such as public recreation facilities, libraries, and so on. Related to the tax rate but even more indicative of clique interests was the whole matter of real property assessment where taxes were a matter of concern. This issue was fraught with extreme bitterness in Dorado and was weighted with almost as much feeling in Hiberna because of major assessment concessions given to wealthy individuals. But property reassessment was a divisive issue in Center City and was emerging as divisive in Floriana. In Eastbourne and Orange Point the fiscal issue was somewhat different: it concerned the method of financing basic public improvements, especially sewers.

Almost as common an issue as the fiscal ones of taxes and property assessment has been that of zoning. But zoning was not an issue in all our cities because it is basically a middle-class and upper-class instrument. For one thing, zoning requires some knowledge of urban patterns of living, of general concepts of land use, of a sense of classification and orderliness, of an ability to articulate a viewpoint in other terms than the real motivation, which is usually simply the desire to hold certain elements and interests at bay. These qualities are lacking in Eastbourne, Estiva, Orange Point, and Floriana, but they are present in marked degree among many persons in Westbourne, Dorado, Hiberna, and even in Center City because of the different socio-economic structure of all these cities. The challenge in zoning has come most frequently from touristic interests and to a less degree from merchandising business interests. Not one of the zoning battles centered around industrialization, a not surprising fact in view of the general scarcity of industry in most Florida cities.

Industrialization was divisive in only one community, a city which was industrialized and which split over the rate of industrialization. But of all other cities, only Westbourne found it inconceivable to think of industry. Floriana, our sole city that divided on the industrialization issue, was torn by both the question of how fast to industrialize and how much industry would be desirable and by the question of whether to regulate existing industry for health reasons.

We come to the question raised in the first chapter — the possibility of developing a framework for the comparative analysis of urban politics. The concepts we have developed and the modest developmental sequence we have proposed are only a first step in the construction of such a framework. Our ideas are subject to considerable refinement. For instance, the concepts of monopolistic and competitive politics are both gross formulations. Can we find meaningful analytical subdivisions within these ideas? Further, we might question the appropriateness of the conceptual framework for really large cities or cities with major industrial complexes under absentee control. Are the concepts useful in explaining politics in large urban centers? Finally, although we have touched upon forces external to the community, such as an inflow of people or money, we have not considered external relations such as those produced by party politics or inter-governmental relations. What are the forces of governmental competition in large metropolitan counties such as those containing several of our cities?

Many of the foregoing questions are not intended to be answered by any of the data presented in preceding chapters. We hope merely that by raising such questions we may stimulate speculation among students regarding the handling of our data and the nature of politics in the real municipal world, among larger as well as smaller cities. The contemplative student may well ask many more questions and push the frontiers of comparative study much further along than this modest effort we have made can conceivably accomplish.

APPENDIX

PUBLIC ADMINISTRATION CLEARING SERVICE

University of Florida

Please return completed questionnaire promptly to:
Professor Gladys M. Kammerer,
Director, PACS, Peabody Hall
University of Florida, Gainesville

All information given on this questionnaire will be KEPT CONFIDENTIAL AND WILL NOT BE DIVULGED.

Questionnaire for Study of the Profession of City Manager in Florida

1. Presently employed as City Manager of _____
2. Date of birth _____
3. Birthplace _____, _____
              City   State
4. Education:
   High School:_____Located at_____Yr. of Grad._____
          Years Attended
   Tech. or
   Bus. School:_____Located at_____Yr. of Grad._____
          Years Attended
   College: _____   Located at_____
   Kind of degree_____   Year of degree_____
   Graduate School_____   Located at_____
   Kind of Degree_____   Year of degree_____
5. Any specialized training in city management? _____
   If so, what?_____
   Use additional sheet if spaces are inadequate for your answers to any questions.
6. *Employment Record Listed From Present Position Back*

Position	Location	Starting Salary	Last Salary	Dates of Employment	Reason For Leaving

7. Do you belong to any organizations or groups in your town? (such as Elks, American Legion, P.T.A., Chamber of Commerce, Kiwanis, board of vestrymen of your church, etc.)
   Yes ☐   No ☐   Please list groups:_____
8. Have you held any offices or committee chairmanships in the above groups?
   Yes ☐   No ☐   If so, please list:_____
9. What is the present population of your city?_____
10. For how many years has your city had council-manager form of government?_____

11. How many managers has your city had since adoption of the plan?____
12. How is the mayor of your community selected? By council ☐
    By voters separately ☐   By highest vote at council election ☐
13. Are there any city department heads not under the jurisdiction of city
    manager? Yes ☐   No ☐   If "yes", please list departments:____
14. City department heads under the city manager are selected in the fol-
    lowing way:
    CHECK ONE
    _____ a. All are appointed by me with virtually automatic approval
    by council.
    _____ b. Some are selected by me with virtually automatic approval
    by council, and the council appoints the rest.
    _____ c. I find out first from council whom they desire, and if that
    person is at all qualified, I appoint him.
    _____ d. The majority faction on council always tells me whom to
    appoint without waiting for me to ask them for suggestions.
15. Are there any utilities that are publicy owned and operated in your
    city? Yes ☐   No ☐
    If "yes", please list:_____
16. My present annual salary is $_____.
17. My original annual starting salary here was $_____.
18. My expense allowance is $_____, per year.
19. For those previously city managers in other cities:
    I accepted my present city manager position and resigned from a pre-
    vious city managership for the following reason:
    CHECK ALL APPROPRIATE ANSWERS:
    _____ a. Higher salary here.
    _____ b. Better opportunity for future salary increases here.
    _____ c. Larger expense allowance over and above salary here.
    _____ d. Conflict with council minority in other city.
    _____ e. Conflict with council majority in other city.
    _____ f. Rejection of budget by city council in other city.
    _____ g. Failure by council to support my program.
    _____ h. Conflict with mayor.
    _____ i. Other reasons which were:
20. I entered the city manager profession for the following reason:
    CHECK ALL APPROPRIATE ANSWERS:
    _____ a. Higher salary than I could earn in private employment.
    _____ b. Higher potential pay in future positions.
    _____ c. More security than in private business.
    _____ d. More opportunity as a city manager to develop my own ideas.
    _____ e. Preference for the public service over private business.
    _____ f. Preference for managerial work to elective public office.
    _____ g. Desire to be an active community leader.
    _____ h. Other reasons: _____
21. My present relationship with my city council can be described as
    follows:
    CHECK ALL APPROPRIATE ANSWERS:
    _____ a. Full confidence of city council.
    _____ b. Support from council on major issues.
    _____ c. Interference by council with city personnel and administration.
    _____ d. Rejection of major recommendations by city council.
    _____ e. Rejection of budget by city council.

_____ f. Conflict with minority group on council.
_____ g. Conflict with majority group on council.
_____ h. Conflict with mayor.
_____ i. Other relationship which is: _____

22. My relationship with the community can best be described as follows:
CHECK ALL APPROPRIATE ANSWERS:
_____ a. Support for my administration from principal organizations and press.
_____ b. Support for my administration from principal organizations but not from press.
_____ c. Support from press, but not from principal organizations.
_____ d. Support from one newspaper, but strong opposition from the other.
_____ e. Support from some of the principal organizations, but strong opposition from others.
_____ f. Indifference from principal organizations and press.

23. With reference to community attitudes, is there a movement in your city to abandon the council-manager plan of government?
Yes ☐   No ☐
a. If so, how strong would you say this movement is? _____
b. What groups are behind it? _____
c. Can any of these groups be fairly described as "lunatic fringe" groups? Yes ☐   No ☐   Which ones? _____

24. Last year, the most important question to be decided in my city was:
On the question, the decision was finally made: (CHECK ONE)
_____ a. By the voters in a referendum election in which I made no public statements and took no stand.
_____ b. By voters in a referendum election in which I urged voters to vote in a particular way.
_____ c. By a council vote in which the majority followed the course I had recommended for the settlement of this issue.
_____ d. By a council vote in which the majority followed in part the course I recommended, but also rejected in part my recommendations to them.
_____ e. By a council vote in which the majority rejected the recommendations I made to them.
_____ f. The council dropped the issue through inability to get a majority to support a particular course of action.
_____ g. By the council delegating the whole issue to me to be settled at my discretion.

25. Would you say most major policy questions are settled in the way you checked above? Yes ☐   No ☐   If not, in what way? Describe:

26. The initiation of policy in my city can best be described as vested in:
CHECK APPROPRIATE ANSWERS:
_____ a. The mayor who tries to lead in all policy proposals and attempts to act like a strong mayor.
_____ b. The council and mayor who jointly propose almost all major policy decisions.
_____ c. The mayor and me.
_____ d. Me, as I propose major policy which is usually adopted by council.
_____ e. The council and myself; we usually propose major policy jointly or alternatively.
_____ f. The council which proposes almost all major policy.

_____ g. The heads of departments not under my control who have strong influence with the council.

27. The greatest influence on policy initiation comes from:
CHECK ONE:

_____ a. Business organizations in town, whose proposals usually get adopted.

_____ b. A few strong political personalities who do not hold office, but who originate most policy proposals on major questions which actually get adopted by the council.

_____ c. Certain department heads under me who have great influence with the council and by-pass me in making major policy proposals which usually get adopted.

_____ d. Civic and good government groups who make most of the major policy proposals which are adopted by the council.

_____ e. The press which originates most of the major policy proposals which are adopted by the council.

28. During my tenure as manager, the politics of my city can best be described as:
CHECK ONE:

_____ a. Very stable, with very few controversial policy questions that divide the community.

_____ b. Stable despite a few controversial questions that divide the community.

_____ c. Subject to marked changes in groups controlling city government from one election to another as a result of major controversies.

_____ d. Subject to change of control from one election to another based upon personalities of candidates and not related to policy disagreements.

29. My future plans can be described as follows:
CHECK ONE:

_____ a. I like this city and my associates and plan to stay indefinitely.

_____ b. I do not like this city and am looking for another city managership.

_____ c. My family does not like this city and, therefore, I am looking for another city managership.

_____ d. I plan to leave city management for some more lucrative work as soon as I get the right offer.

_____ e. Although I find the salary adequate, I plan to leave city management for some more congenial type of work as soon as I get the right offer.

_____ f. I like this city, but I hope to move on to a larger city as manager in the not too distant future.

30. Why did your predecessor as city manager leave his position in your city?
CHECK ALL APPROPRIATE ANSWERS:

_____ a. Higher salary offered as city manager of another Florida city.

_____ b. Higher salary offered as city manager of a city in another state.

_____ c. Higher fringe benefits as city manager of another city.

_____ d. Decided to enter private employment.

_____ e. Moved into another type of position in the public management field.

_____ f. Opposition by city council minority.

_____ g. Opposition by city council majority.

_____ h. Rejection of budget by city council.
_____ i. Conflict between him and mayor.
_____ j. Dismissed by council or resigned for any other reason, which was:

31. My predecessor had the following relationship with the council:
    CHECK ALL APPROPRIATE ANSWERS:
    _____ a. Full confidence of the city council.
    _____ b. Support from council on major issues.
    _____ c. Interference by council with city personnel and administration.
    _____ d. Rejection of major recommendations by council.
    _____ e. Rejection of budget by city council.
    _____ f. Conflict with minority group on council.
    _____ g. Conflict with majority group on council.
    _____ h. Conflict with the mayor.
    _____ i. Other relationship which was

HAVING ASKED YOU MANY QUESTIONS ABOUT YOURSELF IN REFERENCE TO YOUR WORK AND YOUR CITY, WE WISH TO ASK YOU SOME QUESTIONS ABOUT YOUR PHILOSOPHY OF COUNCIL-MANAGER GOVERNMENT.

32. Do you think it wise for a city manager to remain in one city for a time or is it better policy for him to move to a new city periodically?
    Yes ☐   No ☐   Reason:
33. Do you think a city manager should play a leading role in policy-making in his community? Yes ☐   No ☐   Give reason for your answer.
34. It is often said that continuity for administration is achieved under the manager plan. Do you think this is true in view of the fact that managers change their positions frequently? Yes ☐   No ☐ Why?
35. Do you think city managers should belong to the International City Managers Association? Yes ☐   No ☐   Why?
36. In presenting recommendations to city councils, which of the following approaches do you consider most desirable?
    CHECK ALL APPROPRIATE ANSWERS:
    _____ a. Present the major alternatives with facts supporting each, with no specific recommendation from the manager.
    _____ b. Present the major alternatives with facts supporting each, with the manager's choice as to the best solution indicated.
    _____ c. Present only the manager's recommended solution with supporting facts, because the inclusion of alternative solutions simply confuses the councils.
    _____ d. Present the manager's recommended solution with little or no supporting facts.
37. Which of the following educational backgrounds do you consider most valuable for a manager?
    CHECK ONE:
    _____ a. Engineering
    _____ b. Architecture
    _____ c. Business administration
    _____ d. Political science with major emphasis on public administration with courses in politics.
    _____ e. Specialized curriculum in city management
    _____ f. Other
38. Now, finally, we want to ask you some questions about your philosophy of life.

CHECK IN THE APPROPRIATE BOX: (headed *Agree Strongly, Agree Somewhat, Agree Slightly, Disagree Slightly, Disagree Somewhat, Disagree Strongly.*)

A. Labor unions should become stronger and have more influence generally.

B. Most government controls over business should continue.

C. America may not be perfect, but the American way has brought us about as close as human beings can get to a perfect society.

D. The best political candidate to vote for is the man whose greatest interest is in fighting vice and graft.

E. It is up to the government to make sure that everyone has a secure job and good standard of living.

F. The government should own and operate all public utilities (transportation, gas, and electricity, etc.)

G. Depressions can be prevented by proper government planning.

H. Poverty could be almost entirely done away with if we made certain basic changes in our social and economic system.

I. Men like Henry Ford or J. P. Morgan who overcame all competition on the road to success are models for all people to admire and imitate.

J. In general, the best way of aiding our fellow men is to give time or money to some worthy charity.

K. The highest form of government is a democracy and the highest form of a democracy is a government run by those who are most intelligent.

L. Even though freedom of speech for all groups is a worthwhile goal, it is unfortunately necessary to restrict the freedom of certain political groups.

M. In times like these it is often necessary to be more on guard against ideas put out by people or groups in one's own camp than by those in the opposing camp.

N. A group which tolerates too much difference of opinion among its members cannot exist for long.

O. In the long run the best way to live is to pick friends and associates whose tastes and beliefs are the same as one's own.

P. Unfortunately, a good many people with whom I have discussed important social and moral problems don't really understand what's going on.

Q. It is only when a person devotes himself to an ideal or cause that life becomes meaningful.

R. Of all the different philosophies which exist in this world, there is probably only one which is correct.

S. A person who gets enthusiastic about many causes is likely to be a pretty wishy-washy sort of person.

T. A person who thinks primarily about his own happiness is beneath contempt.

U. Fundamentally, the world we live in is a pretty lonesome place.

V. There is so much to be done and so little time to do it.

W. The main thing in life is for a person to want to do something important.

Interview Guide

I. Issues — General

General probe. Let respondent exhaust his own stock of community issues before producing our check list.

1. What have been the major problems faced by the city of —— since the end of World War II? Any others?

2. How has the town been changing in the last 15 years? (New population? New industry? Same kind of people getting elected to the council?)

3. Here are some issues that many Florida cities have faced in the last 15 years. Have any of these come up in ——?

a. Land-use and planning
b. Urban renewal and public housing
c. Tax sources
d. Reassessment
e. Annexation
f. Public works
g. Religion
h. Labor
i. Industrialization
j. Northerners vs. Southerners
k. Retired people
l. Shopping centers
m. Race
n. Recreation facilities
o. Demos vs. Repubs.
p. Form of govt.
q. Liquor, gambling, etc.
r. Trying to get manager fired

4. Which *five* of those you mentioned and others you picked from the list I read would you say have been the most important five?

II. Issues — Specific

1. All right, you mentioned —— as an issue. What groups (what people) were interested in that?

a. Do any particular individuals lead that group? What individuals? What occupations?

b. What stand(s) did they take on the issue(s)?

c. Any other groups (people) take a stand? Who were they? What stands(s)? Any connection between these people (bus. soc. others?)

2. How did the city council decide the issue?

a. (If settled outside council, or not settled) Who won?

b. By the way, what line of work is each councilman in?

3. How about the mayor — did he take a stand?

a. What stand?

b. Who was the mayor at that time?

4. How about the manager — did he take a stand?

a. What stand?

b. Who was the manager then?

c. Did this have anything to do with the manager's leaving (where appropriate)?

5. Has this issue finally been settled, or does it still come up?

6. OK. The next issue you mentioned was ——.

III. Manager Turn-over

1. (If high turnover) Why has there been such a large number of city managers in ——?

(If low turnover) In many Florida cities, city managers don't last long. —— seems to be different. Why do you think it has worked out that way here?

2. (using list of managers) Why did —— leave? (Repeat for all managers) (Check election data vs. manager turnover).
   a. What kind of person was ——?
   b. What kind of politician was he?
   c. What kind of manager was he?
   d. Anything else?
   e. Why did he leave?
3. Firing the present manager.

IV. Groups
   Ask each respondent the following questions concerning the manager, the mayor, the council, and the department head(s).
   1. Are there any people who follow closely the action of the council (manager)?
      a. Who are they? Occupation? What groups or organizations do they belong to?
      b. What sorts of people do they work with on local problems?
   2. Are there any people whom the manager (mayor) (council) (department head) practically never listens to? Why is that?
   3. (If appropriate) What groups does the department head work with?
   4. Has it always been this way?

V. Institutional Relations
   A. What part does the mayor play in deciding what needs to be done in the city?
   B. What part does the mayor play in the day-to-day administration of the city?
   C. What part does the council play in hiring and firing? As a matter of courtesy, do you ordinarily consult councilmen before hiring a department head?
   D. What part does the council play in the preparation of the budget? What part do you think it should play?
   E. Is there any trouble between you and independent department heads?
   F. What does the council expect of you in regard to decisions about what needs to be done in the city? What do you expect of them?
   G. (Manager only) Have you ever encouraged qualified people to run for the council?

VI. Structure
   1. From what we have been saying, would it be fair to say that any one individual or group runs this town?
      a. (If yes) Who?
      b. (If no) How does the town run, then?
   2. Are there any groups in —— who are interested in almost all the issues?
      a. Who are they?
      b. Do they usually win?
   3. (If no to 2) Would you say that different groups or people are interested in different issues? Could you give me some examples?
   4. In your judgment, is the outcome of an issue dependent upon which group is interested in it?
      a. Could you give me some examples?

INDEX